Regulatory Bureaucracy

Regulatory Bureaucracy

MIT Studies in American Politics and Public Policy
Martha Weinberg and Benjamin Page, general editors

1. *The Implementation Game: What Happens After a Bill Becomes a Law,* Eugene Bardach, 1977.

2. *Decision to Prosecute: Organization and Public Policy in the Antitrust Division,* Suzanne Weaver, 1977.

3. *The Ungovernable City: The Politics of Urban Problems and Policy Making,* Douglas Yates, 1977.

4. *American Politics and Public Policy,* edited by Walter Dean Burnham and Martha Wagner Weinberg, 1978.

5. *Reforming Special Education: Policy Implementation from State Level to Street Level,* Richard A. Weatherley, 1979.

6. *Regulatory Bureaucracy: The Federal Trade Commission and Antitrust Policy,* Robert A. Katzmann, 1980.

Regulatory Bureaucracy:
The Federal Trade Commission and Antitrust Policy

Robert A. Katzmann

The MIT Press
Cambridge, Massachusetts, and London, England

Copyright © 1980 by The Massachusetts Institute of Technology

This book was set in Optima by Allied Systems, Inc., and printed and bound by The Alpine Press Inc., in the United States of America.

Library of Congress Cataloging in Publication Data

Katzmann, Robert A
  Regulatory bureaucracy.
  (MIT studies in American politics and public policy; 6)
  Includes index.
  1. Antitrust law—United States.   2. United States. Federal Trade Commission.   3. Antitrust law—Economic aspects—United States.
I. Title.   II. Series: Massachusetts Institute of Technology. MIT studies in American politics and public policy; 6.
KF1652.K37   353.008'2   79-22017
ISBN 0-262-11072-5

For my parents,
John and Sylvia Katzmann

Contents

Series Foreword

Social scientists have increasingly directed their attention toward defining and understanding the field of public policy. Until recently public policy was considered to be a product of the actions of public institutions and as such was treated as the end point in analysis of the governmental process. But in recent years it has become clear that the public policymaking process is infinitely more complex than much of the literature of social science would imply. Government institutions do not act in isolation from each other, nor is their behavior independent of the substance of the policies with which they deal. Furthermore, arenas of public policy do not remain static; they respond to changes in their political, organizational, and technical environments. As a result, the process of making public policy can best be understood as one that involves a complicated interaction among government institutions, actors, and the particular characteristics of substantive policy areas.

The MIT Press series, *American Politics and Public Policy,* is made up of books that combine concerns for the substance of public policies with insights into the working of American political institutions. The series aims at broadening and enriching the literature on specific institutions and policy areas. But rather than focusing on either institutions or policies in isolation, the series features those studies that help describe and explain the environment in which policies are set. It includes books that examine policies at all stages of their development—formulation, execution, and implementation. In addition, the series features studies of public actors—executives, legislatures, courts, bureaucracies, professionals, and the media—that emphasize the political and organizational constraints under which they operate. Finally, the series includes books that treat public policy making as a process and help explain how policy unfolds over time.

In this study of antitrust decisionmaking in the Federal Trade Commission, Robert Katzmann analyzes how the organizational and professional norms of the lawyers and economists who work in the antitrust division affect policy considerations and policy outcomes. He shows that personnel of an agency governed by a complicated and explicit body of law enjoy considerable leeway and discretion in their enforcement of federal antitrust policy. He calls into question a widely held assumption underlying much of the government's regulatory policy, that legal processes can and should be used to resolve economic problems, and assesses various proposals to reform antitrust regulation.

In analyzing both the organizational and professional constraints that affect the decisions of policymakers, Katzmann not only provides insights into the behavior of the Federal Trade Commission but also raises important questions about the impact of institutional and bureaucratic norms on the regulatory process.

Robert A. Katzmann received his Ph.D. from the Department of Government, Harvard University, and is a candidate for the J.D. degree at Yale Law School where he is an Articles and Book Review Editor of the *Yale Law Journal.*

Martha Wagner Weinberg

Acknowledgments

The experience of studying and writing about organizational decision-making was particularly worthwhile and memorable because of the many people who provided encouragement and wise counsel. I will always feel privileged to have had the good fortune to learn from these concerned individuals, and it is with great pleasure that I acknowledge my debt to them.

James Q. Wilson of Harvard University supervised this project from the outset and aided me during every phase. For his valuable criticisms and advice, as well as for his arrangements for financial support, I am most grateful. Richard E. Neustadt of Harvard University and Martha W. Weinberg of MIT also offered many helpful comments on various versions of this manuscript; I am very appreciative of their efforts. A seasoned FTC attorney, whose anonymity I preserve at his request, carefully scrutinized the book and saved me from errors in detail; I should like to thank him as well. Gary Katzmann read parts of the study and offered many useful suggestions.

Moreover, I am grateful to the Governmental Studies Program of the Brookings Institution, where I was a Guest Scholar during the time that I conducted field research in Washington, D.C. The research and writing of this book was made possible by financial support from the Alfred Sloan Foundation through its grant to Harvard University to promote the study of public management; in the absence of such aid, I could not have hoped to do this study.

Of course, special thanks are due to the over one hundred persons who were interviewed. Within the commission, they included the economists and lawyers of the Bureau of Economics and the Bureau of Competition, the bureau directors, assistant directors, chairmen, commissioners, the executive director, administrative law judges, and the secretary. I am also grateful to Capitol Hill staff, OMB examiners, and members of the private bar for sharing their thoughts with me. Without the generous cooperation of these informed practitioners, I could never have undertaken this project.

Most of the interviews were conducted in the summer of 1975. In subsequent years (through 1978), I made brief trips to Washington to collect data. Then FTC Executive Director Richard T.

McNamar provided me with full access to commission personnel; he gave me the freedom to marinate in the agency. I scheduled interviews myself; each lasted for about two hours and covered every dimension of the antitrust case-selection process. In fulfillment of a promise made to every interviewee, I will not name anyone in the following chapters, except where attributed quotations and information are taken from public sources. (Of course, in addition to field research, I relied upon many public sources, including congressional hearings and reports, budget documents, speeches of agency officials, periodicals, FTC reports and complaints, as well as the secondary literature.)

Field research focused on the decision to issue complaints—the decision to prosecute. It was not possible to study the process of case settlement through consent decrees—a process that results in the disposition of many cases—because the delicate and confidential nature of negotiations must exclude parties not involved in the case. I could not, at the executive director's instructions, ask the staff to specifically identify ongoing cases. For my purposes it was not necessary that I have such information; in any event I became quite aware of the names of cases simply because I spent quite a lot of time around the commission.

In the postinterview phase I sought to secure relevant nonpublic documents. I made use of the Freedom of Information Act and also appealed formally to the commission to gain access to data bearing upon case-selection matters. In 1975 and 1977, the commission granted access to a number of documents on the case load, including memoranda of the Bureau of Competition and the Bureau of Economics that dealt with opening and closing of investigations and the issuance of complaints. These memoranda provided solid evidence of the often clashing perspectives of the lawyer and economist; moreover, they were valuable because they discussed the kinds of issues the commissioners address in their deliberations. In accordance with the grant of access, I will not state the names of cases, individuals, or corporations mentioned in the memoranda. It is clear to me that such disclosures would not add anything of substance to this study. I am very grateful to all those who supported my requests for nonpublic documents—the commissioners, the attorney advisers, the executive director, the staffs of the bureaus, the Office of the General Counsel, and the Office of the Secretary.

My interest in government was encouraged as an undergraduate at Columbia College and later as a graduate student at Harvard University. During the years I spent on this study, I enjoyed working with faculty and students at Harvard. As a teaching fellow in government and as a graduate student, I had the good luck to be exposed to many fine professors in various fields with diverse perspectives. My appreciation extends to Lawrence Brown, Martha Derthick, Doris Kearns Goodwin, Stanley Hoffmann, Christopher Leman, Arthur Maass, Daniel P. Moynihan, and Nadav Safran. I am also grateful for the hospitality of Masters William and Mary Lee Bossert of Lowell House at Harvard while I was a resident house tutor in government.

I am appreciative of the efforts of those who played important roles in the production of this book; in particular, Beverly Cedarbaum who typed the manuscript with great skill and diligence.

Finally, it is impossible to look back upon these past years without making note of the special and profound contributions of my family to this project. I am deeply grateful to my family—to my parents, my brothers Gary and Martin, and to my sister Susan. Their encouragement, warmth, and caring were vital and sustaining forces.

Regulatory Bureaucracy

1
Introduction

"The antitrust movement is one of the faded passions of American reform," wrote Richard Hofstadter scarcely fifteen years ago.[1] Yet, he continued, "the antitrust enterprise has more significance in contemporary society than it had in the days of T. R. or Wilson, or even in the heyday of Thurman Arnold."[2] While public attention has waxed and waned, antitrust has endured. Today antitrust is once again in the public spotlight, in part because the issues on which it touches—the extent to which the state should regulate business, the nexus between corporate wealth and political influence, the effect of market concentration on economic problems—are still very much debated.

Antitrust is a banner under which many march, but for different reasons: politicians interested in combating inflation, consumer groups convinced that large manufacturers charge excessive prices, populists fearful that corporate giants corrupt the political process, businessmen threatened by the anticompetitive behavior of others, private attorneys dependent on antitrust practice as a source of income, and economists concerned with the welfare costs of monopoly and the estimated consumer gains from its elimination. Whatever their policy objectives—social, political, economic—these sundry groups and persons closely monitor the activities of those public agencies that largely set antitrust policy. This book examines how one such agency, the Federal Trade Commission (FTC), selects cases for antitrust action, and analyzes some of the problems the agency confronts in performing its duties.

The FTC, established in 1914, administers both antitrust and trade regulation laws.[3] In recent years, the commission has used its broad powers to launch significant actions against major economic interests, among them the oil, breakfast foods, and business copying industries. Such efforts have immersed the agency in controversy. In the view of its critics, at least some of the FTC's cases are "antibusiness" and injurious to consumer welfare.[4] To others, the agency has not been vigorous enough; in their judgment, we need more antitrust action against large industries.[5] The debate over whether the FTC either does "too much" or "too little" raises the fundamental question of *why* the agency has

pursued the kinds of antitrust cases that have characterized its
enforcement effort in these past years.

Consideration of the role of the commission as an engine of
antitrust policy is particularly appropriate now that politicians
from all points on the political spectrum see antitrust enforcement
as a major weapon in the battle against inflation. The dramatic
increases in the commission's antitrust budget ($30.299 million for
fiscal 1979 is more than double the amount appropriated by
Congress for fiscal 1975) have coincided with the mounting
problems of inflation.[6] The FTC, itself, in a typical budget request
stated that it believed that "increased commitments of antitrust
resources . . . contrary to the rule generally applicable to any
government expenditure—*will directly aid in the battle against
high prices.*"[7]

Not all commentators agree, however, that the commission is in
fact equipped to deal with complex problems such as inflation.[8] In
the aftermath of an organizational crisis in the late sixties, when a
wide range of persons and groups—including the American Bar
Association (ABA), Ralph Nader, and President Richard Nixon—
severely criticized the commission's performance, the agency
engaged in major efforts to improve the quality of its case-load
and decision-making processes. Institutional reforms were implemented, and there were high hopes that they would achieve
their purposes. The *Exxon* case, a suit directed against the eight
major oil companies, is representative of the agency's recent
attempts to pursue the "big" case by attacking structural weak-
nesses in the market and thereby enhancing consumer welfare.
Despite its best efforts, the FTC has encountered severe difficulties in prosecuting such cases. The turnover rate among staff
attorneys assigned to them has been so high that many doubt the
commission's capacity to handle such mammoth cases. More
generally, the FTC's problems raise questions about the suitability
of legal processes and institutions to attack economic ills.

The FTC: Its Antitrust Duties and Powers

Among its many antitrust responsibilities, derived principally from
the Federal Trade Commission Act[9] and the Clayton Act,[10] the

FTC is charged with preventing unfair methods of competition and unfair or deceptive acts or practices in, or affecting, commerce and with forestalling mergers or acquisitions that might substantially lessen competition or tend to create a monopoly. Moreover, the commission is to prevent unscrupulous buyers from using their economic power to exact discriminatory prices from suppliers to the disadvantage of less powerful buyers and to prohibit suppliers from securing an unfair advantage over their competitors by discriminating among buyers.[11] To these ends, the FTC conducts investigations of alleged violations of the antitrust acts; monitors the implementation of antitrust decrees; investigates the organization, business, conduct, practices, and management of corporations engaged in commerce (except where statutorily exempted); and makes reports and recommendations to Congress.

The agency has broad powers to fashion appropriate relief if the laws have been violated.[12] The commission may issue a cease and desist order prohibiting the continuation of acts judged illegal, and it may seek to restore competitive conditions by mandating relief that attacks structural imperfections in the market. For example, the agency can order respondents to dispose of illegally acquired companies or make trademarks, patents, trade secrets, or expertise available to competitors at reasonable royalties, or even without royalties.

The Goals of the FTC's Antitrust Policy

The breadth of the agency's activities is largely due to the ambiguous wording of the statutes that grant the FTC's authority. What constitutes "unfair methods of competition in commerce and unfair or deceptive acts or practices in commerce" is not self-evident. To state, as does section 7 of the Clayton Act, that a practice is unlawful when its "effect may be to substantially lessen competition or tend to create a monopoly" says little; the meaning of the phrases "may be," "substantially lessen," and "tend to create" demand definition.

Unclear statutory language exacerbates the problem of determining what end (or ends) the commission should pursue and fuels the debate about the direction of the agency's antitrust policy. Antitrust could serve many purposes, some competing and others complementary: (1) the achievement of desirable levels of economic performance by individual firms and ultimately by the economy as a whole; (2) the limitation of the power of big business; (3) the maintenance of a fair standard of business conduct; and (4) the nurturing of competitive market processes as an end in itself.[13]

Realization of the first goal would presumably yield economic growth at a relatively stable rate, full employment, price stability, an equitable distribution of income, efficiency, and progress.[14] Of these results, antitrust is thought to most easily affect efficiency and progressiveness.

The second goal reflects a desire to control unchecked power. This aim arises from a fear of bigness and is based on the assumption that size correlates with power, regardless of whether size is in fact synonymous with market control. The proponents of this goal maintain that "great industrial consolidations are inherently undesirable, regardless of their economic results."[15] Many believe that while higher prices may result from the maintenance of inefficient firms or decentralized and fragmented industries, such costs are worth bearing. Populists, in particular, champion the small independent businessman whose existence, they argue, must be preserved, lest large corporations damage the social and political fabric of the nation.

Fair dealing, an essentially social goal, is concerned not with the existence of power per se, but with the way in which power is wielded. Those who advocate fair dealing place a premium on the individual's opportunity to engage in enterprise and argue that merit will be determined in the free market. Fair dealing is a goal worth pursuing, its proponents contend, even if added economic benefit does not result (and conceivably, fewer opportunities could yield equally efficient economic results in some circumstances).[16]

The fourth goal views competition as nearly an end in itself, rather than as a means to achieve desired economic objectives. Those who stress this goal argue that self-regulating market processes are preferable to either of two main alternatives—control by government bureaucracy or by private monopolies. If the market is to remain relatively free of government regulation, then some means should be devised to place limits on unreasonable market power, which stifles structural competition.[17]

The lack of precision in statutory language and the absence of unambiguous directives with respect to policy ends are the sources of wide discretionary authority for the FTC. The extent of this discretion is illustrated by the changes in the commission case load during the last few years. The agency has placed increasing emphasis on *structural cases*, which are intended to attack fundamental market imperfections that facilitate anticompetitive activity among the dominant firms in an industry. Such cases, which often require the investment of considerable resources, are intended to yield substantial economic benefits—for instance, reductions in price levels—to the consuming public. In fiscal 1978, for example, the commission allocated 59 percent of its antitrust budget to what have been described as structural programs in the energy, health care, transportation, chemical, and food industries.[18] Fewer resources have been devoted to simple *conduct cases*, which deal with particular business practices and not with the underlying structural conditions that might foster anticompetitive behavior—especially those that do not have economic objectives. Conduct cases usually have social and political ends —for example, the preservation of small business. Indicative perhaps of the shifting emphasis in approach to antitrust enforcement has been the decrease in Robinson-Patman actions—cases whose effect is usually, although not necessarily, to maintain small, inefficient businesses at the expense of competition. In fiscal 1976, the agency approved only 6 Robinson-Patman investigations; in 1967, 173.[19]

Explaining Outcomes: The Conventional Wisdom

Many commentators have sought to explain the behavior of government organizations that regulate business. Some theorists maintain that bureaucracies are rational actors attempting to maximize organizational self-interest; bureaucrats, they contend, are motivated fundamentally by a desire to maximize budgets or power.[20] Other writers, including such unlikely kinsmen as conservative economists,[21] populists,[22] and radical historians,[23] argue that public agencies serve the very economic interests that they are charged with regulating; thus these organizations are not likely to pursue policies that protect the consuming public. One political scientist, writing specifically about the Federal Trade Commission, explains the regulatory body's case load by focusing upon the statutes that are the sources of the agency's authority; commission policies, he states, promote both competition and stability because the Federal Trade Commission Act and the Clayton Act enshrine these contradictory impulses.[24]

Economists who have analyzed the Antitrust Division of the Justice Department and the Federal Trade Commission commonly concentrate upon the economic determinants of antitrust activity.[25] Building upon economic models, they have attempted to relate antitrust cases to the economic characteristics of industries by inferring from the historical distribution of prosecutions the criteria—for example, the industry volume of sales, profitability, concentration, or welfare loss—that were decisive in the case-selection process.

In this book I will show that these accounts do not fully explain FTC behavior. The flaws in some of these studies are readily apparent. For instance, the finding that the Federal Trade Commission is inconsistent in its policies because of contradictory purposes embodied in the statutes does not explain how the agency allocates its resources or why the mix of cases has changed over time. Moreover, it does not account for the many factors affecting prosecutorial determinations (such as the demands of organizational maintenance).

Economists who have focused on the economic determinants of antitrust activity have failed to consider other explanations of an agency's behavior. Because they have linked the selection of antitrust cases to the economic characteristics of industries, economists have tended to foreclose the possibility that there may be other important, or even more significant, factors in accounting for the ways in which antitrust agencies determine their case loads. Indeed, this work will suggest that the determinants of antitrust activity are not necessarily or primarily economic. In deciding whether to bring a case, the antitrust agencies are in many situations more concerned with the probability of success than with ultimate economic effects. The FTC might decide to prosecute, even though substantial economic benefits are unlikely, because the particular case provides an apt vehicle for establishing an important precedent or because of the presumed deterrence value generally associated with prosecutions.

Those who charge that government serves the economic interests it is supposed to regulate or that agency outcomes reflect the desire of public officials to maximize power or budgets tend to make sweeping generalizations. Their studies are often unsupported by evidence. Along with the scholars whose approaches were described above, they fail to examine closely the actual operations of government organizations.[26] Some assume that goverment is little more than a black box, the policy outcomes of which are entirely a function of the resources or environment of the agency. Others concede that internal processes may be important but assume that all members of the organization have a simple, even identical, set of motives—personal self-interest, usually portrayed in pecuniary terms.

Antitrust Decision Making in the FTC: A Study in Bureaucracy

My central assumption is that the outcomes of governmental bodies can best be understood by examining the many organizational factors affecting the exercise of discretion. Organizational arrangements have much to do with determining how power is distributed among participants in the decision-making process, the manner in which information is gathered, the types of data that are collected, the kinds of policy issues that are discussed, the choices that are made, and the ways in which decisions are implemented. The various professional norms and personal objectives of the actors—executives, managers, and operators—also affect the decisions of organizations. Moreover, external actors (for example, the president, congressional committees, and interest groups) may also influence agency behavior.

This study explains how the FTC chooses its case load and why the agency has had problems in prosecuting big structural cases by focusing upon the organizational dynamics of its antitrust components. I will argue that in the period studied, from 1970 to 1976, the case load of the commission was mainly the product of the interaction between two bureaus and the five commissioners (see appendix A). These two bureaus, the Bureau of Competition (the lawyers' unit) and the Bureau of Economics (the economists' unit), were separate and coequal. The personnel of each had their own conception of the kinds of antitrust goals and cases that the agency should pursue. One bureau competed with the other for commission approval of its viewpoint.

An organizational study of the FTC tells us much about the impact of professionalism on the commission's antitrust activity. The FTC often tolerated intense disagreements between professionals—lawyers and economists—whose different career objectives and training led to conflicting views about antitrust policy. That the FTC should have encouraged such competition is surprising; one might have expected that the agency because of the "need for morale, for a sense of mission and distinctive competence" would have sought to impose a single governing ethos. But it is clear from observing the competition between lawyers and economists at the FTC that how the balance is struck between professionals with different norms and goals often significantly affects, and sometimes even determines, the definition of antitrust activity.

In order to evaluate the impact of lawyers and economists on case-load decisions, I will examine how the Bureau of Competition is run; how and why the Bureau of Economics affects prosecutorial choices; how the staff attorneys with limited expertise and experience influence case load decisions; and the ways in which the demands of organizational maintenance and the need to satisfy the aspirations of the staff attorneys affect the decisions of bureau executives.

Because it has limited resources, the commission cannot pursue every conceivable violation. The case load of the agency reflects the outcome of an informal debate, waged mainly at the bureau level, on setting the investigation agenda. Basically, there are two approaches to antitrust policy making. The *reactive approach* looks to the *mailbag* (consisting of letters of complaint from businessmen, public interest groups, and congressmen) as the source of antitrust investigations. The *proactive perspective* relies upon planning mechanisms as a means of initiating enforcement actions.[27] The policy consequences of the two approaches differ quite dramatically; each perspective is examined closely.

In order to explain FTC policy, it is also necessary to analyze the role of the commissioners, to assess the effects of the commission form of governance on case-load outcomes. Critics of commission government charge that collegiality spawns compromises that are antithetical to the setting of coherent policy. They contend that commissions are ill-equipped to manage bureaucracies and that collegial bodies foster irresponsibility by cloaking individual decision makers in anonymity. I argue that collegial decision making, at least in the case of the FTC, is not inherently unworkable and that the single-headed form of administration is not necessarily more effective.

In their efforts to shape policy outcomes, executives seek to control the process by which decisions are reached. They try to establish and maintain an organizational setting conducive to the achievement of their preferences. In the course of describing how commission officials sought to change the character of the case load in the period from 1970 to 1976, I examine the means used to accomplish their purposes—reorganization and quality control mechanisms—and assess the impact of such devices on staff behavior and, ultimately, on outcomes.

The decisions of public bureaucracies, though very heavily influenced by internal organizational factors, may be affected by other variables as well. Governmental agencies operate in a political environment; hence, various outside actors—the president, the Office of Management and Budget (OMB), congressional committees, public interest groups, and representatives of private interests—may have some bearing on FTC decisions. Therefore I will attempt to analyze the effect that outside forces have on the commission's case-selection process at the pre-complaint stage.

It is only after undertaking this empirical study of the commission organization that the capacity of the agency to prosecute big structural cases designed to yield substantial benefits to the consuming public can be assessed. Understanding the effect of organizational constraints on outcomes should also help in evaluating the fitness of legal processes to resolve economic questions and in discussing remedies proposed to treat the commission's problems. Analysis of the various dimensions of the commission's organizational behavior will enable us to assess the FTC's major attempts to upgrade its case load, to explain the difficulty of fulfilling the expectations of the early seventies, and to explore the role of the agency as a protector of competition.

Notes

1
Richard Hofstadter, "What Happened to the Antitrust Movement?" in *The Paranoid Style in American Politics and Other Essays* (New York: Vintage Books, 1965), p. 188.

2
Ibid., p. 189.

3
For works dealing with the creation of the Federal Trade Commission, see: G. Cullom Davis, "The Transformation of the FTC, 1914–1929," *Mississippi Valley Historical Review* 49 (1962): 437–445; George Rublee, "The Original Plan and Early History of the Federal Trade Commission," *Academy of Political Science Preceedings*, 11 (1926): 666–672; Gerald Leinwand, "A History of the United States Federal Bureau of Corporations" (Ph.D diss. New York University, 1962); James C. Lang, "The Legislative History of the Federal Trade Commission Act," *Washburn Law Journal* 13 (1974): 6–25; Arthur S. Link, *Wilson: The New Freedom* (Princeton: Princeton University Press, 1956); Gabriel Kolko, *The Triumph of Conservatism* (New York: Free Press, 1963); Gerard C. Henderson, *The Federal Trade Commission* (New Haven: Yale University Press, 1924); Thomas C. Blaisdell, Jr., *The Federal Trade Commission* (New York: AMS Press, 1967) (first published in 1932); Alan Stone, *Economic Regulation in the Public Interest: The Federal Trade Commission in Theory and Practice* (Ithaca; Cornell University Press, 1977),ch. 2; Douglas Walter Jaenicke, "Herbert Croly, Progressive Ideology, and the FTC Act," *Political Science Quarterly* 93 (Fall 1978): 471–495.

4
For an argument that antitrust activity against concentrated industries is misplaced, see J. Fred Weston, "Statement of J. Fred Weston," in U.S., Congress, Senate, Committee on the Judiciary, Subcommittee on Antitrust and Monopoly, *Hearings on Oversight of Antitrust Enforcement*, 95th Cong., 1st sess., 1977, pp. 558–565, 569–571 (hereafter *Oversight*

Hearings); also see Yale Brozen, "Antitrust Witch Hunt," *National Review* 30 (24 November 1978): 1470–1477.

5
Mark Green, Beverly C. Moore, Jr., and Bruce Wasserstein *The Closed Enterprise System: Ralph Nader's Study Group on Antitrust Enforcement* (New York: Grossman Publishers, 1972). Compare this book with Richard Posner's "Antitrust Policy and the Consumer Movement," *Antitrust Bulletin* 15 (1970): 361; Posner holds that attempts to press antitrust into the service of the consumer movement are essentially opportunistic.

6
U.S., Congress, House, Committee on Appropriations, *Hearings on Department of State, Justice and Commerce, the Judiciary and Related Agencies, Appropriations F.Y. 1976*, part 7, 94th Cong., 1st sess., 1975, p. 7 (hereafter *Appropriations Hearings FY '76*); U.S., Congress, Senate, Committee on Appropriations, *Report No. 95–1043*, 95th Cong., 2nd Sess., 1978, pp. 72–73; U.S., Congress, House, Committee on Appropriations, Report No. 95–1565, 95th Cong., 2nd sess., 1978, pp. 23–24.

7
U.S., Congress, House, Committee on Appropriations, *Appropriations Hearings FY '76*, p. 17.

8
Dean Ernest Gellhorn, "Statement of Ernest Gellhorn," *Oversight Hearings*, pp. 617–631.

9
38 Stat. 717 (1914), as amended, 15 U.S.C.A., sections 41–58 (1976).

10
38 Stat. 730 (1914), as amended, 15 U.S.C.A., sections 12–27 (1973). Besides exercising jurisdiction in cases arising under the Federal Trade Commission Act (FTCA) and the Clayton Act, the commission also has authority over cases that might be considered Sherman Act (and therefore Department of Justice) matters. The courts have ruled that conduct violative of that act is also an "unfair method of competition" and is thus subject to commission action under Section 5 of the FTCA.

11
49 Stat. 1526 (1936), 15 U.S.C.A. 13 (1973). For historical background on the Robinson-Patman Act, see Joseph C. Palamountain, Jr., *The Politics of Distribution* (Cambridge, Mass.: Harvard University Press, 1962), and Merle Fainsod, Lincoln Gordon, and Joseph Palamountain, Jr, *Government and the Economy* (New York: Norton, 1959).

12
In affecting the behavior of business, the five commissioners need not resort to adjudicatory proceedings. The agency's methods include trade

practice conferences, guides, and advisory opinions. These means are seldom used in antitrust proceedings; see Earl Kintner, *An Antitrust Primer*, 2nd ed. (New York: Macmillan Co., 1973), pp. 143–137.

Should the agency decide that a complaint may be in order—that is, that the commission, upon the recommendations of staff attorneys, and occasionally economists, should prosecute—then the respondent can indicate its willingness to sign a *consent order*, a formal document by which the business or company certifies that the challenged practices will be discontinued. The consent order is negotiated with various members of the staff. If the commission rejects the consent settlement, the matter is adjudicated through the normal processes: a hearing held before an administrative law judge. His initial decision, delivered upon the conclusion of the hearings, becomes the commission's final order, unless appealed within thirty days. In reviewing an appeal, the commissioners may affirm, modify, or reverse the judge's decision. The commission's decision is appealable in federal court.

13
This section is based on Carl Kaysen and Donald F. Turner's *Antitrust Policy: An Economic and Legal Analysis* (Cambridge, Mass.: Harvard University Press, 1959), pp. 11–18.

14
Ibid., p. 11.

15
United States v. Aluminum Company of America, 148 F 2d 416 (2nd Cir. 1945).

16
Support for the triumph of the ideal of the dispersal of power over that of economic benefit was expressed by Chief Justice Warren:

We cannot fail to recognize Congress' desire to promote competition through the protection of viable, small, locally owned businesses. Congress appreciated that occasional higher costs and prices might result from the maintenance of fragmented industries and markets. It resolved these competing considerations in favor of decentralization. We must give effect to that decision. *Brown Shoe Co. v. United States*, 370 U.S. 297 344 (1962)

17
The proposed Hart Industrial Reorganization Act was a deconcentration measure; see Harvey J. Goldschmid, H. Michael Mann, and J. Fred Weston, eds., *Industrial Concentration: the New Learning* (Boston: Little, Brown and Company, 1974), ch. 7.

18
U.S., Congress, Senate, Committee on Appropriations, *Hearings on Department of State, Justice and Commerce, the Judiciary and Related*

Agencies, Appropriations, F.Y. 1978, Justifications, part 3, 95th Cong., 1st sess., 1977, p. 339.

19
U.S., Congress, House, Committee on Small Business, Ad Hoc Subcommittee on Antitrust, the Robinson-Patman Act and Related Matters of the House Committee on Small Business, *Hearings on Recent Efforts to Amend or Repeal the Robinson-Patman Act,* part 2, 94th Cong., 1st sess., 1975, pp. 186–191. Also, Richard A. Posner, *The Robinson-Patman Act: Federal Regulation of Price Differences* (Washington, D.C.: American Enterprise Institute for Public Policy Research, 1976).

20
See William A. Niskanen, Jr., *Bureaucracy and Representative Government* (Chicago: Aldine Press, 1971); George Stigler, "The Process of Economic Regulation," *The Antitrust Bulletin* 17 (1972): 207–235; Richard Posner, "The Federal Trade Commission," *University of Chicago Review* 39 (1969): 47–89.

21
See, George Stigler, "The Theory of Economic Regulation," *Bell Journal of Economics and Management Science* 2 (1971): 3–21.

22
See Ralph Nader's introduction to Green, Moore, and Wasserstein, *Closed Enterprise System,* p. viii.

23
Gabriel Kolko, *Railroad and Regulation 1877–1916* (Princeton: Princeton University Press, 1966), and Kolko, *Triumph of Conservatism.*

24
Stone, *Economic Regulation.*

25
Long, Schramm, and Tollison concluded that economic variables do account for variations in Department of Justice cases across industries. They inferred that the most prominent determinant is industry sales and that variables more closely measuring performance—concentration, aggregate welfare losses, and profit rate on sales—play a secondary role (William F. Long, Richard Schramm, and Robert Tollison, "The Economic Determinants of Antitrust Activity," *Journal of Law and Economics* 16 (1973): 351–364 [based on data collected by Richard Posner in "A Statistical Study of Antitrust Enforcement," *Journal of Law and Economics* 13 (1970): 365–426]).

Siegfried, using different statistical measures, disputed the findings of Long, Schramm, and Tollison. He found that economic variables have little influence on the case-selection process (John J. Siegfried, "The

Determinants of Antitrust Activity," *Journal of Law and Economics* 18 (1975): 559–574.

In another study economist Peter Asch, employing still different statistical techniques, concluded (after surveying Federal Trade Commission and Department of Justice cases) that even statistically significant relationships between industry characteristics and antitrust cases do not indicate that the criteria underlying case selection can be unambiguously inferred. Moreover, "even if clearer inferences could be drawn, it might not be possible to proceed to very specific conclusions about policy effects" (Peter Asch, "The Determinants and Effects of Antitrust Activity," *Journal of Law and Economics* 18 (1975): 575–581).

26
An exception is political scientist Suzanne Weaver's *Decision to Prosecute: Organization and Public Policy in the Antitrust Division* (Cambridge, Mass.: MIT Press, 1977).

27
Albert J. Reiss, Jr., first used the terms "reactive" and "proactive" in describing the operation of police departments. When it responds to citizen requests, for example, the police department may be described as a "reactive organization." When the department intervenes in the lives of citizens on its own initiative, it serves as a "proactive organization." See Albert J. Reiss, Jr., *The Police and the Public* (New Haven: Yale University Press, 1971).

2
The Bureau of Competition: The Lawyers' Unit

"In political government," Richard E. Neustadt has written, "the means can matter quite as much as ends; they often matter more."[1] If organizational structures affect case-load outcomes, then it is necessary to describe the operations of the Bureau of Competition, the unit central to antitrust decision making because it initiates investigations and largely determines the cases upon which the commissioners will eventually have to deliberate. The purpose of this description of the bureau through 1977 is simply to provide the background needed to understand the subsequent chapters, which deal with the factors affecting case-load decisions.

The Key Actors: The Bureau Director and the Assistant Directors

A bureau director is appointed by the FTC chairman, with the approval of at least two other members, to head the Bureau of Competition; he is responsible for supervising a staff of 200 attorneys.[2] With the possible exception of the chairman of the commission, the bureau director has a better opportunity to shape the character of the case load than any other decision maker. His influence stems from his strategic position in the case-selection process and his regular involvement in every important decision.

His authority to decide which matters should be investigated is at the heart of his power. No staff attorney or assistant director can devote resources to an investigation without the approval of the bureau director. While the bureau director usually solicits the advice of the Evaluation Committee (a unit consisting of assistant directors as well as key officials of the Bureau of Economics), he is not bound by its recommendations. "The ultimate decision," former Assistant Director for Evaluation Harry Garfield remarked, "directly or indirectly, is for the bureau director, based on the best advice that he can get from his staff."[3]

The bureau director's influence on the antitrust case load does not end with the decision to open or close an investigation. He can further affect case outcomes by shaping investigations and dictating strategy and tactics to his assistant directors. He can fashion a theory for the case, set deadlines, decide if and when an investigational hearing should be held, determine whether the bureau should seek broad investigational authority from the commissioners, and to some extent censor the work of the bureau staff. With the aid of a computerized case-tracking system the bureau director can monitor the progress of an investigation.

Several assistant directors for litigation report directly to the bureau director in matters concerning case prosecutions. (The bureau director is also aided by an assistant director for evaluation, who is not concerned with directing litigational activities but with managing the case-assessment process.) However extensive his involvement in bureau matters, the bureau director cannot personally supervise every detail of each case. He must rely on his assistant directors for litigation to oversee most of the investigations. Because he needs their cooperation to accomplish his purposes, the bureau director usually takes into account the views of the assistant directors and attempts to anticipate their reactions to his policy pronouncements before making a significant decision.

The ability of the assistant director to affect the course of an investigation stems in part from his access to and control of information that flows through his *shop* of twenty to thirty lawyers. (Every unit handles a variety of matters, although each tends to retain proprietary interests over specific areas—for example, food or energy.) He is the first to read the mailbag complaints that the Evaluation Office forwards to his shop for analysis; he has the right to review all incoming correspondence directed to the staff attorneys; he can examine all documents that the staff lawyers have gathered; he can review letters of inquiry from his staff to firms involved in an investigation; he can edit communications that the staff might direct to the bureau director and the commissioners; and he serves as the intermediary between the bureau hierarchy (principally the bureau director) and the staff, conveying the views and desires of one party to the other.

The assistant director also selects the staff for most cases besides supervising bureau investigations (other than the choice matters the bureau director handles). While the depth of his involvement in a case depends upon his interest in the matter, he almost always reviews the work product of the staff and presides over general strategy sessions. He might offer suggestions with respect to both the substantive and procedural aspects of the case; his advice is typically wide ranging and may have to do with the theoretical foundations of the case, as well as staff strategy and tactics. He may be concerned with the ways in which the staff should deal with the parties involved in the investigation, the timing of subpoenas, the desirability of holding investigational hearings, and the charting of strategy to secure the support of the commissioners. The assistant director also makes sure that deadlines are met.

Quite clearly, the success of an investigation reflects, to a considerable extent, the skill of the assistant director in choosing staff and selecting appropriate strategies. Whether the Bureau of Competition will be able to recommend that a complaint should issue and convince the commissioners of the correctness of its position usually depends in large part upon the evidence that the assistant director and his staff uncover.

The influence of an assistant director, however, extends beyond a particular case. He can fundamentally affect bureau affairs by molding the professional skills and norms of young attorneys. His perspectives are likely to affect the views of the new recruit with respect to such basic concerns as the goals of antitrust enforcement, the kinds of cases that should be pursued, and the desirability of economic input. The breadth of the novice's vision largely depends on how the assistant director exposes him to antitrust matters. Whether the young staff lawyer will become a skillful investigator and litigator is to a significant degree contingent upon the pedagogical abilities of the assistant director and the senior attorneys appointed by the assistant director. How well the assistant director shapes young talent is of utmost importance because the staff attorneys, by dint of their professional norms, skills, and career objectives, can severely limit what the bureau executives can accomplish.

The Office of Evaluation

Many actors participate in Evaluation Committee and Merger Screening Committee meetings at which decisions are made regarding the approval of preliminary or formal investigations; the director of the Bureau of Competition, his assistant directors, the bureau's liaison with the Antitrust Division, the deputy director of the Bureau of Economics, and the assistant director for economic evidence are key members of the cast. The Evaluation Committee handles all matters not related to merger activity—the bailiwick of the Merger Screening Committee. Servicing the evaluation committees is an Office of Evaluation that screens virtually all incoming correspondence and distributes information to bureau executives.

In the period studied, an assistant director for evaluation and four full-time staff attorneys manned the office. The tasks of the assistant director include preparing the budget justification, overseeing resource expenditure, and monitoring the work load. With the aid of his staff, he also drafts comments having to do with proposed and existing legislation and regulations. Moreover, he serves as a liaison with other government agencies involved in antitrust matters. The assistant director also helps the bureau director identify and generate antitrust initiatives for Evaluation Committee and Merger Screening Committee consideration. (It is in this regard that the Evaluation Office staff review complaints charging that the laws have been violated.)

Complaints from outside sources and decisions of the Evaluation Committee to study industries whose profit rates seem unusually high are the sources for the antitrust investigations of the Bureau of Competition. In any given week the Office of Evaluation receives about fifty letters, alleging that an antitrust violation has been committed.[4] These complaints typically come from competitors of the firm or firms accused of illegal conduct, trade journals, financial newspapers, congressmen, public interest groups, concerned citizens, and Washington lawyers who represent the aggrieved parties. Not infrequently, the complainants write directly to the commission chairman or other commissioners. Mailbag correspondence is quickly directed to the Bureau of Competition. An attorney sorts the mail, reads every piece of correspondence, and logs the complaints in a register. The attorney then checks the computerized case-tracking system in order to determine whether a similar kind of matter is presently under investigation within the bureau. As a general rule, all correspondence related to cases under investigation or in litigation are directed to the attention of the attorneys involved in such cases. These attorneys will prepare responses to the complainants for the signature of the assistant director of evaluation.

In many instances, however, the complaints are not related to current cases. Some clearly do not constitute violations of the antitrust laws. These complaints, which comprise most of the mailbag correspondence, are submitted by business competitors, consumer groups, and congressmen. As one Evaluation Office attorney stated: "Mostly we get 'gripe' letters—the parties believe that they have been wronged but aren't quite sure what to do about it. . . . So they write us a letter, assuming that the antitrust laws are the appropriate remedies. But more often than not the complaints . . . prove unfounded." The Office of Evaluation attempts to answer such complaints by explaining why the problem is not covered by the antitrust laws. Congressional inquiries receive immediate and possibly more careful attention, although they usually do not otherwise carry special weight. The assistant director for evaluation is quick to emphasize that his office employs attorneys "skilled in the art of saying 'no' to congressmen." He commented that "to say that Congress never has influence would be foolish. Their influence is sometimes felt at the early stages of the case-selection process, but by and large, we try to be informative, tough but polite."

Often the description of an alleged abuse is vague and the Evaluation Office must ask for more information from the complainant. After more data have been supplied, the Evaluation Office may conclude that evidence of illegal behavior does not exist or that the claims of the complainant—often a competitor of the would-be respondent—are greatly exaggerated.

There are, to be sure, some mailbag complaints that do have merit. Frequently the volume of complaints regarding the same product line or business enterprise is a cue for investigation. The sheer number of complaints does not necessarily mean that a firm has violated the law, but it often indicates to the Evaluation Office that further examination would be appropriate. As has already been noted, if the complaint is related to a pending matter, then it is directed to the attorneys who are charged with investigating the problem. Otherwise an Evaluation Office attorney, at the direction of the assistant director for evaluation, will perform a pre-preliminary investigation. He will spend several hours checking a variety of public sources to get a general knowledge of the product market. He will examine trade journals, for example, in order to learn about the sales volume, profitability rates, concentration ratios, and barriers to entry in the industry of which the accused firm is a part. Should the attorney conclude that a reasonable possibility of anticompetitive conduct exists (as revealed, perhaps, by unusually high concentration ratios and the excessive profits of the firm), then he will write a memorandum to the assistant director and recommend that greater resources be devoted to an investigation of the possible violation. If the assistant director agrees with the attorney's assessment, he will probably place the matter on the next Evaluation Committee agenda, so that the bureau director and other agency officials can decide whether a more in-depth inquiry is warranted.

The Evaluation Office handles merger cases separately from other kinds of antitrust matters. A small unit of economists in the Bureau of Economics are attached to the Evaluation Office and the Merger Screening Committee, and they gather information about possible merger cases. Raw data are usually culled from the *Wall Street Journal,* Standard Corporation Reports, the Standard Industrial Classification system (SIC), *Moody's,* and *Standard and Poors.* By the time that law firms representing competitors of firms that plan to unite contact the commission about the impending merger, the merger screening unit has usually already uncovered the information from the standard sources.

When firms do contact the Federal Trade Commission, they are asked to provide basic data about both the acquiring and the acquired companies: the nature of the product lines, the degree of concentration in the industry, the market share of the companies involved in the merger, net income, total assets, and the rate of return on the stockholder's equity. When the commission learns of a proposed merger from a public source, like a trade journal, the merger screening unit obtains the necessary data by dispatching an economist to the library for several hours of research. He will list all pertinent data on a Merger Information Sheet.

In certain situations the commission is automatically notified of an impending merger by the acquiring and acquired firms. According to the Pre-Merger Notification Program, acquiring companies with sales or assets of $100 million or more and acquired companies of $10 million or more are required to inform the commission of the impending merger at least thirty days before it is consummated.[5] When the merger screening unit receives notice of the merger, it sends a Special Report form to the companies for basic data about the merger.

While the merger screening unit is aware of virtually all mergers, it does not scrutinize every transaction. As a general rule, the commission will not devote its resources to a merger that does not meet a minimum (undisclosed) figure for industry. Because most transactions do not reach this figure, the work load of the merger screening unit is not burdensome. Every week the economist who heads the merger study unit compiles the Merger Information Sheets, Special Report forms, and other relevant data that are distributed to the members of the Merger Screening Committee.

Once the Evaluation Office has completed its preparatory work in merger and other kinds of antitrust cases, the two decision-making bodies it serves—the Evaluation Committee and the Merger Screening Committee—are ready to deliberate.

The Merger Screening Committee

The Merger Screening Committee handles merger matters exclusively and consists of the director of the Bureau of Competition, the assistant director for evaluation, a staff attorney with experience in merger affairs, the assistant director for economic evidence, and the economists of the Merger Screening Unit. Because mergers involve economic factors, attorneys readily accept, and rely upon, the participation of the Bureau of Economics in deliberations having to do with section 7 of the Clayton Act.

As in other types of matters, bureau decision makers must determine whether there is reason to believe that the law has been violated and whether commission action would be in the public interest. For those mergers that are investigated the lawyers and economists examine certain standard economic features. The decision makers define the relevant product and geographic markets. (The former may consist of one or a number of products or services supplied by either the acquired or acquiring firm, while the latter is determined by ascertaining the area in which the acquired and acquiring companies operate.) Then they focus upon the proportion of the relevant market held by the companies, the trend of the industry toward concentration, the existence of entry barriers, and the economic size and strength of the acquiring company with respect to the particular market under study. If the merger would probably create impenetrable barriers to entry, then the economists and lawyers will recommend a formal investigation or the issuance of a complaint. The evaluation criteria will vary with the type of merger—vertical, horizontal, product extension, or market extension.

The Evaluation Committee

The bureau director, the deputy bureau director,[6] and the assistant directors (or their surrogates) represent the Bureau of Competition at Evaluation Committee meetings; the deputy bureau director, the assistant director for economic evidence, and a few staff economists, who participate at the meetings on a rotational basis, represent the Bureau of Economics. The meeting opens with a presentation by an Evaluation Office attorney of a summary of the matters on the agenda. The attorney attempts to highlight the salient issues that the Evaluation Committee will have to weigh. The Evaluation Office or the assistant directors for litigation (through their staff lawyers) have already undertaken a pre-preliminary investigation of the matters on the agenda and decided that the bureau should consider whether to devote more resources to an inquiry to determine if there is "reason to believe" that the law has been violated.

In theory the officials at the meeting should already be familiar with the topics for discussion, since the Evaluation Office sent them all relevant information on the previous day. However, the assistant directors seldom have the time to study carefully the items on the agenda, except for those that relate to their shops, and they usually take their cues from the director of the Bureau of Competition, who is briefed on all matters by his personal staff. The assistant director for economic evidence and the deputy bureau director of the Bureau of Economics make a special effort to examine all matters that will be discussed at Evaluation Committee deliberations.

The tenor of the meeting reflects in large measure the personality of the bureau director of competition. In its history the bureau has been guided by directors who have encouraged the participation of their assistant directors at Evaluation Committee meetings and have been influenced by their views. (Influence, of course, may be reciprocal. Some assistant directors, who would like the bureau director to charge them with supervising the prosecution of attractive cases, attempt to anticipate the positions of the bureau director. At the Evaluation Committee meetings, these assistant directors will support those cases that they believe the bureau director will favor.) Other bureau directors, however, have singly decided the position of the Bureau of Competition, and have not valued the input from the assistant directors. Under such "boss-slave" regimes (the description of an assistant director), the Evaluation Committee meetings are essentially bargaining and strategy sessions in which the bureau director of competition and the assistant director for Economic Evidence of the Bureau of Economics are the main participants. While the assistant directors for litigation might state their positions, they do not determine the course the Bureau of Competition will pursue.

At the Evaluation Committee meetings the topics of discussion are varied: whether to open a preliminary or formal investigation, whether to ask the commissioners to grant compulsory process or approve an industrywide investigation, or how to respond to a letter from an influential congressman. Preliminary investigations are "short, informal inquiries, conducted to dispose of relatively minor matters and to determine whether formal 7-digit investigations should be initiated."[7] Such investigations are opened only when it is necessary to "go beyond the original public complaint or other sources for the purposes of securing information," and the matter appears to "involve both a possible violation of Commission-enforced law and sufficient relative public interest to warrant the expected time and expense of pursuing it."[8] Preliminary investigations will be initiated "when and only when" research and investigative efforts conducted with regard to such circumstances are expected to exceed an aggregate of sixteen man-hours (or two man-days).[9]

The bureau director may approve the opening of the preliminary investigation only after consultation with officials of the Antitrust Division of the Department of Justice. This consultation between the two agencies is designed to ensure that the commission and the Antitrust Division do not duplicate each other's work. Once initiated, a preliminary investigation should be completed "as early as possible in favor of the opening of a formal investigation."[10] The bureau is to close a preliminary investigation when corrective action is unnecessary or impossible, the apparent violation was minor and has been corrected, or when the matter has been transferred to a local or another federal authority.

Formal investigations (also known as *7-digit investigations* because their file numbers have seven digits) are comprehensive inquiries into possible violations of the laws that the commission is charged with enforcing. These investigations involve a greater expenditure of commission resources. In addition, the authorization of a formal investigation is a procedural prerequisite for the commissioners to grant Bureau of Competition requests for the use of compulsory process, special investigatory reports (known as *6(b) reports*), subpoenas, and investigational resolutions.

Once the Evaluation Committee has discussed matters relating to the authorization of a formal investigation, its work essentially ends. If an investigation is launched, it proceeds until some determination is made as to whether the Bureau of Competition should recommend that the commissioners issue a complaint. The bureau director might decide to close an investigation before its completion because he perceives that it is unlikely that the attorneys will be able to construct an argument that would justify a complaint recommendation; or at the conclusion of an investigation the bureau director might decide not to urge the commissioners to prosecute. However, because the Bureau of Competition carefully scrutinizes proposals for preliminary and formal investigations before approving the allocation of resources to such inquiries, the bureau director seldom decides not to recommend the issuance of a complaint.

While the *Operating Manual of the Federal Trade Commission* provides a general idea of what constitutes preliminary and formal investigations, it gives little guidance in choosing matters for investigation. The types of matters that are selected as subjects of preliminary or formal investigations are left to the discretion of the director of the Bureau of Competition, in consultation with the other participants in the Evaluation Committee sessions. Former Assistant Director for Evaluation Harry Garfield noted "that no formal criteria for evaluation exists within the Commission."[11] The succeeding chapters explore the factors affecting case-selection decisions.

Notes

1
Richard E. Neustadt, *Presidential Power: The Politics of Leadership* (New York: John Wiley and Sons, 1960), p. 47. See Graham Allison, *Essence of Decision: Explaining the Cuban Missile Crisis* (Boston: Little, Brown and Company, 1971), chs. 3 and 5.

2
Information supplied by Harry Jordan, administrative officer of the FTC, January 1978.

3
Statement of Harry Garfield, U.S., Congress, House, Committee on Small Business, Ad Hoc Subcommittee on Antitrust, the Robinson-Patman Act and Related Matters, *Recent Efforts to Amend or Repeal the Robinson-Patman Act*, part 2, 94th Cong., 1st sess., 1975, p. 160.

4
See statement of Daniel Schwartz, U.S. Congress, House, Committee on Small Business, Ad Hoc Subcommittee on Antitrust, the Robinson-Patman Act and Related Matters, *Recent Efforts to Amend or Repeal the Robinson-Patman Act*, part 3, 94th Cong., 2nd sess., 1976, p. 8. In calendar year 1975, the Bureau of Competition received 2,069 complaints.

5
The Hart-Scott-Rodino Antitrust Improvements Act of 1976 (PL 94–435), 15 U.S.C. 1311, Title II, formally institutionalized the commission's premerger notification procedures, which had been in existence for some time.

6
The deputy bureau director during the period studied performed the same tasks as the assistant directors, and therefore, it is not necessary to examine his role separately.

7
Operating Manual of the Federal Trade Commission (1975), ch. 1, p. 8.

8
Ibid.

9
Ibid. ch. 2, p. 1.

10
Operating Manual, ch. 2, p. 1.

11
Garfield, *Recent Efforts to Amend or Repeal the Robinson-Patman Act*, p. 161.

3
Policy Choices: The Reactive and the Proactive Approaches

Because the commission does not have unlimited resources, the Bureau of Competition cannot pursue every apparent infraction; bureau executives must choose among cases. In recommending the issuance of a complaint, they are required by commission law not only to find that "there is reason to believe" that the law has been violated but also that action would be in the "public interest." There has been much discussion among commission officials and other interested parties as to what kinds of antitrust policies would be in the public interest—a term that, because it is vague, does not mandate that the agency pursue any particular course. In the view of public interest groups the commission should devote more of its resources to structural attacks on oligopolies and shared monopolies. However, others (large corporations, for example) believe that such a policy emphasis could injure the economy. In determining what constitutes action in the public interest, commission officials, quite clearly, are not merely interpreting some abstract provision of law but are setting a course with important implications for public policy.

Debate within the commission about types of public interest cases has focused on two different conceptions of antitrust policy: a reactive and a proactive approach. The *reactive approach* relies upon the mailbag as the source of investigations, supports strict enforcement of the laws, and tends to yield conduct cases. Proponents of the *proactive approach* argue that the Bureau of Competition should not only react to the complaints that are directed to the commission but also plan its prosecutorial efforts; the bureau should assume the initiative and use its scarce resources selectively to attack abuses in those sectors of the economy that most affect the consumer. The proactive perspective frequently leads to a caseload of ambitious and innovative structural matters that seek to eliminate market power. The consequences of each approach in terms of commission policy differ quite dramatically, and I think it would be fruitful to examine each one in depth.[1]

The Reactive Approach

The reactive approach maintains that the Bureau of Competition should pursue virtually every apparent violation of the law that is reported to its attorneys, no matter how minor the infraction might seem. This strict-law-enforcement-view holds that a decision not to investigate, when there is some indication that a violation has been committed, is nothing less than an abdication of responsibility. It is a signal to business that the law need not be obeyed because there is little chance that (in a phrase often heard in the bureau) "the commission will slap wrists." The criterion to be followed in choosing cases should be legal precedent, not economic argument. In discharging his tasks the attorney should be guided by legal doctrine, because "cases are won in courts of law, not at meetings of the American Economic Association."

Advocates of the reactive approach contend that dependence on the mailbag has distinct advantages. The mailbag generally produces conduct cases, which are usually easier to prosecute than complex structural matters. Conduct prosecutions focus upon the behavior of the firms and not on the underlying conditions that promote such activity. Thus, all that is essentially needed in court is evidence that the defendants actually engaged in the prohibited acts (for example, pricefixing, tying contracts). A structural case of the proactive kind is far more difficult, so its detractors argue, because it is concerned less with the acts themselves than with the fundamental economic imperfections (for instance, an anticompetitive market structure on the buying side, the selling side, or both) of which the various aspects of business conduct are merely symptoms. Generally, a conduct case, as one attorney noted,

is more cut and dry. You just have to be concerned with the barest economic data. . . . We can be fairly certain that it will "go" in court, because we're following established criteria, laid down by judges. Structural cases [often] involve complicated economic arguments, which have not been swallowed whole by the courts. Consequently, with a structural case . . . you're always on pins and needles, worrying that the court may not buy your argument.

The proponents of the reactive approach deny that little consumer benefit results from conduct cases, which concern business practices rather than market structure. The lines of causality do not always run from structure to conduct to performance, they are quick to argue; there are many situations in which the line of causation is the reverse—from conduct back to structure. For example, predatory or exclusionary practices and merger activity could conceivably change the structure of an industry by transforming a competitive structure into a monopolistic or oligopolistic structure. Thus, by attacking conduct violations the commission could preserve structural competition. It should be noted, however, that the defenders of conduct cases seldom stress the potential economic benefits resulting from the prosecution of such matters. For them, the antitrust statutes are concerned primarily with achieving fairness in the market place and not consumer benefit. Not surprisingly many reactive approach supporters are vigorous advocates of those sections of the Robinson-Patman Act that seek to maintain small business firms.

Proponents of the reactive approach reject the claim that the commission does not have the resources to prosecute every violation. They do not feel that it is necessary or advisable for the Bureau of Competition to concentrate its efforts on a few ambitious structural cases. They contend that even if big structural cases do yield substantial consumer benefit, as proactive approach supporters maintain, it cannot be denied that such cases are difficult to prosecute: they are technically complex and uncertain of success (most innovative structural cases involve legal theories that have yet to be tested in the judiciary). Attorneys, who are convinced that their advancement depends on the securing of trial experience, resist assignment to structural matters, which generally do not reach the courtroom for several years. Those attorneys who are chosen for such cases quickly become disillusioned and try to disengage themselves from the case. As a result, the turnover rate among attorneys on these cases is very high.

A striking example of the problems of prosecuting complex structural cases is the *Exxon* matter. Heralded by the commission as the nation's most significant antitrust matter, the *Exxon* litigation charged the eight largest oil companies with having limited and weakened competition at all levels of the petroleum industry by monopolizing refining. The commission left open the possibility that it would seek a drastic restructuring of the petroleum industry. There have been serious obstacles, however, to prosecuting the case. Since the filing of the case on 18 July 1973, forty attorneys have been assigned (as of 1 March 1976) to work part- or full-time on the *Exxon* matter.[2] Of the original staff, only one attorney remained on the case, and only four others were still working in the Bureau of Competition. The average period of involvement of the attorneys assigned to the case was approximately twelve months. Critics of the big case argue that the commission cannot expect to succeed if the coherence and continuity of an investigation are undermined by a a high turnover rate.

Moreover, the proponents of the reactive approach are not that confident that economic benefits will flow from mammoth structural cases. By the time a case is finally resolved, they claim, market conditions in the particular industry may have changed so dramatically as to render the original remedy inappropriate. In short, the commission may spend years and millions of dollars without achieving substantial results. (The *Exxon* case, for example, consumes between 12 and 14 percent of the budget each year but may not be concluded in the foreseeable future.)[3]

For reasons similar to those advanced in opposition to the big structural cases, the defenders of mailbag conduct matters are critical of the commission's industrywide investigations. The source of such inquiries is the consumer price index and other consumer surveys, the targets for investigation are highly-concentrated industries, and the scope is wide. (The commission will delve into the practices of numerous firms at all levels of operation.) Even firms that have not been the object of consumer and business complaints will be investigated, if their market shares and profitability are unusually high.

Presumably, the industrywide approach, which is supported by the proponents of the proactive perspective, is a rational way of determining how to allocate resources. Supporters of the reactive approach charge, however, that such efforts are fraught with problems. There is a tendency in industrywide investigations, so the argument proceeds, to "go on fishing expeditions" in order to uncover violations that will justify the substantial resources devoted to such inquiries. Since Congress (the source of the agency's funding) is thought to measure commission performance in antitrust enforcement largely in terms of the number of cases and investigations that are underway, bureau officials may feel pressure to manufacture cases. Industrywide investigations pose special risks, because they are announced with great fanfare. As one Bureau of Competition official noted:

Once you announce that there is going to be a big industrywide investigation into the food industry, for example, then everyone will be looking to see how many cases having to do with the food industry result from the investigation. You can't come up short—then Congress will say that you've failed. So, you have to squeeze cases of dubious value out of the investigation. On the other hand, if you concentrate on mailbag cases and just investigate whatever comes up, then there is no special pressure to come up with a case. No one in Congress knows what's in the mailbag, so you can open and close at will.[4]

Industrywide investigations also have many of the same problems as big structural cases—staffing (young attorneys do not like to be assigned to protracted investigations that may not reach trial), technical complexity (it is often a lengthy and difficult process to secure and interpret complex economic variables), and uncertainty of result (both in terms of judicial success and economic benefit).

The Proactive Perspective

Only a minority of Bureau of Competition executives favor the reactive approach. Most, including the director, maintain that attention must be given to the planning and evaluation of antitrust efforts. As one official stated:

We simply do not have the resources to fully investigate every possible violation of the law which we learn about. Accordingly, we must constantly make hard choices among alternatives in order to maximize the effect of our enforcement activity. We try to select cases which will result in maximum benefit to consumers and to the competitive process in relation to the enforcement dollars invested. We also attempt to select cases which will have maximum deterrent effect.[5]

Advocates of planning in antitrust enforcement are critical of a reactive ad hoc approach, because they believe it wastes commission resources. As a result of devotion to the mailbag and the absence of planning, the Bureau of Restraint of Trade (as the commission's antitrust arm was known before it was reconstituted in the 1970 reorganization as the Bureau of Competition) tended to bring trivial cases.[6] Moreover, the commission devoted much time to investigations of generally competitive sectors, since mailbag complaints often emanate from businessmen in such industries. In order to create a balance among the various kinds of antitrust matters, Bureau of Competition officials created an evaluation committee case-selection process in 1972. As former Assistant Director for Evaluation Harry Garfield stated:

The purpose of the evaluation process is not to permit the individual participants to select cases by applying their own personal biases. Quite the opposite. The trouble in the old days was that case openings were effectively determined by individuals who promptly clogged the pipeline with their own choices.[7]

Proponents of the proactive approach do not suggest that the mailbag should be ignored; the bureau should closely monitor the mailbag and use it as an early warning system, an indicator of possible problem areas. Some reactive cases are valuable because, as a former bureau director noted:

It is important for a law enforcement agency to maintain an element of unpredictability as to what cases it will bring. Particularly since our budget is not large enough to permit us to challenge every violation brought to our attention, the deterrent effect of the Commission's presence would be lost unless some uncertainty existed as to what violations would be prosecuted.[8]

An enforcement effort, however, that reacts only to specific problems flowing from the mailbag and fails to develop broad enforcement plans, the bureau director continued, can only be ineffective. In short, what is needed, the supporters of the proactive approach believe, is a balance between conduct and structural cases.

Advocates of antitrust planning assume that conduct cases usually have less value to the consumer than do structural prosecutions. Though certain business practices are unfair and illegal, they are incapable of altering the structural composition of the industry, since they are the products and not the causes of market imperfections that lead to anticompetitive behavior. While the bureau would probably succeed in halting the particular practice, its actions would not deal with the real source of competitive problems (market or financial power) and thus would probably not restore competition. It may be necessary to analyze the source of power that allows predatory and unfair practices to continue.[9] For having undertaken a structural examination, the staff attorneys may then be able to fashion relief that attacks market power at its source.

Supporters of the proactive perspective freely admit that big structural cases and industrywide investigations are much more difficult to prosecute than are most conduct violations; many of these cases raise new legal questions and deliberately seek to blaze untrodden paths. It may very well be true that the Bureau of Competition will be denied victory, yet the need to attempt such cases is strongly felt among many of the bureau executives. Whether the courts or the commissioners will accept their arguments will never be known unless such cases are attempted, they explain. The outside observer frequently hears that "the problem with antitrust enforcement is that it has never been tried in a big way."

An analysis of the case load of the Federal Trade Commission indicates that the agency has decided to devote more of its resources to what are essentially planned efforts. In fiscal 1978, for instance, the commission allocated 59 percent of its antitrust resources to programs concerned with the energy, transportation, health care, food, and chemical industries.[10] Reactive cases—especially of the Robinson-Patman variety—command far less attention from the commission than they did a decade ago. Why the commission, given its apparent discretion, does not devote all of its resources to proactive investigations is not immediately obvious; why the agency still chooses to bring other kinds of cases (at least through the regime of Calvin Collier) despite the stated economic objectives of its policy, is not clear.

The following chapters explain the factors, connected with the case-selection process, that affect the way in which resources are allocated between proactive and reactive cases. The character of the case load—the kinds of actions undertaken—can in some sense be understood as a reflection of the views expressed in the debate between advocates of the two approaches to antitrust enforcement.

Notes

1
As has been noted previously (ch. 1, n. 27), the terms "proactive" and "reactive" were first used by Albert J. Reiss, Jr., in his *The Police and the Public* (New Haven: Yale University Press, 1971). These terms provide useful handles for grasping two kinds of mentalities, or styles, of decision making. I do not mean, however, to apply them too tightly or to imply that they represent pure types. The proactive approach involves planning and generally yields structural vehicles (for example, oligopoly cases) designed to attack market power. Nevertheless, not all structural matters —for example, standard merger cases that the commission has prosecuted for years—are the products of the proactive approach (that is, involve extensive planning, cost/benefit analysis, etc.).

Generally speaking, when the term "structural" is used in connection with the proactive approach, I am referring to the mammoth, innovative investigations (for instance, *Exxon* or the cereal case). Moreover, it should be noted that in the course of an investigation of the proactive type attorneys may uncover apparent conduct violations which they may pursue.

Finally, although conduct cases that are the products of the reactive approach generally do not have economic ends, their prosecution sometimes benefits consumers.

2
U.S., Congress, House, Committee on Foreign and Interstate Commerce, Subcommittee on Oversight and Investigations, *Hearings on Regulatory Reform*, vol. 4, 94th Cong., 2nd sess., 1976, p. 625.

3
U.S., Congress, Senate, Committee on Appropriations, *Hearings on Department of State, Justice and Related Agencies, Appropriations, F.Y. 1978*, part 3, 95th Cong. 1st sess., 1977, p. 344.

4
When a public agency announces its plans, it may not only heighten the expectations of its supporters but also invite the opposition of those who seek to thwart the agency. See Edward C. Banfield, "Ends and Means in Planning," in *Concepts and Issues in Administrative Behavior,* ed. Sidney Mailick and E. Van Ness (Englewood Cliffs, N.J.: Prentice-Hall, 1962), pp. 70–80.

5
James T. Halverson, "F.T.C. and the Food Industries—1974's Major Antitrust Emphasis" (Paper delivered at the Eighth Annual Antitrust Institute of the Ohio State Bar Association, Antitrust Law Section, Columbus, Ohio, 18 October 1974), p. 1.
6
Report of the American Bar Association Commission to Study the Federal Trade Commission (1969), pp. 15, 77. For earlier criticisms of a similar nature, see Gerard Henderson, The Federal Trade Commission: A Study in Administrative Law and Procedure (New Haven: Yale University Press, 1924), and Gerald Auerbach, "The Federal Trade Commission," Minnesota Law Review 48 (1964): 393.
7
Statement of Harry Garfield, U.S. Congress House, Committee on Small Business, Ad Hoc Subcommittee on Antitrust, the Robinson-Patman Act and Related Matters, Hearings on Recent Efforts to Amend or Repeal the Robinson-Patman Act, part 2, 94th Cong., 1st sess., 1975, p. 160.
8
Halverson, "F.T.C. and the Food Industries," p. 3.
9
Carl Kaysen and Donald Turner, Antitrust Policy: An Economic and Legal Analysis (Cambridge, Mass.: Harvard University Press, 1959), p. 17.
10
U.S., Congress, Senate, Committee on Appropriations, Hearings on Departments of State, Justice and Commerce, the Judiciary and Related Agencies, Appropriations, 1978, Justifications, part 3, 95th Cong., 1st sess., 1977, p. 339.

4
Professional Economists and the Case Load:
The Impact of the Bureau of Economics

To open an investigation or recommend that the commissioners issue a complaint, the director of the Bureau of Competition needs only to decide whether there is reason to believe that the law has been violated and commission action would be in the public interest. In reaching his decision, however, he does consider other factors, such as the reaction of the Bureau of Economics to his bureau's recommendation. That the policy preferences of the Bureau of Economics should affect case-load choices may at first glance seem surprising. Neither the *Operating Manual* (at least during the period studied) nor the *Rules and Practices of the Commission* defined a formal role for the Bureau of Economics in the case-selection process; no organization chart mentioned an Evaluation Committee, the forum at which representatives of the Bureau of Economics participate in the case-selection process.

An examination of the interaction between lawyers and economists shows how professionalism can affect policy choices; the antitrust case load in a sense represents the outcome of often intense competition between lawyers and economists whose different norms, goals, and training lead to disputes about the kind of antitrust policy that the FTC should pursue. That a unit of economists dedicated to preventing "wasteful" cases should thrive in an agency of lawyers determined to prosecute seems curious; few organizations can operate effectively, if competing norms exist, threatening morale, mission, and a sense of distinctive competence.[1]

In discussing the role of the Bureau of Economics in antitrust affairs, this chapter describes the operations of the Division of Economic Evidence, examines the ways in which the economists conceive of their tasks, explains how and why economists and lawyers differ in their interpretation of data, devotes attention to the ways in which the Bureau of Competition attorneys perceive the economists, and assesses the effect of the economists on case-selection decisions.

The Division of Economic Evidence and the Case-Selection Process: An Overview

The Bureau of Economics advises the commission on broad policy questions, concerning suspect business practices and relationships, the evaluation of proposed remedies, and the formulation of legislative recommendations. The Division of Economic Evidence of the Bureau of Economics has a number of opportunities to intervene in the case-selection process. When the director of the Bureau of Competition is deciding whether to open an investigation, he will seek the judgment of the assistant director for economic evidence of the Bureau of Economics; during the course of an investigation, economists, upon the request of the Bureau of Competition, will work with the attorneys; and when the Bureau of Competition has completed its investigation and makes its recommendation to the commissioners, the economists can set forth their own views on the lawyers' position.

The assistant director for the Division of Economic Evidence is the key member of the Bureau of Economics in the case-selection process. Though formally under the direction of the director and the deputy director of the Bureau of Economics, he is "responsible for *all* economic work of the Commission relating to legal cases involving unlawful corporate mergers and other violations."[2] In addition, he "exercises wide discretion in planning, organizing and directing the economic investigation and analysis of legal cases."[3] He also controls the assignments of cases to the division's forty staff members, guides the staff on matters of policy and economic strategy, and scrutinizes the staff's reports and recommendations in order to ensure that they are consistent with agency policy. He is also responsible for training the division staff, evaluating their performance, and recommending promotions. Finally, as the bureau's spokesman and decision maker in antitrust matters, the assistant director for the Division of Economic Evidence is in frequent contact with the director of the Bureau of Competition.

The economists, under the assistant director, can be divided into two groups: those who entered the commission before the 1970 reorganization (which lead to major changes in agency operations discussed in Chapter 8) and those who have joined in the succeeding years, when the Bureau of Economics' impact on case-load decisions increased substantially. (In 1977, only six out of the forty economists in the division belonged to the first group.)

Almost without exception, those who joined the commission shortly after the end of World War II, did so because they could not find comparable financial security and opportunities for advancement in the private sector; lacking Ph.D.s in economics, the economists did not seek careers in academia. They had little difficulty, however, in securing employment with the agency, because the commission of the period did not set rigid standards for appointment. Although they had no particular interest in antitrust matters they soon found the work to be interesting, because it dealt with a wide range of manufacturing industries. Uncertain at the outset about an agency career, these economists are content to be still with the commission.

The economists who joined the commission after the 1970 reorganization, a period when funding for the Bureau of Economics substantially increased, are better educated than their more senior colleagues. The superior credentials of these economists reflect the concerted efforts of Bureau of Economic officials to attract well-educated economists. (In the 1969 report of the American Bar Association (ABA) commission, the quality of economic input came under attack.) Nearly all of the more recent economists in the FTC have passed their Ph.D. preliminary examinations,[4] and about half have completed their dissertations. With only a few exceptions, these economists stated that they did not originally intend to work for the government upon completion of their graduate school courses. Their ambition was to become college professors, but the prospects of academic careers dimmed with the tightening job market. To be sure, there were some economists who were disenchanted with academic life or simply desired some government experience. For these persons a commission post was a welcome opportunity and not a last resort. For the most part, however, the Division of Economic Evidence economist is on the government payroll because he was unable to secure an attractive academic position.

In most instances Bureau of Economics officials recruited the staff economists at professional gatherings (for example, meetings of the American Economic Association). Most of the staff attended institutions that are generally described as satellites of the University of Chicago, a school whose economists tend to have a deep faith in an unfettered market. All are well trained in microeconomics. Bureau of Economics executives prefer candidates who have mastered some facet of industrial organization and/or whose specialties are related to FTC activities (for example, in the health or energy fields). They seek economists who are good technicians and sophisticated analysts. Since they interact with the attorneys, economists must also demonstrate oral proficiency.

Although most of the recent recruits were orginally uncertain about their future in government service, few regret having joined the Bureau of Economics. The material benefits the agency provides are far superior to those of academia. The typical staff economist has remained with the Bureau of Economics because it satisfies many of his professional interests. (However, as other government organizations—for example, the Congressional Budget Office, regulatory agencies, cabinet departments—upgrade their units of economic analysis and provide benefits similar to those the commission offers, the attraction that the Bureau of Economics holds for economists could very well diminish. The existence of other employment choices could also lead to an increased turnover rate within the Division of Economic Evidence.)

For the economist who sought a university life, the Division of Economic Evidence's think-tank environment provides an atmosphere that is conducive to scholarly pursuits. One economist expressed it well when he said,

Why shouldn't we be happy? This bureau has a greater number of industrial organization economists than any other establishment in the country. . . . We're assigned to such a wide variety of matters that we have a chance to become experts in areas that we might not have ordinarily studied. We're also graced by the presence of some of the country's leading microeconomists—people like Mike Scherer.

The assistant director for economic evidence has successfully maintained a high level of morale by fostering an environment that stresses professional competence. He encourages the economists to think of themselves as independent decision makers

rather than subordinates of the attorneys. "Attorneys and economists are each housed in separate buildings about a mile and a half
apart, and that's the way we want it," commented one economist.

At whatever point they are involved in the decision-making
process, the economists who participate in case-selection matters
believe that it is the responsibility of their unit to render advice
based on economic principles.[5] In short, it is their task to determine whether the business behavior under scrutiny is anticompetitive. If the economists conclude that such behavior
results in a misallocation of resources, then the Bureau of Economics will recommend, depending on the stage the matter has
reached, that a preliminary or formal investigation be approved or
a complaint be issued. What the law states, the assistant director
and deputy director of the Bureau of Economics claim, should be
of no concern to the Division of Economic Evidence.

The economists insist that they will not perform any task that
would place them under the direction of the attorneys. With the
exception of a few veterans, the staff economists expressed their
unwillingness to undertake the same kinds of investigative tasks
the attorneys perform—fact-finding, data gathering, and the reviewing of company records. "We're not staff support for the
attorney and we're not hired to draw up statistical tables,"
declared an economist. In rejecting the attorneys' position that
the Division of Economic Evidence should aid the lawyers in
proving cases, one representative economist commented:

I'm a professional economist, which means that I'm a dispassionate searcher for truth. Professional integrity demands that
I analyze data, free of bias. The attorney, on the other hand, wants
to find data, which support his case. Were I to aid him in finding
data for his purposes, I would no longer be a dispassionate social
scientist.

Economists are willing to participate in investigations if they are
given the freedom to chart their own course and preserve their
sense of autonomy. For example, many economists are willing to
formulate questions that will be asked of industry officials at
investigational hearings and to help compose 6(b) questionnaires,
which frequently deal with complex economic matters. Economists often find it necessary to become involved in commission

investigations, because they do not have enough information about the industry or because a deeper understanding of the industry under investigation could aid the economist in designing and evaluating appropriate remedial measures. Since unsound relief can impose severe costs upon society (just as adequate relief can produce substantial benefits), economists are particularly interested in developing antitrust remedies. In some recent significant cases the economists played a primary role in constructing antitrust relief.

Very likely, the Division of Economic Evidence would have difficulty retaining many of its academically oriented economists if the bureau executives did not provide an environment that fosters standards of professional integrity and independence. Were the economists to become merely staff support of the attorneys, then the Division of Economic Evidence might no longer be so attractive to those persons who sought employment with the Bureau of Economics because of its reputation for promoting scholarly economic research.

The assistant director for economic evidence also has had little difficulty in maintaining morale, because many of the economists in the division—those who have joined the commission since its revitalization—are convinced that without their presence the agency would engage in what they perceive to be a dangerous and relentless assault on American business. (The more senior colleagues have greater sympathy for a governmental role in solving social and economic problems.) "We are saviors of the free market, contending against forces bent on governmental intervention," exclaimed one typical young economist.

Division of Economic Evidence staffers believe they must prevent attorneys from interfering with the market. In the words of one economist: "The Federal Trade Commission is really a lawyer's agency. . . . The thrust, therefore, is towards bringing cases. It is our job to apply the brakes to such activity; to say, 'Hey, you're bringing a case just for the sake of bringing it. Let's look at the economic benefit to the consumer.' " For the economists, there is nothing more gratifying than to oppose the Bureau of Competition successfully at the commission table. (The conservative cast of the Division of Economic Evidence may change:

Chairman Michael Pertschuk, who took office in 1977, has criticized recent commissions for uncritically accepting the positions of the "Chicago school." How his views will affect recruitment remains to be seen.)

The Policy Preferences of the Economists in Antitrust Enforcement

The economists are opposed to most conduct cases principally because there is often little benefit to the consumer gained from the prosecution of such matters. In general they disapprove of Bureau of Competition efforts, which are directed against vertical and conglomerate mergers, franchise arrangements, tying requirements, and price discrimination cases (Robinson-Patman matters), because such actions do little to maintain vigorous competition. Economists particularly dislike Robinson-Patman Act matters, while attorneys who support the reactive approach favor them because of the ease with which they can be prosecuted. "You could put all pro-Robinson-Patman economists in a Volkswagen," commented a Bureau of Economics official, "and still have room for a chauffeur." The Bureau of Economics' opposition to such matters was perhaps best explained by Bureau Director Frederic M. Scherer:

Most economists believe that long-run viability of competition is not enhanced by preserving or protecting individual competitors whose operations are inefficient and whose costs therefore are so high that they continue to exist only at the sufferance of the industry's more efficient members. . . .
The facts are often obscure, and how one comes out in a particular complex factual situation is likely to be influenced by how sanguine one is about the likelihood that vigorous competition will in fact survive the exit of competitors. A typical economists's study of numerous industrial histories is apt to induce somewhat more optimism on such matters than that which the drafters of the Robinson-Patman Act . . . manifested. . . . Our biases in this respect are freely acknowledged by us and well known to the Commission.[6]

Given the limited resources of the FTC, the executives of the Bureau of Economics believe that energies should be devoted to those cases that will most benefit consumers. Although a supporter of the structural case and a proactive approach to enforcement activity, the assistant director for economic evidence was quick to emphasize that there are few areas of the economy that merit commission attention. Along with most of his staff, he stated that he was unsympathetic to the notion that government solutions to social and economic problems are more effective than market mechanisms. While he conceded that vigorous antitrust activity is sometimes necessary (in the health care industry, for example), he argued that for the most part antitrust action can only make a marginal contribution. Antitrust enforcement is useful, he claimed, in that it probably appeases some individuals who would otherwise demand greater state regulation (and perhaps ownership) of private enterprise. He warned however that misplaced antitrust activity could harm the economy by interfering with market processes and by harassing businessmen, who "are simply responding in a rational way to their environment."

Economist and Lawyer: Differences in Data Interpretation

For their part, the attorneys in the Bureau of Competition contend that the opposition of the Bureau of Economics to their cases is often unfounded. Certainly, the reluctance of many staff economists to participate in Bureau of Competition investigations casts doubt upon their claims of dispassionateness and objectivity.[7] Several attorneys recounted cases in which intensive fact-finding efforts revealed that the economists had drawn groundless conclusions. A seasoned attorney offered an illustration:

Some years ago, we looked at the plywood industry and saw that a few firms had a very substantial share of the market. At about that time, a new process was developed which facilitated the conversion of southern pine wood into plywood. . . . Generally speaking, it seemed as if anyone who wanted to make plywood and could bear the relatively small capital costs [needed to build factories] would be able to enter the market. The economists argued that because of the seeming availability of the southern pine and of the new conversion process, entry barriers were low. . . . Therefore, they said we shouldn't bring a case. I took a few lawyers on an investigation to make sure. . . . We did a lot of digging. . . . We found that much of the southern pine was not suited for the conversion process, and more importantly, that most pine was already committed to lumber and paper. . . . It was clear that we had a case, even if the economists refused to look at the evidence.

Even when they do carefully analyze the data the attorneys have collected, the economists tend to interpret the information in a manner that argues against government action. In other words, the attorneys and economists draw opposite conclusions from the same data. The zones of dispute involve a number of areas: market definition, concentration ratios, conditions of entry, and performance and policy preferences.[8]

Market Definition

Both economist and lawyer search for information relating to market power and market performance. *Market power* can be defined as the "possession by a firm (or group of firms acting jointly) of the ability to behave over fairly long periods of time in a way different from the way a firm in the economist's model of a competitive market facing the same cost and demand conditions would be forced to behave by the pressures of competition."[9]

A judgment concerning the degree of market power possessed by a firm, or group of firms, acting jointly requires the proper definition of the market and "consideration of what set of near substitutes should be considered as the 'product' traded in the market."[10] Defining the relevant market is a prerequisite for determining the degree of market concentration of the company, or firms, under investigation. The narrower the definition (the fewer the number of companies in the market), the greater the degree of market concentration of each firm in the market.

The staff attorney is inclined to include fewer buyers and sellers in his definition of the relevant market, since the higher the concentration ratio, the greater the presumption that the market is not workably competitive. The staff economist is less likely to define the market narrowly or to limit the number of product substitutes (or near substitutes). By including a wider range of substitutes in the market definition and reducing the concentration ratios of the firms under investigation, the economist weakens the lawyer's case for antitrust action.

A case involving the baking industry illustrates how their differences in defining the relevant market can lead lawyers and economists to reach opposite conclusions. The Bureau of Competition charged that ITT Continental Baking Company had attempted to monopolize the wholesale bread-baking industry through predatory pricing practices (as well as through other anticompetitive tactics of lesser significance).[11] The lawyers argued that in order to achieve dominance in wholesale baking in all relevant markets, ITT Continental Baking sought to exclude or eliminate rivals by selling bread below cost or at predatory prices in the various markets where competitors entered.[12] The company would subsidize such sales by selling bread at higher prices in less competitive areas or by taking advantage of its dominant position in the sale of Hostess snack cakes. Presumably, many small wholesale bakers would be forced to discontinue the production and sale of bread, and the growth of the wholesale baking industry would thus be inhibited. After having substantially lessened, eliminated, injured, and/or foreclosed actual and potential competition in wholesale baking, the ITT Continental Baking Company would raise prices—as firms possessing monopoly power often do—to an excessively high level in those markets where it had excluded or eliminated competition through below-cost or predatory pricing.

Quite clearly, defining the relevant product market as the "baking, sale and distribution of bread by *wholesale* bakers" was essential to the lawyers' case. The Bureau of Competition could easily present data indicating the trends toward concentration in wholesale baking and the dearth of rival wholesale baking firms, that could effectively compete with ITT Continental Baking. By limiting the market definition to wholesale bakers, the attorneys could dramatically point to the market power of ITT—a power that could enable the company to set prices almost at will, absent wholesale competition.

The economists of the Bureau of Economics, however, strongly took issue with the attorneys of the Bureau of Competition and argued that ITT Continental Baking would not secure the power to overcharge the consuming public.[13] They contended that the attorneys had erred in limiting the relevant product market to wholesale bakers. However much ITT Continental succeeded in eliminating its wholesale baker competitors, the corporation still faced price competition from regional grocery chains that bake and market their own in-house (captive) brands of bread. Should ITT Continental attempt to raise the price of its products after having excluded rival wholesalers, the grocery chains, the economists claimed, would simply expand the output of their own bakeries and assume an even greater share of the local bread market. As the most vigorous and effective competition in the baking industry comes from the in-house bakeries of the retail grocery chains, they should have been included in the relevant product market. In providing a broader definition of the relevant product market than the staff attorneys, the economists challenged the lawyers' claim that ITT Continental Baking was exercising effective monopoly power. Because ITT, in the view of the economists, was hardly immune from competition, the commissioners were advised not to issue a complaint. Ultimately, however, the lawyers' judgment prevailed.[14]

Concentration Ratios

Economists are more likely than lawyers to find justifications for high concentration. It may result not from anticompetitive behavior but from a high degree of technical expertise that only a few firms possess or from high economies of scale. A dying industry may only be able to support a few firms while a young one may still not have attracted entry. Moreover, while the market share of the companies under investigation may be high, analyses of four firm concentration ratios over a period of years might reveal a decline. If a firm's share of the market has declined, then this may indicate that the barriers to entry are not high and that other firms in the market are competitive.

The Conditions of Entry

The market power of imperfect competitors may be temporary, if other firms can penetrate their markets, take away their sales from them, and thereby restore competition.[15] Whether these firms will be able to enter the market depends in large measure upon the height of the barriers to entry. In the course of the preliminary and formal inquiry, the investigator will attempt to secure information on four main sources affecting entry: (1) blocked access, (2) capital requirements, (3) scale economies, and (4) product differentiation.

When lawyers and economists differ about conditions of entry, the latter usually argue that no significant barriers hinder competition. Because easy entry would make it difficult, or impossible, for the firms under investigation to impose losses upon consumers, antitrust action in such a situation would yield little or no benefit to the public.

Disputes arise between lawyer and economist because each focuses on different conditions of entry. For example, the economist might evaluate such factors as capital costs, advertising, product differentiation, and scale economies. Should he conclude that capital costs are not high, advertising not heavy, scale economies inconsequential, and patents unimportant, then he would probably recommend that the commission not issue a complaint. The staff attorney, concerned with conditions that make entry difficult, might contend that the shortage of competent personnel and the highly technical nature of the industry imposed significant barriers to entry.

Performance

Assessing the workability of competition is not an easy task.[16] It is difficult to judge what constitutes abnormally high profits, excessive selling costs, chronic excess capacity, or the absence of progressiveness. Joe Bain has written that "any economist's assessment of the workability of competition is likely to have a highly provisional and even personal character and is likely to rest heavily on the ad hoc assessment of obvious alternatives in given situations."[17]

In making these subjective assessments the economist is more likely than the staff attorney to argue that workable competition exists. For example, while the attorney might claim that the firms under investigation are earning supranormal profits, the economist might very well contend that the lawyer has misinterpreted statistical data and conclude that profits are not markedly higher than the industry average. When he agrees with the attorney's finding that profits are very high, the economist might not assume that the companies under investigation were engaging in practices that violate the antitrust laws. He might attempt to determine whether such returns could be attributed to such factors as managerial skill or rapidly growing demand.

Policy Preferences

The economists will oppose the issuance of a complaint when they believe that the attorneys have failed to demonstrate that the market is not functioning properly or when they are convinced that antitrust action would interfere with policy objectives that they deem desirable. An especially illustrative case involved the reporting methods of natural gas producers and the policy debate about natural gas deregulation.

After a four-and-one-half-year investigation the Bureau of Competition charged that the American Gas Association and eleven producers had deliberately underreported gas reserves in order to obtain higher wellhead prices from the Federal Power Commission (FPC). The bureau urged the commissioners to issue a complaint. The economists, however, who were forceful advocates of natural gas deregulation, argued that commission action would be ill-advised:

If the FTC were to issue a complaint at this point, it would surely cloud the public-policy debate on regulation which is presently taking place. Supporters of continued regulation would be able to point to the complaint as proof that the natural gas shortage was a contrivance of the producers. . . . The result might be continued FPC regulation into the distant future. At a time when the FTC at the insistence of its Chairman is engaging in a thoughtful review of the efficacy of various regulatory institutions, the FTC might be taking steps which would entrench one of those institutions.[18]

In response the director of the Bureau of Competition sought to separate the public-policy issues from law enforcement concerns:

At this point I should emphasize that this is not a case about natural gas deregulation. . . . This complaint will not, and indeed, it is not, designed to answer the important questions of whether the gas industry is structured competitively and whether there are obstacles to effective competition in the production sector of the industry should deregulation occur.[19]

The head of the Bureau of Competition also criticized the economists for not confining themselves to economic arguments:

"To a large extent, the Bureau of Economics has, because it believes a complaint in this matter would threaten to cloud the policy debate concerning natural gas deregulation, in an uncharacteristic manner assumed the role of legal advocate and has . . . sought to join issue with the legal staff."[20]

The Strategy of the Division of Economic Evidence

The natural gas case notwithstanding, Bureau of Economics officials argue that they do not consider noneconomic criteria when they oppose the Bureau of Competition. Discussing the accomplishments of his unit, the assistant director for economic evidence commented that as a result of the influence of the Bureau of Economics, executives in the Bureau of Competition often base their decisions on economic criteria. "It wasn't too long ago that the lawyers would only ask: 'what does the law say?' . . . Now, economic principles are usually controlling, even among the attorneys. The Bureau of Competition has become keenly interested in such questions as 'Is there enough size?'" Because of their professional training, it is not surprising that the attorneys do inject noneconomic criteria into the case-selection process (notably legal precedent).

There is some debate within the Bureau of Economics as to whether the economists should contest the attorneys on all matters on which they disagree. Some officials maintained that the Bureau of Economics should not compromise its economic principles and should defend its position before the commissioners, if necessary, in every instance of dispute. Adopting a more pragmatic view, other officials stated that the Bureau of Economics should object to most, but not all, cases that it deems unworthy of FTC resources. Opposition to every "worthless" case could only heighten the antagonism between the two bureaus, and the Bureau of Economics might soon find itself under investigation by congressional committees clamoring for more vigorous antitrust enforcement. The commissioners themselves would find it impossible to support the Bureau of Economics consistently, mainly because there would be very few cases under investigation, if the perspective of the economists were adopted.

Should the commissioners accept the Bureau of Economics' position, then Congress, consumer groups, the media, and the private bar (whose livelihood is linked to the level of commission activity) might accuse them of slackening the agency's antitrust effort. In short, they would be creating a politically intolerable situation.

The Bureau of Competition's Perception of the Bureau of Economics

That the Bureau of Economics should decide as a matter of strategy not to oppose every Bureau of Competition recommendation that it deems unworthy of commission attention is of little consolation to the attorneys, who would prefer not to encounter any opposition to their case-investigation proposals. The economists are accused of "economic God-playing," of making assumptions that have no basis in reality. Stated one Bureau of Competition assistant director, "They're dogmatic, they make all kinds of inferences, but are unwilling to roll up their sleeves and do some investigating to see whether there are facts to support those inferences." In focusing on economic performance, the Bureau of Economics, so the assistant directors charge, cares little about the language of congressional intent, judicial opinion, or antitrust laws. The economists are viewed by many as conservative ideologues who are hostile to government intervention in the economy. Rather than support the Bureau of Competition in its efforts to prosecute violations, the economists are accused of being "case-killers," regularly justifying the behavior of business firms as not only rational, but also appropriate.

Bureau of Competition executives disagree about the desirability of having an autonomous economics division involved in the case-selection process. Reactive approach supporters declared that the Division of Economic Evidence should be dissolved and that the economists charged with tasks relating to antitrust enforcement should assume staff support roles within the Bureau of Competition. Such a step would greatly reduce the role of the economists in the decision-making process by depriving them of an independent voice. Supporters of a balanced antitrust effort believe that the tension between the lawyer and the economist is caused not so much by the existence of an autonomous economics division as it is by the kind of economist currently staffing the Bureau of Economics. The work product of their attorneys is probably better, they commented, because of the competition the Division of Economic Evidence provides. Friction between the bureaus would be reduced, these assistant directors claim, if more "liberal" economists were to join the commission. An economist who is sympathetic to the notion that government intervention in the economy is sometimes necessary is more likely to favor antitrust action as a means to correct what the attorneys perceive to be market abuses than a free-market oriented economist.

Why Lawyers and Economists Disagree

In part, disputes between lawyer and economist arise because of legitimate differences about how data should be interpreted. Often the industries under investigation are so complex that it is difficult to determine the effect that each of their many factors might have on the market. In addition, the reference points of the lawyer and economist are not the same; the economist is not concerned with legal criteria when making case-selection recommendations.

More fundamentally, however, disagreements between the Bureau of Competition and the Bureau of Economics exist because lawyers and economists have different professional norms and personal goals. By training, the economist is wary of interference with the market mechanism; he perceives his task as the prevention of unwarranted government action. To the extent that he uncritically sanctions such intervention, his professional prestige and career advancement are likely to suffer.

In contrast to the economist, the lawyer is trained to be prosecution-minded; his career prospects depend upon his securing trial experience. Thus, the attorney views the economists who oppose cases that could reach the trial stage within a brief period of time as obstacles to the realization of professional rewards.

The Bureau of Economics: Its Influence in Case-Selection Matters

If the the Bureau of Economics does not have a formally defined role in the case-selection process and the director of the Bureau of Competition has sole authority to open and close investigations, then perhaps the power of the economists is not as great as the attorneys believe.

Indeed, Bureau of Competition executives were not especially attentive to the positions of the Bureau of Economics until the commissioners became receptive to the economists' arguments. With increasing frequency, the commissioners requested the Bureau of Economics to review the economic effects of the attorneys' proposals. On several occasions, the Bureau of Economics successfully contested the complaint recommendations of the Bureau of Competition at the commission table. For example, though the commissioners still accepted the attorneys' view that a particular merger might violate a legal standard, they began to oppose prosecution as not being in the public interest, given the agency's limited resources, if the economists showed that concentration was declining in the relevant markets and that entry barriers would not rise as a result of the union of the firms under investigation.

Instances of the kind just described were signals to the head of the Bureau of Competition that he could not expect the commissioners to support his position routinely. As the Bureau of Economics' views prevailed at the expense of the Bureau of Competition's recommendations, the attorneys became concerned about their credibility. Many of the bureau executives strongly feared losing to the Bureau of Economics at the commission table. From the perspective of a bureau executive, eager to impress his constituency, there were rather compelling incentives for the attorneys to establish a good working relationship with the economists, whose successful opposition could tarnish the attorneys' reputation.

In order to reduce the number of setbacks at the commission table, the director of the Bureau of Competition made a conscious effort to develop closer ties with the economists. By 1973, both economists and lawyers were participating at Evaluation Committee meetings. Such gatherings, the Bureau of Competition executives hoped, would enable them to learn of the views of the economists early in the decision-making process. Should the Bureau of Economics strongly oppose a proposal to open a formal or preliminary investigation, then the bureau director might decide not to pursue the matter, knowing that someday the economists might succeed in dissuading the commissioners from issuing a complaint.

The Evaluation Committee was created not only because the executives of the Bureau of Competition wanted to be alerted as soon as possible about the views of the economists, but also because they realized that complex cases that might benefit the consumer could not be prosecuted without substantial economic input. As a result of the regular exchange of ideas between the two bureaus, the economists were able to convince many of the assistant directors of the need for innovative structural cases and planning in antitrust enforcement.

The notion then that the Bureau of Economics is principally engaged in "case killing" is overstated. Ultimately, it is the commissioners who decide whether a complaint should issue, not the Bureau of Economics. Whatever influence the Bureau of Economics has in the case-selection process results from its ability to secure the support of a majority of the commissioners for its views on any given matter, the inclination of the Bureau of Competition director to accommodate the Bureau of Economics when he fears that the position of the economists might very well prevail in arguments before the commissioners, and the capacity of the economists to educate the attorneys as to the correctness of their views. Should some future commission be less respectful of the Bureau of Economics perspective, then it is conceivable that the Bureau of Competition might not be quite so attentive to the economists' positions.

Conclusion

The increasing emphasis on structural cases is in many ways attributable to the influence of Bureau of Economics economists who have argued that the commission should shift its attention from conduct actions to matters that could yield substantial economic benefits to the consumer. Moreover, the certainty of an independent evaluation by the Bureau of Economics forced the Bureau of Competition to give careful thought to the proposals for investigations. As a result, the bureau director seldom approves investigations without solid evidence justifying an allocation of resources. At the end of an investigation he is usually able to recommend that the commissioners issue a complaint. Institutionalized conflict between the Bureau of Competition and the Bureau of Economics, it may be concluded, has resulted in more thoughtful decisions. As a former assistant director for evaluation of the Bureau of Competition stated in 1975:

While there are many instances where there have been disagreements between economists and lawyers, one of the great improvements that has come about at the Commission is the increased cooperation between the two Bureaus. . . . This does not mean, however, that the Bureau of Economics dictates what cases shall be opened or closed or that the analysis of the economists is the whole determinant of such actions. . . . But it is obvious to anyone who has lived with the Commission in recent years that the Bureau of Economics has a profound influence in the ultimate determinations of what cases shall be brought and what matters shall be investigated.[21]

Notes

1
The concept of organizational mission is well examined in the works of Philip Selznick and James Q. Wilson.

2
"Position Description of Assistant Bureau Director for Economic Evidence" (1975), p. 1. Michael Glassman, who studied at the University of Chicago, was a staff economist and then assistant director for economic evidence when economists gained influence in the case-selection process. An aggressive and articulate leader, Glassman set the independent path the economists have followed. In 1977, Glassman left the commission to become a private consultant.

3
Ibid., p. 2.

4
Data furnished by Deputy Director James M. Folsom, August 1976.

5

For a discussion of the role of the economist in the policy-making process, see Joseph Pechman, "Making Economic Policy: The Role of the Economist," in *Handbook of Political Science*, ed. Fred Greenstein and Nelson W. Polsby, 8 vols. (Reading, Mass.: Addison-Wesley Publishing Company, 1975), 6: 23–79; Joseph Lekachman, *Economists at Bay: Why the Experts Will Never Solve Your Problems* (New York: McGraw-Hill, 1976); Harold Demsetz, "Economics as a Guide to Antitrust Regulation," *Journal of Law and Economics*, 19, no. 2 (1976): 371–384; and Kenneth W. Dam, "Comment," *Journal of Law and Economics* 19, no. 2 (1976): 385–389.

6

Statement of Frederic M. Scherer, U.S., Congress, House, Committee on Small Business, Ad Hoc Subcommittee on Antitrust, the Robinson-Patman Act and Related Matters, *Recent Efforts to Amend or Repeal the Robinson-Patman Act*, part 2, 94th Cong., 1st sess., 1975, p. 145.

7

Robert L. Heilbroner, "Economics as a Value Free Science," *Social Research*, (Spring 1973): 129–143; Robert M. Solow, "Science and Ideology in Economics," *Public Interest*, no. 21 (Fall 1970): 99–107.

8

There are many works dealing with the economics of antitrust law, for example: Carl Kaysen and Donald Turner, *Antitrust Policy: An Economic and Legal Analysis* (Cambridge, Mass.: Harvard University Press, 1959); Carl Kaysen, *United States v. United Shoe Machinery Corporation: An Economic Analysis of an Antitrust Case* (Cambridge, Mass.: Harvard University Press, 1950); Ernest Gellhorn, *Antitrust Law and Economics in a Nutshell* (St. Paul: West Publishing Company, 1976); Harvey J. Goldschmid, H. Michael Mann, and J. Fred Weston, eds., *Industrial Concentration: The New Learning* (Boston: Little, Brown and Company, 1974); Frederic M. Scherer, *Industrial Performance and Market Structure* (Chicago: Rand-McNally, 1970); Phillip Areeda and Donald Turner, *Antitrust Law: An Analysis of Antitrust Principles and their Application* (Boston: Little, Brown and Company, 1978); Richard Posner, *Antitrust Law: An Economic Perspective* (Chicago: University of Chicago Press, 1976).

9

Kaysen, *U.S. v. United States Shoe Machinery Corporation*, p. 16.

10

Areeda, *Antitrust Analysis*, p. 197.

11

In the Matter of ITT Corp. and ITT Continental Baking Co., Inc., D. 9000 (1974).

12
See *Antitrust and Trade Regulation Report*, no. 693, 17 December 1977, p. F-1.

13
Ibid., p. F-4.

14
In a dissenting opinion, which was supportive of the Bureau of Economics' position, Commissioner Mayo Thompson captured the essence of the dispute between the lawyers and economists:

Our lawyers say that we must act to deprive the consumer of the short-run benefits of these lower prices in order to spare him the burden of having to pay a "monopoly" price in the future. Our economists suspect, however, that the short-run and the long-run will not be too much different thanks (as noted) to the competition that will remain from the captive bakeries of the retail chain stores. In the economists' view, therefore, this lawsuit is very likely to have anticonsumer effects, i.e., to produce a higher rather than a lower price for bread in the cities affected by it. (Ibid)

15
Areeda, *Antitrust Analysis*, pp. 18–23; Kaysen and Turner, *Antitrust Policy*, pp. 71–75; Scherer, *Industrial Market Structure*, pp. 96–97, 341–345.

16
Areeda, *Antitrust Analysis*, p. 38.

17
Joe Bain, "Workable Competition in Oligopoly: Theoretical Considerations and Some Empirical Evidence," *American Economic Review* 40 (1950): 37.

18
Memorandum to the commission from F.M. Scherer, director; James M. Folsom, deputy director; and Michael L. Glassman, assistant director for economic evidence, Bureau of Economics, regarding American Gas Association, reprinted in U.S., Congress, House, Committee on Interstate and Foreign Commerce, *Hearings Before the Subcommittee on Oversight and Investigations on Natural Gas Supplies*, vol 1, part 1, 94th Cong., 1st sess., 1975, p. 615.

19
Memorandum of James Halverson to the Bureau of Competition, ibid, p. 752.

20
Ibid., p. 751.

21
Statement of Harry Garfield, U.S., Congress, House, Committee on Small Business, Ad Hoc Subcommittee on Antitrust, the Robinson-Patman Act and Related Matters *Hearings on Recent Efforts to Amend or Repeal the Robinson-Patman Act*, part 2, 94th Cong., 1st sess., 1975, p. 160.

5
Attorney Tasks, Expertise, and the Case-Selection Process

In the abstract, Bureau of Competition executives could easily make case-load decisions without interference from the staff attorneys. After all, they have devised mechanisms (the Evaluation Committee, for instance) that centralize their authority. When the typical Bureau of Competition staff attorney is questioned about his tasks, he is apt to respond that he really has no role in choosing matters for investigation and prosecution. He is at the mercy of his bureau executives and subject to the whim of economists. The assistant directors believe, however, that the staff attorneys can greatly constrain the Bureau of Competition executive in choosing cases. Commented one such official:

The staff attorney makes or breaks an investigation. Before we can do anything, we have to assess the skills and reactions of the staff. You can't have a caseload consisting totally of complicated matters if you don't have a staff which is sophisticated in gathering data or that doesn't know about the complexities and structural characteristics of an industry. It is we who often feel powerless.

This descriptive chapter examines the tasks of the staff attorney in the precomplaint stages.[1] By focusing upon the complexities of investigations of the proactive variety, it shows that however much his superiors might constrain him, the attorney—because of the limits of his expertise and experience—affects the kinds of enforcement actions that the Bureau of Competition can undertake.

The Staff Lawyer Constrained

The staff attorney does not have the authority to open investigations nor does he routinely have access to all the complaints that the Bureau of Competition receives. Even when he learns of a possible violation of the law, the staff attorney is not free to devote his time to the matter without securing his assistant director's approval. It is the Evaluation Office that first sifts information about possible illegal activity, the assistant director who assigns staff to undertake a pre-preliminary investigation, and the bureau director, with the aid of the Evaluation Committee, who decides whether to approve a preliminary or formal investigation or a recommendation that the commission should issue a complaint.

To be sure, the staff attorney may, if he chooses, recommend that the Bureau of Competition open an investigation. However, the Evaluation Committee is not likely to take his suggestion seriously if it does not have the support of the staff attorney's assistant director. Because he is not present at Evaluation Committee deliberations, the staff attorney is at a distinct disadvantage compared with the assistant director; obviously, he cannot respond to questions and arguments that the bureau executives might pose. The assistant director is usually able to dissuade the staff attorney from sending a memorandum contesting his judgment to the Evaluation Committee. The staff attorney, who owes his future assignments and promotions to the assistant director, is reluctant to risk incurring his disfavor.

While it is apparent that the bureau executives can greatly circumscribe his role in the decision-making process, the staff attorney does play an important part in the conduct of bureau investigations. Should the staff attorney conclude after a pre-preliminary review that further action is not warranted, the assistant director will probably accept his judgment. While the assistant director and the bureau director are generally not so quick to accept a recommendation that the bureau devote additional resources to an investigation, their ultimate determination regarding the authorization of a preliminary or formal inquiry is partly dependent upon how well the staff lawyer can justify his position. Similarly, the level of staff expertise affects the ease with which the bureau director is able to defend a recommendation that a complaint should issue. The commissioners' decision is likely to hinge upon how well the staff attorneys can marshal evidence to support their case. Clearly, if the staff attorney does have a significant role to play, then it is necessary to examine the way in which he performs his tasks.

Information Gathering

In building a case, the staff attorney devotes much of his time to gathering data having to do with concentration ratios, profitability, barriers to entry, the structure of the industry, and business practices—all of the key areas involved in antitrust prosecutions. Such information is not always readily available and can take several months or years to obtain. Since attorneys use a variety of techniques to secure data, I will examine their data-collection techniques at the various junctures of an inquiry—pre-preliminary, preliminary, and formal. An effort will be made to compare the level of difficulty in pursuing investigations of the reactive and proactive types.

The Pre-Preliminary and Preliminary Investigation

The Beginning of the Reactive Investigation The investigation of mailbag (or reactive) matters begins when the Evaluation Office distributes to the litigation shops complaints about areas in which it has little expertise. The assistant director for litigation, who assigns staff to review such matters, will indicate to his attorney the importance that he attaches to the pre-preliminary investigation. The staff attorney will not expend much energy on a matter his superior thinks unimportant. Usually, all that the assistant director will demand is a letter to the complainant stating why commission action would not be appropriate.

If the assistant director is interested in a case, then he will instruct his staff attorney to delve more deeply into the complaint. At the outset of a pre-preliminary investigation, the attorney's knowledge of the matter might be based solely upon the complainant's letter. In an industrywide investigation he may only have the instructions of the Evaluation Committee to learn as much as he can about the structure of the industry. A pre-preliminary investigation entails several hours of research in the FTC library. After quickly surveying standard sources (for example, the *Wall Street Journal*, Moody's Industrial Report, or the forms of the Security and Exchange Commission), the attorney is generally in a position to determine whether there is reason to recommend a preliminary investigation.

At the pre-preliminary stage the staff lawyer searches for clues —often connected with concentration ratios or market shares— that could aid him in determining whether further investigation is warranted. As one attorney commented: "When you find that one company has 60 percent of the market, then a little light goes on. You know that you're on to something."

Nearly every lawyer who was interviewed stated that he tries to uncover evidence that could justify the expenditure of additional resources. As one representative attorney noted: "For me, each complaint is an opportunity, a vehicle which someday could take me into the courtroom. I want to go to trial so badly that there are times when I overstate the possibilities which the particular matter might offer." Such exaggerations, most staff attorneys and assistant directors maintain, are both rare and easily uncovered. An attorney who is anxious for choice assignments acts unwisely if he risks losing his assistant director's respect.

Should an attorney believe that the evidence suggests that a firm (or firms) has violated the antitrust laws and a preliminary investigation is in order, then he will write a brief memo to that effect to his assistant director. The assistant director, if he supports the recommendation, will then ask the Evaluation Office to place the matter on the agenda of a forthcoming Evaluation Committee (or Merger Screening Committee) meeting. If the Evaluation Committee authorizes a preliminary investigation, the bureau will assign three or four attorneys to the case.

Unlike a pre-preliminary investigation, which essentially involves several hours of library research and perhaps a few telephone calls to the complainant, a preliminary investigation may entail two or three arduous months of fact finding. Of course sometimes a preliminary investigation may require less effort because soon after commencing their inquiry the staff attorneys may uncover sufficient evidence to merit recommending the issuing of a complaint or the opening of a formal investigation. Other times, the clear lack of evidence may lead the lawyers to urge the closing of the case.

Although the staff lawyers might invest much time in the investigation of mailbag complaints, they generally have little difficulty in determining the scope of the targets of the inquiry. The complainants themselves provide the attorneys with a ready source of information. Commenting about the relative ease with which lawyers commence investigations emanating from the reactive approach, one assistant director stated: "You usually don't have to be too worried about assigning someone who is rather inexperienced. Of course, we try to have him work with a more senior lawyer. In any event, the attorney's job is pretty clearly laid out—he knows who to talk to, what to look for."

The Beginning of the Proactive Investigation The problem of determining where to start is particularly acute in the large-scale industrywide investigations produced by the proactive approach. In such investigations, which originate from the consumer price index rather than from specific complaints, attorneys seek out firms willing to discuss the illegal activities of competitors. At the outset of a preliminary investigation, the attorneys usually have merely a general understanding of the situation surrounding the inquiry and a vague idea about the legal theory the case entails. One experienced Bureau of Competition attorney described the first days and weeks of an investigation as a period of uncertainty:

It's really hit-or-miss. . . . You just keep calling up companies, send out letters of inquiry and hope that a few firms will respond. One or two leads could be quite helpful. Sometimes you don't come up with anything. Maybe that's because in the industrywide cases, you're never sure what to look for. The industries are so big and have so many facets.

Not surprisingly, the attorneys preferred the mailbag case to the industrywide investigation because it is easier to find evidence of a violation when a complainant specifies which firm to examine and supplies the relevant data. Advocates of the reactive approach are quick to argue that the proactive view is impractical and causes the bureau to expend considerable resources before lawyers uncover leads.

At the outset of the preliminary investigation the attorney tries to obtain a thorough knowledge of the industry in which alleged violations of the antitrust laws have occurred. Commission lawyers believe that they are at a great disadvantage compared with their adversaries, who have easy access to company records. The lawyers fear that they will not have enough information to build a case, that the other side possesses superior data, and that opposing counsel are of higher quality. To compensate for these handicaps, the staff attorneys engage in a thorough and unyielding search for data. In the beginning of an investigation, before the legal theories have been shaped, the Bureau of Competition attorney gropes for every bit of information related to the case.

The lawyer considers the volume of data he accumulates as a measure of his seriousness of purpose and his investigative skills. Many staff attorneys are convinced that the assistant directors judge their performance on the basis of their ability to amass information simply because they have little else on which to evaluate the work product of the staff. Few attorneys, after all, are involved in trial activity. Most are occupied with investigative tasks. Thus, because an attorney believes that promotion and future assignments depend on projecting the image of the skilled investigator, he tries to collect as much information as possible.

Securing the Voluntary Cooperation of Parties Involved in an Investigation In his attempts to obtain data, the Bureau of Competition attorney tries to secure the voluntary cooperation of the firm under investigation, as well as its competitors. The government lawyer can learn much simply by conversing with businessmen and trade association officials, especially at the outset of an investigation. Commented one staff attorney:

In the beginning we ask a lot of stupid questions, mainly because we don't have enough knowledge, needed to ask intelligent questions. But with each passing day, our questions become more sophisticated . . . until we reach a point where we're ready to develop a theory to support the case.

The attorneys can coerce the companies into releasing needed information only pursuant to a formal investigation. If at the beginning of a case the bureau director decides to forego a preliminary investigation and devote resources to a formal investigation, the attorneys can then ask the commissioners to issue a subpoena, "directing that person named therein to appear before a designated time and place to testify or to produce documentary evidence, or both, relating to any matter under investigation by the Commission."[2] Similarly, the authorization of a formal investigation is a prerequisite for the issuance of a commission order, requiring the corporations under investigation to give agency economists and attorneys access to company documents or to supply them with written answers to questions.

Bureau of Competition attorneys prefer not to coerce the companies into releasing information unless efforts to secure voluntary cooperation have failed or the firms have complied only in part with commission requests. Attempts to force information sometimes prove counterproductive. At the outset of an investigation when the attorneys often do not have enough knowledge to pose pointed questions, a subpoena is of little use because the commission does not yet have a clear idea of which documents it needs and could seal valuable informal lines of communication between the commission attorneys and industry sources. The companies feel threatened by subpoenas and usually respond with all of the legal devices at their disposal in an attempt to block the agency. Not infrequently, the companies will file a series of motions and countermotions to quash government subpoenas and requests for documents. For its part, the Bureau of Competition must expend considerable resources in order to meet the challenges posed by the companies. Such resources might be better channeled into the actual investigation. Thus, in mapping their investigative strategy, the staff attorneys will first attempt to induce the companies to cooperate with the commission before using coercive means to obtain data.

Such a strategy often works rather well. Companies under investigation (and competitors who are asked to comment about the behavior of the accused firms) are aware that the commission has the authority to compel the release of data. Anticipating that the commission will almost certainly issue subpoenas should they steadfastly refuse to cooperate, the firms will try to satisfy to some degree the demands of the government in the hope that the Bureau of Competition will decide not to press for subpoena powers. Several attorneys noted that an effective tactic in securing at least partial cooperation is to inform the company (or companies) that unless the firm (or firms) shows some willingness to comply with data requests of the commission, the agency will have no choice but to compel them to supply the information. Smaller-sized firms, which do not have their own legal departments and are often unable to bear the costs of protracted legal confrontations, may decide to be responsive to the commission. Larger corporations, however, which do have specialized legal staffs and are therefore in a position to contest commission attorneys, may not be as likely to be as forthcoming as the smaller-sized companies.

Staff attorneys attribute the resistance of the larger corporations to a variety of factors: the firms' conviction that business records should remain confidential; their belief that they will successfully block commission attempts to secure records; and their sense that they will ultimately prevail because their will to persevere is greater than that of the agency, whose existence (unlike the corporation's) does not depend upon the outcome of the case. While many of these large firms, in the view of the staff attorneys, do not seriously intend to release data until legally required to do so, they often profess their willingness to cooperate with the agency. Commented one staff attorney: "They'll stall for time, hoping to wear us down. As soon as they've readied their own case, which they'll present in the event we serve a subpoena, they'll drop the pretense of cooperation."

In the end, bureau attorneys might be forced to use their subpoena power. Sometimes a firm that had been helpful decides that it is no longer in its interest to provide more assistance. Not infrequently, competitors of firms under investigation state that they want to cooperate with the Federal Trade Commission but will not do so unless legally compelled to respond to agency demands. Such firms are usually small in size, are not in a position to make deep inroads into the business of their competitors, and would like nothing more than to expose the illegal practices of those competitors. They are fearful, however, that their competitors would retaliate against them—perhaps even attempt to eliminate them from the market—were they to offer information gratuitously about the practices of the firms under investigation. To protect themselves from the wrath of their competitors, the smaller firms may insist that the Bureau of Competition serve them with subpoenas so that they can claim that they had no choice but to comply with commission demands.

The Formal Investigation

With the approval of a majority of the commissioners, staff attorneys can invoke *compulsory process*—a term that describes the power of the Federal Trade Commission to require companies to supply data and respond to questions. Commission authorization of the use of subpoena powers (of compulsory process) takes the form of an investigational resolution. The attorney who wants to employ such powers either because a company refuses to produce information or because a subpoena would "provide the most economical or efficient means of obtaining information or evidence"[3] drafts a resolution with a supporting memorandum. The assistant director and the bureau director review the resolution, make revisions, and then seek commission approval.[4] (The attorneys have a variety of devices to compel companies to release information, including subpoenas, investigational hearings, and 6(b) reports.)

When the commission approves the investigational resolution for compulsory process, it delegates authority to the directors of the bureaus of Competition and Economics and to the assistant directors of the two bureaus to issue subpoenas to companies involved in the investigation.[5] In practice, the staff attorneys working on the case merely ask the assistant director to sign the documents authorizing the subpoenas. Companies served with subpoenas may have to supply specific books or documents or dispatch executives to testify at investigational hearings conducted by commission officials. At such hearings the attorneys from the Bureau of Competition and economists from the Bureau of Economics (if economists have been assigned to the investigation) will question company officials or their competitors. At the conclusion of the hearings, the investigators might possess a wealth of data. On occasion the Bureau of Competition has recommended the issuance of complaints almost solely on the basis of data secured in the course of the investigational hearings.[6]

Besides the hearings, the staff attorneys can make use of the very extensive powers of investigation that section 6 of the Federal Trade Commission Act vests in the commission.[7] Section 6(b) allows the agency to undertake intensive industrywide investigations without having to use its own staff to conduct file searches of the companies under investigation. The 6(b) reports could compel the companies to examine their internal records, evaluate raw data, and to construct specific answers to commission questions at their own expense.

Commission attorneys are not assured of collecting needed information simply because they have various means to secure it. Through legal action in federal court, for example, the firms from which information is sought could prevent the commission from compelling the release of data. To a large extent, however, whether the attorneys will secure the information that they deem relevant depends on the skill with which they use the devices to exact data. They must have a sense of when to use the hearings, 6(b) reports, or the various kinds of subpoenas.[8] The lawyers must have the ability to determine the order in which witnesses should be called at investigational hearings. They must be crafty interrogators who can orchestrate events in an effort to pressure the companies into responding to agency demands. Whether the attorney is effective is largely a function of the length of his experience (though to be sure, there are some characteristics of the investigator that are not always acquirable—common sense, judgment).

Quite obviously, those lawyers who have been involved in many kinds of situations tend to be better equipped to deal with complex cases than those who have had limited training. In deciding whether to allocate resources to big cases—those that involve both substantive and procedural complexities—bureau executives ascertain if the available attorneys have the requisite expertise. Decisions about simple conduct cases do not involve such judgments, since the degree of sophistication needed to pursue such matters does not approach that required to prosecute complex structural vehicles.

The Type of Data That the Attorney Seeks
The investigative tasks, discussed in the preceding pages, define in large measure the working day of the Bureau of Competition lawyer. Since the type of data sought in structural investigations— market definition, concentration ratios, conditions of entry, and

market performance—are often economic in nature, the Bureau of Competition attorney is handicapped (at least during the period of this study) by not being especially well trained in economics. In a recent survey 89 percent of commission attorneys (including lawyers from both the Bureau of Competition and Bureau of Consumer Protection) indicated that they needed more training in economic studies.[9]

The attorney assigned to a conduct case is not so much concerned with abstract economic concepts as he is with securing concrete data that may indicate that there is reason to believe that the laws have been violated. The lawyer attempts to secure company memoranda and records as well as oral testimony detailing company practices from officials of the firm under investigation to learn how the firm makes its production and marketing decisions, particularly with respect to prices and out-put. (It is rare, of course, that company officials explicitly declare their intention to violate the law.) If the information establishes that each firm does not make its decisions independently and that the companies try to exclude or eliminate rivals through such anticompetitive means as price discrimination, predatory pricing, or tie-ins, then the attorney will probably have little difficulty convincing the Bureau of Competition executives to recommend the issuance of a complaint. Partly because the kind of data sought in a conduct case tends to be tangible and intellectually ac-cessible, the attorney prefers such matters to complex structural investigations.

Recommending a Course of Action

Once the attorney has gathered the data and completed his investigation, he writes a memorandum to the assistant director and bureau director stating his views about the course the bureau should pursue. The soundness of the memorandum largely de-pends on the attorney's ability to collect and interpret data. If the lawyer does not adequately perform the tasks associated with the conduct of an investigation, then the quality of his recommenda-tion is likely to suffer. To the extent that there is a shortage of attorneys with the skills required to guide an investigation in the precomplaint stages to its conclusion (the memo represents the culmination of that effort), the bureau will have difficulty pursuing complex cases.

Their distance from the case means that bureau officials often have to rely upon the staff lawyer's data, although they may question his conclusions. It should be emphasized that the staff attorney's influence is not unlimited. In the first instance, the bureau director and the Evaluation Committee determine, usually after careful deliberation, whether to launch a preliminary or formal investigation. They generally choose to devote resources to an inquiry when they think that there is some evidence indicating that the laws have been violated. Thus, when the staff attorney concludes that a complaint should issue, he is in a sense confirming the initial prediction of the bureau director and the assistant directors. Second, although the staff attorney has much latitude in performing his daily tasks, he does have to report periodically to his superiors. His work is subject to general review; the extent to which it is censored depends on the style of the assistant director and the nature of the case. Third, though the staff attorney is free to send his memoranda to the commissioners, regardless of how his superiors evaluate his work, he tends to accept the criticisms of the assistant director and the bureau director. He does so because he knows that the commissioners are likely to reject his recommendations if they do not command the support of his superiors.

In the memorandum the staff attorney must address two issues: (1) whether there is reason to believe that the antitrust laws have been violated and (2) whether the issuance of a complaint would be in the public interest. He considers both economic and legal criteria. Besides recognizing the relevance of economics, the attorney appreciates the influence of the Bureau of Economics in the case-selection process. Since the economists challenge actions on the grounds that they are unlikely to yield substantial consumer benefits, the attorneys try to counter the position of the Bureau of Economics with their own economic analyses.

The lawyer's attention to legal criteria is easily explained. He is trained in the legal profession. Moreover, since the courts evaluate the commission's decision in terms of judicial precedent, the attorney seeks to show in his memoranda that the case conforms to the corpus of legal opinion.

Legal precedent provides the lawyer with broad guidelines; the laws themselves prohibit activities the "*may* tend to lessen competition"—there need not be absolute proof that the effect will be to lessen competition. Supreme Court decisions, for example, have given the commission attorney, at least in theory, wide discretion in determining what constitutes a violation of section 5 of the Federal Trade Commission Act: "The Federal Trade Commission does not arrogate excessive power to itself if . . . it . . . considers public values beyond simply those enshrined in the letter or encompassed in the spirit of the antitrust laws."[10] There are, the Court has said, several factors which the commission may consider in determining whether a practice that is neither in violation of the antitrust laws nor deceptive is nonetheless unfair: (1) whether the practice, without necessarily having been considered unlawful, offends public policy as it has been established by statutes, the common law, or otherwise—whether it is within at least the penumbra of some common law, statutory, or other established concept of unfairness; (2) whether it is immoral, unethical, oppressive, or unscrupulous; and (3) whether it causes substantial injury to consumers (or competitors or other businessmen).[11] Judicial precedent also recognizes that the Federal Trade Commission Act not only provides a means of attacking established monopolies but also enables reaching monopoly in its incipiency. Attorneys cite such Supreme Court opinions to bolster their argument that the aim of antitrust policy should not be limited to the promotion of economic benefit (as the economists would prefer) but should also seek to foster other values (for example, the dispersal of power or the maintenance of small independent businesses).

As is the case with the Bureau of Competition executives, the personal goals of the staff attorney and his perception of what he must do so that he might achieve his objectives influence his decision-making calculus. However, the bureau director and the staff attorney assign different weights to the various factors considered in the case-selection process. Each has a different sense of what he must do in order to attain his own objectives;

therefore, one differs with the other in regard to the degree of importance that should be attached to the decision-making factors.

For a bureau director, eager to preserve his influence, it is imperative that the commissioners consistently approve his recommendations. He is, therefore, likely to weigh carefully the judgment of the Bureau of Economics. If he believes that the economists will probably convince the commissioners that the lawyer's position should not prevail, then he could very well decide not to press ahead in support of his attorneys' recommendation. (He may be more inclined to contest the economists' view if the lawyers assigned to the case are known to command the respect of the commissioners.) Moreover, the bureau director is likely to champion the dramatic structural cases, even those which may prove difficult to prosecute. Apart from the possible merits of such cases, he finds them attractive beause they generate favorable publicity. Should the industrywide investigation fail to produce results, the bureau director who first announced the commission action will probably not be held accountable; by the time the problems of the case are fully realized, he will probably have left the commission and joined a prestigious law firm, which may have been interested in him partly because of the dramatic investigations that he spearheaded.

Because he wants desperately to be involved in a trial, the staff attorney is inclined to interpret the data gathered in the course of an investigation in a manner that will justify the recommendation that a complaint issue. Information that lends credence to the view that the firms under investigation have violated the antitrust laws looms large, while less-supportive data seems not to be as important.

Moreover, the attorney, unlike the bureau director, is not likely to be deterred by opposition from the Bureau of Economics to his position. For him every investigation is a potential trial vehicle; having worked diligently on an investigation, he is averse to abandoning the case, simply because the economists might challenge his recommendation at the commission table. Commented one staff attorney: "If they [the economists] are able to beat us at the commission table, then it's a rough deal. But if we give up, just because the bureau director is afraid to lose, then we surely can't win. Then our effort is wasted; we don't go to trial."

Summary

The skills and level of expertise demanded of an antitrust lawyer depend on the nature of the case. In a simple conduct case or a conventional merger matter, the attorney need only have a basic understanding of the antitrust laws. To prove his case he needs only standard economic data and established legal criteria. Complex structural matters, however require that the lawyer know not only the law but also have some familiarity with industrial organization. He must be a skillful investigator, thoroughly conversant with the various ways of extracting information. He must be able to ask pertinent questions, to know how to interpret complex data, and to fashion a creative theory (particularly when the case seeks to break new ground). The necessary expertise is acquired through years of experience. An organization whose attorneys leave its service before or shortly after acquiring the skills and knowledge needed to prosecute complex matters will have difficulty realizing substantial results.

Notes

1
It is not the purpose of this chapter to explain the administrative processes of the commission. The reader who is interested in administrative law should consult any standard textbook on the subject.

On the importance of "tasks," see James Q. Wilson, *The Investigators: Managing FBI and Narcotics Agents* (New York: Basic Books, Inc., 1978); also Herbert Kaufman, *The Forest Ranger* (Baltimore: Johns Hopkins Press, 1960).

2
Section 2.8 of the *Organization, Procedure and Rules of the Federal Trade Commission*. Part 2 ("Non-Adjudicative Procedure") subpart A ("Investigations"), of *Organization, Procedure and Rules* discusses investigational procedures. In addition, chapter 2 ("Preliminary Investigations") and chapter 3 ("Formal Investigations") of the *Operating Manual of the Federal Trade Commission* (1975) are also instructive.

3
Operating Manual, ch. 3.7.

4

The memorandum supporting the resolution provides background information regarding the general nature of the case: basic data such as the approximate dollar volume of sales of the respondent, the dollar volume of sale of the product or service affected by the alleged practice, the segment of the consuming public that may be affected by the practice; the end which commission action will serve, and an estimate of the resources necessary to undertake the investigation. In addition, the memorandum and resolution state possible areas of inquiry and laws that may have been violated. Usually, the resolution is broadly framed to give the staff attorneys wide latitude in pursing their inquiry, but it should not be overdrawn. The resolution should be drafted precise enough for a court to determine whether: (1) the investigation is within the authority of the commission; (2) the material is relevant to the investigation; and (3) the material sought is reasonable in scope. (*Operating Manual,* ch. 3.7B).

5

There are two kinds of subpoenas: the subpoena ad testificandum and the subpoena duces tecum. The *subpoena ad testificandum* requires persons to testify in an "investigational hearing" conducted by commission officials (*Operating Manual,* 3.8). A *subpoena duces tecum* requires the witness to present to the officials of the Federal Trade Commission (usually the Bureau of Competition attorneys involved in the case) those books, papers, and documents specified in the subpoena itself. The subpoena duces tecum differs from the subpoena ad testificandum in that it does not involve the oral testimony of witnesses at investigational hearings. The subpoena ad testificandum, unlike the subpoena duces tecum, does not seek to compel industry to supply specific written documents.

6

For example, after extensive investigational hearings the bureau concluded that the American Gas Association had deliberately underreported proven gas reserves. In his memorandum to the commission Bureau of Competition Director James T. Halverson recommended that the agency issue a complaint: "I have in my analysis *relied upon testimony of industry witnesses and have at times quoted relevant portions of the transcripts of the investigational hearings"* (U.S., Congress, House, Committee on Interstate and Foreign Commerce, Subcommittee on Oversight and Investigation, *Hearings on Natural Gas Supplies,* vol. 1, part 1, 94th Cong., 1st sess., 1975, p.783; italics mine).

7

In particular, section 6(b) gives the commission the power:
To require, by general or special orders, corporations engaged in

commerce, excepting banks and common carriers subject to the Act to regulate commerce, to file with the Commission in such form as the commission may prescribe . . . reports or answers in writing to specific questions . . . as to the organization, business, conduct, practices, management, and relation to other corporations, partnerships, and individuals of the respective corporations filing such reports or answers in writing. (38 Stat. 717, (1914), as amended, 15 U.S.C. 46 (1976))

Accordingly, questionnaires are sent simultaneously to a number of companies in a particular industry to determine the relevant facts about industry practices and whether antitrust laws have been violated. In general terms the 6(b) reports differ from the subpoena duces tecum in that they do more than simply ask companies to supply those internal records that the commission considers pertinent. A hypothetical example illustrates the limits of the subpoena duces tecum in relation to the 6(b). If the subpoena duces tecum requires the concerned companies to surrender specific data, the firms might respond that they do not maintain records containing such information. A 6(b), however, would order the companies to aggregate raw data and prepare responses to the commission's questions if they do not already have documents containing the requested information.

Because section 6(b) orders are comprehensive and usually highly technical in nature—they are, it should be remembered, directed at an entire industry rather than just a few firms—the Bureau of Competition often enlists the aid of Bureau of Economics staff, accountants, and outside-industry consultants in preparing the resolution.

8

In any investigation it is possible that the Bureau of Competition officials will make use of one or both types of subpoenas. When Bureau of Competition attorneys can identify the specific documents that are needed and conclude, upon receipt of the data, that no further questions have to be asked of company officials, they will only serve a subpoena duces tecum. In those situations in which both subpoenas are used, the order in which they are served may vary. If the staff attorneys do not have enough information to identify those documents necessary to determine whether the company under investigation may have violated the antitrust laws, then they would not serve a subpoena duces tecum first. In order to secure sufficient background data to identify relevant documents (that may be susequently obtained pursuant to a subpoena duces tecum), staff lawyers might decide to hold investigaional hearings. In short, the subpoena ad testificandum would precede the subpoena duces tecum.

Sometimes investigational hearings both precede and follow the serving of the subpoena duces tecum. The first set of investigational hearings may be conducted so that the commission attorneys and economists can familiarize themselves with the various facets of company and industry operations. The responses of witnesses will presumably aid them in identifying specific documents that have to do with the base. In the second round of investigational hearings, which would follow the receipt of the documents that were secured after the serving of the subpoena duces tecum, commission attorneys and economists would question company and industry officials about the content of the data they obtained pursuant to the subpoena.

9
Meredith Associates, *Report to the Chairman, Federal Trade Commission Attorney, Attorney and Attorney Manager, Recruitment, Selection and Retention* (15 July 1976), p. 38.

10
FTC v. Sperry and Hutchinson Co., 405 U.S. 233, 244–245 (1972).

11
Ibid.

6
Attorney Objectives and Case-Load Decisions: The Demands of Organizational Maintenance

Some cases require more cooperative effort from staff attorneys than others. In general, the more complex the matter, the greater the degree of contributive support required. If the bureau director wishes to sustain cooperative activity for the length of time needed to prosecute complex structural cases efficiently, then the bureau director must be able to induce staff attorneys to work on such matters. Without adequate incentives to distribute, the bureau director might encounter problems in pursuing big structural cases and have to devote more time to simpler vehicles (generally conduct cases) that do not demand lengthy periods of cooperative activity. The commission might have to revise its policy objectives, perhaps de-emphasizing the consumer-benefit aspects of complex structural cases and placing greater stress on aims achieved through the prosecution of conduct matters—fair dealing, deterrence, and maintenance of small business.

Judged in terms of turnover rate—a basic measure of the extent to which the executive has managed to secure resources and some degree of contributive effort from staff attorneys over a period of time—the organizational maintenance problems faced by Bureau of Competition officials are severe. Since 1970 the annual turnover rate has ranged from 13 to 25 percent; of those attorneys who leave each year, 90 percent have had tenure of four years or less. At the end of fiscal 1976, there were only 20 of the almost 200 attorneys whose service dated from 1969. Over 89 percent of all attorneys who joined the commission in the period from 1972 to 1975 expected (in July 1976) to leave within two years.[1]

For those who would attempt to analyze organizational decision making or prescribe policy, understanding the causes of the agency's organizational maintenance problem is vital. Ascertaining whether adequate incentives are available to induce attorneys to remain with the commission is of fundamental importance in determining whether the agency can expect to pursue protracted cases effectively.[2] To make such a judgment, it is necessary to examine the aspirations of the Bureau of Competition attorneys. This chapter, therefore, explores the lawyers' personal goals, reasons for joining the commission, and policy preference. It discusses how the attempts of the bureau executive to mitigate dissatisfaction among attorneys assigned to disfavored investigations affects case-load decisions. Whether the efforts of the bureau executive to maintain the organization are likely to succeed is another subject of study.

Characteristics of the Staff Attorney

For the sake of analysis it is useful to divide the Bureau of Competition attorneys into two groups: those whose service preceded the 1970 reorganization (which enabled the new commission leadership, as part of its program to revitalize the agency, to pressure many incompetent attorneys to leave the bureau) and those whose service followed the agency's transformation. Of the 170 attorneys who were on the payroll of the Bureau of Competition in 1975, the few who were with the Federal Trade Commission before 1970 are among the most interesting. For them the era of the old commission is a time fraught with memories— mostly sorrowful, occasionally bitter. Having experienced so much, these twenty attorneys—the "survivors" of the commission's housecleaning efforts of 1970—are in a position to compare the new and old orders. They merit attention, moreover, because as senior attorneys they might be expected to play an important role in training and shaping the young recruits.

Their reasons for joining the commission staff are as diverse as their backgrounds. Some came from small towns where opportunities for practicing law were not appealing. Washington seemed to provide a setting where one could be engaged in lawyerlike activities every day. Others, who journeyed to Washington without law degrees in hand, worked in the federal bureaucracy by day and studied for the bar at night. When they earned their degrees, they chose to remain in government. A few matured during the depression and developed a deep faith in the desirability of government intervention in economic affairs; they believed that there could be no more worthwhile career than that of a government attorney, a protector of the public interest. Before joining the commission staff, one experienced trial attorney had enjoyed a long and distinguished career representing corporate interests. A desire to be on the "right side" prompted him to enter government service, although the change in employers involved considerable financial sacrifice.

There are many government agencies mainly staffed by lawyers. Why the survivors joined the commission is, therefore, hardly obvious. A few stated that they had no particular interest in any one area of law and would have been content to have joined any federal agency. Since the commission offered them employment at a favorable moment, they entered its service. Most, however, indicated that they specifically sought work in the antitrust field, and their first choice was not the commission but the Antitrust Division of the Department of Justice. No other government agency could match the reputation of the Antitrust Division. Some did not apply to the Antitrust Division, while others, who did seek employment with the Justice Department, withdrew their applications once the commission offered them positions; most, however, were rejected by the Antitrust Division.

Whatever their reasons for joining the Commission, few of the survivors intended to remain with the agency for the length of their professional careers. Most of them viewed the commission as a good training ground for the inexperienced attorney who, after mastering the various facets of his job, would move on to a high-salaried position in the private sector. A number of reasons account for their remaining in government serivce. First, the attorneys never received a lucrative offer from the prestigious law firm. Second, the few attorneys who did have promising opportunities decided that the security of government service outweighed the uncertainty of private practice. Although he could probably have earned more in private practice, the commission lawyer felt that, in contrast to his counterparts in the antitrust bar, his tenure was virtually assured (especially if he enjoyed special privileges as a military veteran). Third, a few lawyers commented that they did not take advantage of attractive opportunities, because they were fearful that they would not succeed as members of the private bar. Having graduated from less than prestigious law schools and been rejected by the Antitrust Division of the Justice Department, they lacked self-esteem. Fourth, some argued that it would have been unethical for them to forsake their roles as defenders of the public interest and represent the interests of wealthy corporate interests.

Of these reasons, the first is the most dominant—the offer from a prestigious firm never materialized. What is particularly significant is that the younger lawyers perceive that those who have stayed with the agency for a long period of time have failed professionally. It is common for the young attorney to refer to the lawyer who has worked in the commission for more than five years as a "real loser," a "drone," or a "failure." One junior attorney defined a careerist as any lawyer "who is not good enough to get a job with a private law firm or corporation."

Because the survivor is perceived in such an unflattering manner, he does not serve as a role model for the younger attorneys. There are few career attorneys whom the young lawyer admires or would hope to emulate. In the view of the recent recruit there is little distinction in being a career attorney of the Federal Trade Commission; therefore, a career in the Bureau of Competition is not a goal that many young lawyers seek. The absence of a reputation for professionalism among the senior attorneys has consequences for the bureau executive who wants to maintain cooperative activity for long periods of time. The bureau executive, for example, cannot induce the young attorneys to remain with the commission by arguing that they can learn much from the senior lawyers (though they may in fact benefit from interacting with them) or that they will achieve the respect of the private bar as a result of their association with the survivors. The young attorneys might more readily accept assignment on the complex structural cases, if they were convinced that the senior men were persons of high competence, who could impart to them their knowledge and skills. Moreover, if there were a tradition of excellence, a feeling of pride, and a spirit of comaraderie, then the bureau executive might find it easier to sustain cooperative activity among the attorneys assigned to a structural case.

Since the recent recruits were not attracted to the agency because of the reputation of the staff, it still remains to explain why they joined the Bureau of Competition. The typical young attorney first thought seriously about joining the agency after interviewing with personnel from the Washington or regional headquarters of the agency at his law-school campus. The Bureau of Competition probably offered him a position because of his academic record. In recent years 25 percent of the recruits have been elected to Phi Beta Kappa, 33 percent were members of their law reviews, and 80 percent graduated in the top one-third of their law-school classes.[3] They are drawn from every part of the country, reflecting the wide-ranging efforts of commission recruiters. In the last few years FTC personnel have visited between thirty and forty law schools each year throughout the nation.

While most of the recent recruits joined the commission because they were interested in antitrust law, only a small minority view the agency as a permanent employer. This minority is sympathetic to populist ideals and believes that the government should curb corporate power; they would never consider working for any organization except a government agency or a public interest group. The overwhelming majority of Bureau of Competition recruits, however, entered commission service with the intention of leaving within four or five years. For them government employment offered the opportunity to gain responsibility and experience at a far earlier time in their careers than would have been possible had they first joined a private law firm or corporation. In short, they viewed goverment service not as an ultimate career objective, but as a means to an end—a career in the private bar.

Statistics indicate that those attorneys who entered commission service with the intention of leaving within a few years have remained true to their plans.[4] If the staff attorney is determined to exit from the agency after a few years, then there may be little that the bureau executive can do. Still, the bureau director could conceivably take certain actions to induce the staff lawyer to remain somewhat longer.

The bureau director could promise to assign staff attorneys to cases that they believe have important public-policy implications. Such a measure, however, could affect only a few of the attorneys, since most do not have strong convictions about the public-policy objectives that antitrust enforcement should pursue. Only a distinct minority have seriously considered the goals of antitrust policy and have recognized the tension between various objectives. When queried about their views on antitrust policy, these attorneys respond with generalizations—"Antitrust is necessary if capitalism is to survive," "We cannot have competition without vigorous enforcement," or "Business needs the help of government to ensure that the market is allowed to work." Whether the end of antitrust enforcement should seek to assure economic competition or whether economic competition is to be viewed as a means to some other goal (for example, the redistribution of income) are matters that do not preoccupy the attention of the Bureau of Competition attorney.

The absence of passionate conviction about the goals of antitrust enforcement means that the bureau director cannot appeal to a sense of devotion to public service. Most staff attorneys have no compunction about working for a private firm; they harbor no ill will towards big business or the private bar. As one staff lawyer commented: "With a little bit of luck, I'll be out of this dump in a few years and will be on the way to a partnership in some classy law firm."

Perhaps the bureau executive could induce attorneys to remain by not assigning them to what they view as choice cases, which may reach the trial stage within a short period of time, until they have served the commission for a number of years. Above all else, it is important to understand that the staff attorney wants trial experience. He is prosecution-minded and will not consider himself to be a consummate lawyer until he has argued a case in a courtroom. Exclaimed one typical staff lawyer: "You're not a real attorney unless you've been to trial, matched wits with the big boys of the big firms and won." Most of the attorneys chose law as their vocation precisely because they thought that someday they would spend a good deal of time in the courtroom. Moreover, the typical staff lawyer is eager for trial work because he thinks that private law firms will not be interested in him unless he has courtroom experience. He has visions of facing the counsel of a distinguished law firm, of impressing him with his wit and expertise, and of ultimately securing employment in the private bar.

It is questionable, however, whether the bureau executive would refrain from assigning junior attorneys to trial work, since he could not hope to have a well-trained staff if he deprived the young recruit of the opportunity to learn from the seasoned courtroom lawyer. In addition, the commission would probably be unable to attract talented young attorneys if the agency had a reputation for not assigning junior lawyers to trial cases.

If it is assumed that the attorney becomes attractive to the private bar only after he attains a certain grade level, indicative of a high degree of expertise, then perhaps the bureau executive could induce the staff lawyer to remain in the agency by lengthening the time intervals between promotions. Promotion control, however, is not likely to be effective because the typical attorney is more concerned with gaining trial experience than with securing a promotion. He believes that his rating as a GS–11 or GS–13 is less important to the law firm than his courtroom record. The attorney would rather have trial experience and be a GS–11 than have no courtroom exposure and be a GS–14.

Raising salaries might also seem to be a way to reduce the turnover rate. Current wages and benefits are quite attractive—a GS–16, for example, earns $47,500 per year. However, the government simply cannot compete with the larger law firms for talent because the private bar offers higher salaries. A prestigious law firm may offer its attorneys a starting wage of close to $30,000, which is nearly 50 percent more than a commission recruit can expect to earn at the outset of his career. A recent survey indicated that only 3 percent of commission attorneys expected to make less than $35,000 (in current dollars) at the peak of their careers and that 66 percent of them believed that they will surpass this level within five years.[5] Thus, unless the commission raises its salaries to what many would consider exorbitant levels, it cannot hope to retain its staff for more than a few years.

Summary and Conclusion

According to Chester Barnard, an executive must do more than just assure the survival of an organization; he should also provide a system of communication, formulate and define purposes, and secure the essential contribution of effort and resources.[6] In securing this cooperative effort, the executive seeks to minimize organizational strain, which, as James Q. Wilson writes, may be caused by the "withdrawal of valued members, a decrease in the supply of available incentives, serious conflict over purpose, the challenge of a rival organization, excessive demands on the time and energy of key personnel and a loss of morale or of a sense of corporate identity."[7]

Given the Bureau of Competition's organizational problems, it is perhaps inevitable that the bureau director, regardless of his preference for the mammoth structural case and industrywide investigations or his desire to secure the goodwill of the Bureau of Economics, will approve the opening of a number of easily prosecuted matters, which may have little value to the consumer (although to be sure, there are simple conduct matters that do yield economic benefits) in an effort to satisfy the staff's perceived needs.

Structural matters and industrywide cases threaten the morale of the staff attorneys because they often involve years of tedious investigation before they reach the trial stage. (On many occasions, such matters are eventually resolved without the need for a trial.) For staff attorneys who perceive that they will not achieve their career goals (usually a job in a prestigious law firm) unless they gain courtroom experience, such cases are the sources of much unhappiness. In an attempt to accommodate the staff attorney, bureau executives make a conscious effort to assign them not only to industrywide cases but also to smaller matters which might very well reach the trial stage within a relatively brief period of time (perhaps one to two years). Indeed, a few assistant directors admitted that they sometimes support such cases precisely because they believe that the morale and performance of attorneys on the more complex matters will improve, if they are also assigned to vehicles that they think will further their career objectives.

Prosecution of conventional antitrust cases may also be essential to the meeting of the expectations of those few experienced attorneys, without whom the FTC would find it difficult to win cases and train young lawyers. In the course of interviews, it was apparent that the senior men intensely disliked the industrywide investigations and the more innovative structural cases. One such attorney commented: "I would go out of my mind if all I had to do was to work on these economics-oriented cases. . . . I get itchy when I'm not on a case which will go to trial very soon. Besides, I don't have to work with the economists on the simple mailbag cases." Recognizing the aversion of the more experienced attorneys to the ambitious structural matters, an assistant director stated:

If we eliminated the conduct cases, the Robinson-Patman matters and the more conventional merger cases from the menu of cases, we might find ourselves without any experienced trial attorneys. If they left, who would train our newcomers? Who would we rely upon to win cases? As it is, we have a severe shortage of experienced, talented senior men.

It is interesting to note that the Federal Trade Commission has often been criticized for prosecuting worthless cases of little economic value and for not vigorously attacking structural imperfections in the economy. Critics of the commission overlook the fact that the allocation of resources to investigations with minimal potential value to the consumer may be an inevitable cost of maintaining the morale and developing the skill of the attorneys.

Despite the bureau executives' efforts to induce the staff to remain, it should be emphasized that assigning lawyers to simple conduct matters is not likely to solve the chronic turnover problems. While an attorney might remain with the commission for a somewhat longer period of time if he were involved in a case that had a good chance of reaching trial, his tenure would probably not be lengthy. For the bureau director who would hope to prosecute protracted structural matters, the high turnover rate would seem to pose great obstacles to undertaking ambitious cases. The prosecution of complex matters, which requires years of cooperative effort, is especially difficult when the staff attorneys cannot be induced to remain with the commission for more than a short period of time. Quite clearly, the costs of a high turnover rate are considerable. The Bureau of Competition must continually invest its scarce resources to train attorneys, who leave the case (and, not infrequently, the commission as well) soon after acquiring valuable expertise. Moreover, constant changes in personnel could threaten the intellectual coherence of the case—changes in senior attorneys could disrupt the rhythm of an investigation and also result in dramatic shifts in tactics.

Notes

1
These statistics were provided by the Office of the Executive Director. See also Meredith Associates, Inc., *Report to the Chairman, Federal Trade Commission, Attorney and Attorney Manager, Recruitment, Selection and Retention,* (15 July 1976), pp. 12–14; this report is essentially a statistical survey with little analysis.

2
For a discussion of organizational maintenance and incentives, see James Q. Wilson, *Political Organizations* (New York: Basic Books, Inc., 1973), ch. 3.

3
Data supplied by the Office of the Executive Director.

4
Meredith Associates, *Report,* p. 13.

5
Ibid., p. 30.

6
Chester Barnard, *The Functions of the Executive* (Cambridge, Mass.: Harvard University Press, 1968) (first published in 1938), pp. 72, 212.

7
Wilson, *Political Organizations,* p. 31.

7
The Role of the Commissioners

The five commissioners are charged with making policy. They allocate resources among the various kinds of cases, determine whether a complaint should issue, promulgate rules and guidelines, and review the decisions of administrative law judges. On the basis of the evidence presented thus far, it is not at all clear, however, that the commissioners are actively involved in setting policy at the case-selection stage. Rather, they appear to respond to actions taken in the operating bureaus. The commissioners judge whether a complaint should issue, but the bureaus (the Bureau of Competition and the Bureau of Economics) choose which cases are to be developed. Perhaps such an observation is oversimplified. Closer study might reveal that the commissioners do not merely play a reactive role in the policy process. Knowing that the commissioners could ultimately decide not to issue a complaint, the executives of the bureaus might choose to investigate only those matters which they believe a majority of the commission would approve.

Quite clearly, a simple study of the criteria that the commissioners use in making decisions about antitrust matters may fail to explain adequately the extent to which those who are formally charged with setting policy affect case outcomes. If the commissioners have passive roles in the decision-making process, for example, then a discussion focusing on the factors that influence prosecutorial determinations would be misleading because it would imply that the antitrust case load simply results from the choices made by the five commissioners. Thus, before examining the variables affecting the commissioners' case-load decisions (a central component of the theme of this book), this chapter will explore the roles of the commissioners throughout the case-selection process. It will study the ways in which a commissioner can affect the behavior of his colleagues and bureau actors in an effort to further his objectives. After analyzing the case-selection process at the commission plateau, the chapter concludes with an assessment of collegial decision making. It questions whether the commission form of decision making is necessarily ineffective, as its critics maintain.

The Commission Chairman

A cursory review of the rules and statutes governing the commission might lead an observer to conclude that the other four
commissioners are equal in authority to the chairman, who is
appointed by the president. After all, each commissioner casts a
vote of equal weight in determining whether a complaint should
issue, whether compulsory process is in order, if a consent decree
settlement is acceptable, the manner in which an appeal should
be resolved, or how commission resources should be allocated.
The equality that appears to characterize the relationship among
the five commissioners is illusory, however; while the other
commissioners mostly react to what the Bureau of Competition
and the Bureau of Economics have done, the chairman can make
the staff attorneys and economists respond to his own policy
preferences.

The source of his power lies in Reorganization Plan Number 8 of
1950,[1] which vests the chairman with executive and administrative
powers, "including functions of the Commission with respect to
(1) the appointment and supervision of personnel employed
under the Commission, (2) the distribution of business among
such personnel and among administrative units of the Commission, and (3) the use and expenditure of funds.[2] Subsection b
of the plan, however, appears to constrain the chairman's power.
Under it the general policies and other determinations of the
commission are to guide the agency head; moreover, the individual commissioners are free to choose the personnel (including
attorney advisers who aid them in performing their tasks) who
work in their immediate offices. Finally, the chairman's nominees
to head the major divisions and bureaus must secure the approval
of a majority of the commissioners. In reality, these limitations are
not effective checks upon the chairman's power. What follows is
an attempt to explain how the chairman can manipulate outcomes
through his control of appointments, management, and the
budget.

The Chairman's Control of the Case Load
through Key Appointees

While major appointments—the executive director, general counsel, secretary, director of policy planning and evaluation, director of public information, and the directors of the Bureaus of Competition, Economics, and Consumer Protection—are subject to full commission approval, there is little doubt among the commissioners that the nominees are the chairman's people. The criterion for evaluating a nominee is competence; if the candidate is qualified, then he will almost certainly be approved. Only on rare occasions has a majority of the commission rejected the chairman's nominee, because he was judged not to have the necessary experience and expertise. While they believe that a bureau head should follow their suggestions regarding case investigations as diligently as he would heed the directives of the chairman, the commissioners recognize that their hopes are not likely to be realized.

That the bureau director should take his marching orders from the chairman rather than from the other commissioners is understandable. Without the support of the chairman, he would never have been chosen bureau director. Moreover, strong chairmen generally reach an understanding with their would-be appointees whereby the bureau chief consults the agency head before undertaking major antitrust initiatives and agrees to follow his instructions with respect to the conduct of investigations. A chairman who wants to maintain his dominant role in the decision-making process will be wary of attempts made by other commissioners to intervene in bureau affairs. Thus, it is likely that the chairman (assuming that he intends to have an active part) made certain that the nominee would keep him informed of all major communications that the other commissioners have directed to bureau officials. He will want to be sure that none of his colleagues secures positions of influence in the decision-making processes of the bureaus, which would enable them to challenge effectively his control of the commission. Commenting upon the ability of the chairman to manipulate the staff, Commissioner, and former chairman, Paul Rand Dixon recently stated:

"The Chairman has got them all by the 'nape of the neck'; don't let anybody kid you that he doesn't."[3]

Through his ability to affect the behavior of the bureau executives, the chairman can have an important impact on the character of the antitrust case load. By examining his relationship with the bureau heads who are involved in antitrust decision making and with the executive director, we can better appreciate how the chairman can use his position to advance his policy objectives at the bureau level and discover the reasons for the difficulty that the other commissioners generally have in determining bureau policy.

The Chairman and the Director of the Bureau of Competition
Because the bureau director will find it hard to achieve his own objectives (the enhancement of his professional reputation, the desire to affect changes in the corpus of antitrust law, and so on) without the support of the chairman, the bureau director is likely to conclude, it was revealed in the course of interviews, that it is in his interest to cooperate with the chairman.

A bureau director is usually an ambitious attorney, who was recruited from private practice and intends to stay in government service for only a few years. Within that limited time he hopes to shape an image as an aggressive prosecutor, who has gained the respect and confidence of the commissioners. A good reputation will undoubtedly make him attractive to his constituency (the business, legal, or academic community). For obvious reasons a corporation or law firm, for example, would like nothing better than to employ an attorney who is not only knowledgeable about the rules and practices of the commission, but who also has the trust and respect of the agency's decision makers. In order to cultivate his image, the bureau director must prosecute significant cases and have a winning record at the commission table (that is, the commissioners must approve a high percentage of the bureau director's recommendations to prosecute).

If the chairman is not satisfied with the performance of his bureau director, then he can make it difficult for him to achieve his objectives. The chairman can register his displeasure by berating the bureau director at commission meetings or by voting against his recommendations, especially in matters of arguable importance. (To be sure, the chairman is not likely to oppose the bureau director with regard to cases that clearly demand prosecution. To do otherwise would invite criticism about the way in which he handles his responsibilities and also hurt the agency's record.) The failure of the bureau director to secure the support of the chairman (and quite possibly a few of his colleagues as well) will soon become known to the private bar and to the staff attorneys within the Bureau of Competition. It will only be a matter of time before the private bar concludes that the bureau director has lost influence. In such circumstances, his future value to a prestigious law firm or corporation is likely to diminish. Thus, the bureau director will almost certainly consider the consequences of incurring the chairman's wrath. (A bureau director who does not intend to seek employment in the private bar may care little about losing influence within the agency, but in recent years bureau directors have joined private firms that deal with the commission.)

The bureau director also realizes that he could lose control of his staff if he no longer has the support of the chairman. Staff attorneys tend to accept the decisions of the bureau director, however grudgingly, if they believe he has the confidence of the chairman as well as knowledge of how the commissioners are likely to react to various proposals. Thus, should the bureau director reject a staff recommendation because he maintains that the chairman will oppose the proposal, the assistant directors might very well acquiesce in his decision. Once the chairman indicates that such trust is waning, then his appointee might very well encounter stiffer resistance from the staff. The assistant directors might question the bureau director's judgment with ever increasing frequency. With his authority challenged, his credibility weakened, and his effectiveness diminished—largely because of the chairman's withdrawal of support—the bureau director might be forced to resign. Not surprisingly, an ambitious bureau director is not likely to place himself in such an untenable position.

It should be noted that the consequences of a decision to remove an unyielding bureau director may not be without costs for the chairman. He would in effect be admitting, much to his embarrassment, that he had exercised poor judgment in selecting the bureau director. Moreover, the other commissioners might be satisfied with the performance of the bureau director and ally themselves against the chairman. In addition the bureau director could make an issue of his dismissal and use the media to discredit the commission. Should he argue, for example, that he was discharged because he wanted to press ahead with controversial investigations, his accusation—whether true or false—is likely to encourage protests from Capitol Hill, the media, and various public interest groups. It should be emphasized, however, that while disgruntled bureau directors could create problems for commission chairmen, agency heads have not been beset with such difficulties, at least in the recent past.

By capitalizing upon his relationship with the bureau director, the chairman can affect case-load decisions made at the bureau level. Because they desire to leave their imprint on agency affairs and perhaps because the private bar, the media, Congress, the academic community, and consumer groups will probably evaluate their tenure on the basis of prosecutions launched, recent chairmen (at least through Collier) have sought a dominant role in determining broad policy. If a chairman wants to have a substantial impact on the case load, then he must become involved at the earliest stages of bureau decision making, when the Evaluation Committee first decides whether to commit resources to an investigation. By intervening in the decision-making processes of the antitrust bureau through the medium of the bureau director, the chairman can set the general direction that the Bureau of Competition will follow and can act as a catalyst for increased case activities in particular areas. Thus, when the chairman (along with the other commissioners) passes judgment on the merits of a bureau recommendation, he (unlike his colleagues) will most probably already have secured some knowledge of the case at hand and may even have had a part in determining whether the bureau should have devoted resources to the matter at all.

A chairman, who does not become involved early in the decision-making process, will not have a role in choosing cases until the bureau seeks commission approval of a compulsory process resolution or a complaint recommendation. His decision-making role is then reactive—he simply votes for or against the proposal.

The chairman, as has been noted, uses the bureau director to advance his positions at the bureau level. He will tell the bureau director where he thinks resources are warranted and expect him to act accordingly. The chairman's interest in bureau affairs is likely to be especially keen when the case under discussion is of major importance and/or politically controversial. At Evaluation Committee meetings it is not uncommon for a bureau director to preface his remarks about a particular matter or policy with the words: "My sense is that the chairman would like us to. . . ." Usually, the chairman will entrust the bureau director with the responsibility of developing specific cases, strategies, and tactics in those program areas that he believes deserve attention. (He will also involve officials of the Bureau of Economics when economic advice is needed.) Because of the many claims upon his time, the chairman is seldom immersed in routine bureau affairs. For example, while the chairman might very well urge the Bureau of Competition to launch several investigations into the food industry, it is unlikely that he would specify the companies that should be the targets of the inquiry. As one former bureau director commented:

What the chairman wants is a case—preferably a big case, which will make headlines. It may be that a congressional committee has been roasting him about the alleged failure of the commission to act on a problem. Maybe he wants to take the intiative. In any event, he'll ask me to come up with something. . . . I'll present him with various options, outlining the ways in which the commission might proceed and he'll either choose from among them or let me decide.

While he expects the bureau director to agree with him on the general course that the Bureau of Competition should follow, a prudent chairman knows that the bureau director may be more useful to him if he is allowed to disagree with him on occasion at commission meetings. When the bureau director supports a staff recommendation, even if he knows it conflicts with the chairman's position, he gains the respect of his staff attorneys. He can present himself to them as a courageous and independent person, who is willing to defend his staff and risk incurring the wrath of the chairman. A bureau director, who is not thought of as the chairman's jackal, will probably find it easier to secure his staff's acceptance of unpopular decisions, many of which are likely to have been made at the behest of the agency's chief policy maker. Although he may tolerate some disagreement, the chairman will probably attempt to control dissent. He may require that the bureau director inform him in advance of all the criticisms he intends to make at commission meetings. In the words of a former bureau director: "He [the chairman] doesn't want to be caught off guard in front of his colleagues. He knows that there may be times that I feel I have to support the staff and that I'll use strong words. But he doesn't want the words to be *too* strong."

The Chairman and the Director of the Bureau of Economics The chairman's relationship with the director of the Bureau of Economics is quite different. He views the director of the bureau as a skilled economist whose technical expertise aids the commission in passing judgment on various matters and legitimizes the agency's decisions.

The fundamental criterion governing selection of the director of the Bureau of Economics is professional excellence—subject to the constraints of ideological compatibility. Past bureau directors have included Willard Mueller (currently at the University of Wisconsin), H. Michael Mann (currently of the Department of Economics at Boston College), Frederic M. Scherer (author of the leading textbook on industrial organization, *Industrial Market Structure and Market Performance*[4]), and Darius Gaskins (formerly of the University of California, Berkeley).[5] The technical aspects of the bureau director's tasks—overseeing the investigation and analysis of competitive conditions and business conduct in selected industries, collecting and processing economic and financial data, and preparing statistical reports on the performance of various sectors of the economy—require that the chairman nominate an expert, if he wants the Bureau of Economics to operate effectively. Recent bureau directors have been selected largely because their academic writings indicated that they were well equipped to undertake specific projects that the commission intended to pursue. Chairman Engman, for example, sought the services of Scherer because his knowledge of industrial organization seemed especially suited to the task of developing the Line of Business program.[6]

The extent to which the director of the Bureau of Economics is involved in the case-selection process is a matter of personal preference. Recent bureau directors have not chosen to involve themselves in every case-load decision but have decided to concentrate on a few specific cases. The assistant director for economic evidence has assumed most of the responsibilities in case-selection matters. Whatever the degree of his involvement, the bureau director, unlike his counterpart in the Bureau of Competition, is more likely to take positions without regard to the possible reactions of the chairman. Perhaps this is because the personal fortunes of the director of the Bureau of Competition are usually dependent upon maintaining the goodwill of the chairman while the career prospects of the director of the Bureau of Economics are unaffected by the nature of his relationship with the commission head. Above all else, the director of the Bureau of Economics is an established academic, who intends to return to university life following the completion of his tour of government service. Consequently he is loathe to compromise his intellectual integrity and diminish his reputation in the scholarly community. (To be sure, when only minor matters are at issue, the bureau may at times acquiesce in the recommendations of the lawyers to actions that it considers questionable: to always oppose the Bureau of Competition's position would lessen the economists' influence in the commission. The assistant director for economic evidence and the deputy bureau director, not the bureau director, generally make decisions having to do with such minor cases.)

An independent director of the Bureau of Economics does not generally threaten the interests of the chairman like an uncontrollable director of the Bureau of Competition. When the director of the Bureau of Economics supports a position that conflicts with the recommendation of the Bureau of Competition, he usually increases the chairman's freedom to maneuver. The different stances of the bureaus gives the chairman an opportunity to choose the position that best serves his interests. If he accepts the recommendation of the Bureau of Competition, then he could claim that the attorneys presented compelling legal arguments, which should take precedence over economic considerations. However, should he support the economists, he could maintain that whatever the merits of the attorneys' recommendation, the consumer benefit flowing from an enforcement action would probably be so negligible (if not nonexistent) that the commission would do well to allocate its scarce resources to other matters. The opposition of the director of the Bureau of Economics to a Bureau of Competition position could provide the chairman with an expedient justification to argue against commission action in controversial matters he would like to avoid.

Although the chairman's ability to maneuver is generally expanded when the Bureau of Economics contests the Bureau of Competition, there are circumstances in which conflict between the two bureaus could constrain the commission head. A chairman could have difficulty persuading his colleagues to allocate resources to cases that are politically controversial and/or path-breaking if the operating bureaus are in disagreement. In sensitive matters of great significance—an investigation of the auto industry or complaint proceedings against the major oil companies—the chairman seeks the support of both bureaus. If the chairman is backed by the director of the Bureau of Economics, he can claim the support of supposedly dispassionate technical experts.

The Chairman and the Executive Director The executive director, as the agency's chief operating officer, is charged with exercising executive and administrative supervision over the bureaus, staffs, and offices of the commission.[7] He derives his authority from the chairman, who is responsible for discharging the "executive and administrative functions of the Commission."[8] Unlike the heads of the operating bureaus, the executive director does not have a clearly defined role: what he does depends on what the chairman wants him to do. While the other commissioners must approve the chairman's nominee, they recognize that their subsequent control over the executive director will be minimal. Because they perceive that the executive director is not a policy maker but a custodian, the commissioners are willing to accept the notion that his primary loyalties are with the chairman.

The executive director seldom proceeds without first securing the chairman's consent, if only because his future at the commission would be in jeopardy were he to act before obtaining the approval of the agency head. Moreover, should the executive director act without the chairman's backing, he would probably have difficulty persuading the heads of the bureaus to do what they thought undesirable.

The Chairman's Effect on the Nature of the Case Load through his Control of Budget and Management

Management Through the executive director, the chairman can dominate the budgetary and managerial processes of the commission and thereby affect resource allocations among antitrust cases. Chairman Lewis Engman, realizing that control of resource allocation at the bureau level required daily knowledge of developments within the bureaus, brought a management consultant to the commission to develop a sophisticated information system. His executive director, R.T. McNamar, was the first management expert to hold that post. Previous executive directors had been attorneys with no business management or public-policy backgrounds.[9]

McNamar concentrated on upgrading case-monitoring capabilities, improving operational planning and control methods, and revamping accounting procedures. He designed a case tracking and status project to provide the commission with the means to monitor the progress of cases. Prior to the establishment of this system, the chairman had no reliable way of determining whether the Bureau of Competition was meeting deadlines in its investigations.[10] Because of the case tracking and status project, he can rather easily ascertain whether the bureau is meeting scheduled targets; if it is not, then he can ask the bureau director to account for any delays. Should the bureau director fail to provide him with what he considers to be a satisfactory explanation, the chairman can use the means at his disposal to induce the bureau head to follow his directives. Not surprisingly, the director of the Bureau of Competition resisted the efforts of the executive director to institute a case-tracking system, which would enable the chairman to monitor bureau affairs closely.

The Chairman's Domination of the Budgetary Process Theoretically there is no reason why the budget should not be a policy-making instrument of all the commissioners as it must be approved by a majority of the commission. However, the chairman has a major advantage because he can keep abreast of developments throughout the year and can use his executive director to convey his preferences to the operating bureaus, while the other commissioners have only a short time in July and September to review the budget. With limited staff support (each commissioner has only three assistants), they do not have the time to undertake a comprehensive review of commission matters and must limit their evaluations to a few select areas of interest. The Office of Policy Planning and Evaluation, which could assist the commissioners in analyzing agency performance, has not achieved its potential. During the Kirkpatrick years the office suffered from a lack of resources; moreover, the need to effect changes within the bureaus limited the office's opportunities to plan and evaluate. Chairmen Engman and Collier conceived of the office as a gadfly that would contest the positions of the operating bureaus and thereby widen the range of alternatives that the commission could consider. To date, the Office of Policy Planning and Evaluation has not been an integral factor in the process of selecting antitrust cases (although it has made contributions in the consumer protection area).

The Role of the Other Commissioners in the Case-Selection Process

The commissioners seem to be thwarted in setting policy. Although they vote to determine how resources should be allocated, the chairman and the bureau director dominate the budgetary process. Moreover, the commissioners do not appear to have the leverage needed to control the behavior of bureau staffs. Although they approve the chairman's nominees to the most important positions, these appointees usually respond only to the directives of the chairman. The commissioners are reduced to exhorting the staff to move ahead in particular areas, with no guarantee that the bureau heads will heed their pronouncements. As one commissioner stated: "Unless you're the chairman, you're really just a creature of the staff. I can ask the staff to undertake more . . . cases. They'll usually say: 'we'll try to do the best we can for you,' but then will do almost nothing."

What particularly disturbs the commissioners is the extent of the staff's control of the case-selection process. The Evaluation Committee disposes of the great majority of matters at the pre-preliminary stage. The commissioners pass judgment only on those cases that have cleared the Evaluation Committee. Thus, the operating bureaus (and the chairman), through their screening processes, determine which matters merit commission consideration and drastically limit the decision-making role of the commissioners. The commissioners argue that there may be many cases that they might believe worthy of at least a formal investigation, but which never come to their attention because the Evaluation Committee decided not to commit resources for such an inquiry.

In a move designed to curb the staff's discretion and increase their control in the case-selection process, the commissioners unanimously voted in February 1976 to require the heads of the Bureau of Competition and the Bureau of Consumer Protection to provide a bimonthly written explanation of their decisions to open or close investigations. The action, which was taken shortly after the resignation of Chairman Lewis Engman and before the appointment of his replacement, seeks to prevent future commission heads from dominating the policy-making process through his control of the staff and superior access to information about bureau affairs. Paul Rand Dixon, then acting chairman, argued that the requirement was necessary to insure that "the Commission was running the Commission's business, more than just sitting up here and taking what came here."[11]

While their efforts to affect staff behavior have been largely ineffective, the commissioners are not without means to make their preferences known. A commissioner can vote against staff recommendations regarding the disposition of various investigations; moreover, when he is charged with reviewing staff actions and proposing a course of action to the full commission, he leaves his mark on the case load.

The Commissioners: Affecting Outcomes by Veto
No matter how firmly he may control the staff, the chairman cannot achieve his policy objectives if a majority of the commissioners do not support his position. Thus, in a negative sense, the commissioners can affect the development of policy. As one commissioner noted: "We may not be too successful in getting the staff to do what we want them to do, but we sometimes can stop them from doing what they might want to do."

As an instrument of policy making, the veto was frequently used in the late sixties when Commissioners James Nicholson, Philip Elman, and Mary Gardiner Jones joined forces and successfully opposed many of the staff recommendations Chairman Paul Rand Dixon had supported. To be sure, the costs of decision making by veto were considerable. Trapped between the clashing enforcement philosophies of the commissioners, the Bureau of Restraint of Trade (since renamed the Bureau of Competition) was uncertain about the kinds of cases that the attorneys should pursue. On the one hand, bureau executives believed that it was in their interests to take their cues from the chairman because of his ability to affect their career prospects. On the other hand, these attorneys also realized that a majority of the commission did not share the chairman's views and could defeat the recommendations he backed. Were the attorneys to follow the instructions of the chairman, they would expend much time and effort on investigations, which ultimately would not result in commission complaints. The inability of the commission to provide the staff with coherent policy directives only served to heighten frustration at the bureau level. While the commissioners indicated on a case by case basis what the staff could not do, they did not clearly communicate what they believed the bureaus should be doing. Clearly, commission decision making by veto was a poor substitute for active, direct policy making.

The Moving Commissioner and Case Load Decisions

Although a commissioner seldom has an opportunity to directly affect staff behavior in advance of the actual voting, he may exert such influence when he is the *moving commissioner*. A moving commissioner is charged with carefully reviewing staff proposals and with recommending a course of action in advance of full commission deliberation on the matters. The secretary of the commission distributes assignments on a rotational basis. Because the commissioners may have to vote upon several cases in any week, it would be impossible for a commissioner to consider every matter in equal depth. Not infrequently, the bureau staff will support their memoranda with a *buff file*, consisting of thousands of pages of documentary evidence (company records, transcripts of investigational hearings, and so forth). To prevent a severe backlog, which would inevitably result if each commissioner were to examine all cases in detail, the commissioners entrust one of their colleagues with the task of thoroughly studying a particular matter upon which they will soon deliberate and with scrutinizing all facets of the case for its duration. The time that the moving commissioner devotes to his tasks depends on the nature of the case; some complex cases take several weeks. Once the commissioner has completed his work, the case is placed on the agenda for full commission consideration.

The moving commissioner is able to affect the behavior of the staff because his recommendation carries weight with his colleagues. Since he has usually devoted more time to analyzing the case than they have, the other commissioners give serious attention to his arguments. The influence of the moving commissioner is particularly strong in cases of minor importance. Indeed, if he is held in esteem, his colleagues may defer to his judgment. However, where the case at hand is of major significance, the other commissioners are likely to delve deeply into the matter before reaching judgment.

Because the staff attorneys realize that the moving commissioner can often affect how the other commission members will vote, they seek his support. For his part, the moving commissioner recognizes that he is in a position to make that support contingent upon the staff's responsiveness to the various suggestions that he might make. It is rather common for an attorney adviser (a lawyer on the commissioner's staff) to contact the bureau attorneys involved in the case and raise questions and informally indicate the changes that the commissioner deems advisable. Communication between the commissioner's office and the operating bureaus can also begin with the Bureau of Competition attorneys, who once they learn the identity of the moving commissioner, will almost certainly approach his attorney advisers in an effort to determine his views.

Thus, the individual commissioner can shape cases before the commission deliberates. But his influence is usually limited to the minority of cases in which he is the moving commissioner. Moreover, even if he is able to exert some control over the staff, he cannot achieve his policy objectives without the support of at least two colleagues. In fact, there is not much that a commissioner can do to affect the behavior of a fellow decision maker. If he is an antitrust expert, then, he may, of course, influence their thinking by forcefully presenting his views. In addition, it is conceivable that a commissioner would make his vote in support of his colleagues' positions contingent upon their endorsement of his views on particular matters. There is, however, little evidence to suggest that the trading of votes is common.

A commissioner might employ other less potent tactics in a campaign to mobilize support for his policy preferences. He could, for example, contact sympathetic congressmen and urge them to hold hearings which would dramatize the need for commission action. Moreover, he could privately encourage friendly senators and representatives to ask that the commission conduct thorough inquiries into areas which would not have been investigated in the absence of congressional prodding. (According to the terms of section 6(c) of the Federal Trade Commission Act, the commission is required "upon the direction of the President or either House of Congress to investigate and report the facts relating to any alleged violations of the antitrust acts.")[12] In his effort to marshal support, a commissioner might address groups (especially trade associations) that have an interest in commission policies and exhort them to lobby before those who are involved in the antitrust decision-making process; that is, commissioners or legislators. For instance, in a period when Robinson-Patman enforcement decreased sharply, Commissioner Paul Rand Dixon (a strong supporter of Robinson-Patman prosecutions) remarked to the National Retail Merchants Association (another advocate of increased Robinson-Patman activity) that

the FTC is very much a dynamic agency, and that what you know of us today may not be entirely accurate tomorrow. And so I urge you to keep abreast of what we do. In addition, I want to encourage you to let us know what your views are concerning our activities. It can, of course, be very helpful when making decisions to know what the views are of those who are to be affected.[13]

Styles of Decision Making

Up to this point, the discussion has focused upon the ways in which a commissioner might accomplish his policy objectives and has neglected the processes by which a commissioner reaches his decision. Because such processes structure the commissioner's choices, and therefore have much to do with the decisions he makes, it is necessary to examine them.

The most important component of the commissioner's decision-making apparatus is his staff. A commissioner normally has three attorney advisers who aid him in discharging his responsibilities. (The two commissioners who handle motions to quash subpoenas and adjudicative motions have one more aide, and the chairman has one more assistant in addition to the staff support, which the executive director's office provides.) The tasks of the attorney adviser are many: reviewing the buff files (case histories); evaluating staff memoranda; contacting staff economists and attorneys when their memoranda need clarification; writing summaries of the cases for the commissioner; undertaking legal research; providing the commissioner with recommendations as to the course of action that he should pursue; and drafting complaints, opinions, and other memoranda. The commissioner or his senior attorney adviser chooses his personal staff. The attorney advisers are drawn from the bureau staffs, the Office of the General Counsel, and sometimes directly from the graduating classes of prestigious law schools, and they can be divided into two groups. "Career" attorney advisers have worked in the offices of many commissioners, and their thorough knowledge of commission rules and practices provides invaluable support to the commissioner, particularly at the outset of his tenure. Because a commissioner will often have only limited experience with either antitrust or consumer protection laws (not infrequently, a new appointee will be totally unfamiliar with the past work of the agency), the veteran attorney adviser will also have the task of educating him.[14] The second cluster of attorney advisers consists of bright young lawyers, who tend to be graduates of the nation's finest law schools. Uncertain about their ultimate career objectives, these articulate individuals, upon leaving their present positions, plan to consider employment in another part of the agency, with private or public-interest law firms, in academia, Congress, or the executive.

The attorney advisers tend to regard antitrust policy differently from Bureau of Competition lawyers; the latter are more likely to conclude that there is reason to believe that the law has been violated and that the issuance of a complaint would be in the public interest. The perspective of the attorney adviser tends to be much broader than that of the bureau lawyer because the commissioner's aide is charged with evaluating a whole range of commission cases having to do with both consumer protection and antitrust matters. He is in a better position to compare the merits of proposed complaints and to determine which should have priority, given the agency's limited resources. Moreover, because he has not been involved in the investigation and has no personal stake in its outcome, the attorney adviser finds it easier to be dispassionate than does the bureau attorney. Having invested much time and energy in a case, a bureau lawyer quite naturally believes that it is important. Because he wants to secure trial experience, the staff lawyer hopes that the commission will issue a complaint. An attorney adviser, however, is likely to be more skeptical about the merits of proposed complaints because his task is to be critical of the staff's work product and to make certain that the bureaus do not misinterpret data.

Ultimately, the commissioners must make their own judgments on the matters that confront them. They structure the decision-making process within their offices differently. Generally, the commissioner uses his staff according to his personal style, his background in antitrust and consumer protection law, and the matters under consideration. Rarely have there been commissioners who have allowed their attorney advisers to totally dominate them. Such commissioners have generally been unfamiliar with antitrust and/or consumer protection laws and the rules and practices of the agency. But there are others whose very ignorance of commission affairs leads them, upon assuming office, to become involved in virtually every aspect of the staff's work in an effort to educate themselves about the agency's activities.

Some commissioners, especially those who are experts in antitrust law, are their own chiefs of staff. They carefully examine the work load, determine what questions need answering, decide who will perform the necessary tasks, and closely monitor their staff's behavior. They might attempt to undertake most of the work themselves, reducing the staff to a minor role. (Observers of the commission claim that few of the commissioners who have had detailed knowledge of agency affairs have been inclined to devote the considerable effort that such a style of decision making requires.)[15]

Most commissioners are solicitous of their staff's views and look to the attorney advisers to provide them with a full range of options before determining their own positions. They may charge the senior attorney adviser with the task of parceling out the work among other staff members. When they are the moving commissioners, they will immerse themselves in all aspects of the case and scrutinize buff files and memoranda from the Bureaus of Competition and Economics. In those less-than-significant matters, these commissioners will tend to rely upon the recommendation of an attorney adviser or a trusted colleague with whom they generally agree. Moreover, they may choose to concern themselves less with nonagenda matters (which are noncontroversial, do not evoke disagreement at the staff level, involve section 7 Clayton Act case, or pose novel legal questions) and prefer instead to delegate primary responsibility for such cases to attorney advisers. (Every commissioner votes personally on each circulation.)

The Criteria for Determining Whether to Vote to
Issue a Complaint

A commissioner should vote to issue a complaint when (1) there is reason to believe that the laws have been violated and (2) he concludes that commission action would be in the public interest. Because the public interest is not defined in law or statute, the commissioner has the license to consider legal, economic, political, and other factors in reaching his decision. Analyzing how the commission weighs these various criteria is not a simple task for the observer, principally because the complaint itself reveals little about the thought processes of the commissioner. It merely identifies the respondents, states the alleged violations of law, outlines the effects of the possible violations, and sometimes includes a notice of contemplated relief. However, on the basis of analysis of agency budgets, interviews with the decision makers and examination of their public testimony, some remarks can be made about the factors the commissioners consider in the deliberations.

Antitrust enforcement could seek to serve any of several ends. The criteria underlying a commissioner's vote on a particular matter are likely to depend upon the nature of the case. As Commissioner Elizabeth Hanford Dole has noted: "There are not set case-selection formulae. . . . I evaluate each case on the basis of the unique fact situation it presents and the probable benefits to competition and consumers from Commission action."[16]

There are several factors a commissioner may consider when evaluating a complaint recommendation. First, he (or his attorney adviser) will probably ascertain whether successful prosecution of the investigation is likely to yield results that will further his policy preferences. For example, if he thinks that antitrust enforcement should seek to maintain small business, then he will probably support Robinson-Patman action. A commissioner, who thinks that antitrust policy should serve political or social objectives, is less apt to weigh seriously the position of the Bureau of Economics than would a colleague who believes that commission action should promote economic efficiency.

Second, in making his decision about how to vote, the commissioner will probably attempt to judge whether the legal foundation of the case is solid; that is, he will predict the likelihood of the attorneys' satisfying the administrative law judges, the commissioners, and perhaps the appellate courts that the laws have been violated. Should he think that the case may be an appropriate vehicle for the setting of a precedent that he favors, the commissioner is likely to support the issuance of a complaint.

Third, a politically sensitive commissioner might consider the likely reactions of outside actors—Congress, the media, public interest groups, the business community—to a decision to prosecute. There are relatively few occasions when the agency must make controversial decisions. Usually, the commission will hesitate to act if there is deep disagreement between the operating bureaus as to what course the agency should follow. Although the commission might attempt to delay reaching a prosecutorial decision until such time when controversy can be avoided or minimized, the agency ultimately has not been deterred from bringing suit against major economic interests.

In making their determinations most of the commissioners interviewed stated that they did not consider whether the organization has the capacity to prosecute matters. The difficulties in prosecuting complex cases hardly entered into their calculus. Perhaps their lack of knowledge about bureau affairs (the chairman, it should be remembered, is really the only commission member who is thoroughly informed about developments within the Bureau of Competition) accounts for their not evaluating bureaucratic obstacles to the prosecution of antitrust matters.

The Commission Form of Governance

Having examined the case-selection process at the commission level, it is perhaps appropriate that this chapter conclude with some thoughts about collegial decision making. Political scientists and students of public administration commonly write that single-headed agencies operate more effectively than do collegial bodies.

The collegial form of decision making, critics maintain, invites irresponsibility since individual commissioners need not be concerned about being held accountable for their actions.[17] That is, collegiality provides a cloak of anonymity that allows the commissioners to act without fear of public reaction. Moreover, a collegial administration, its detractors continue, has difficulty managing the bureaucracy, because the staff attorneys in the operating bureaus have divided loyalties. In their quest for influence the commissioners are likely to compete with one another for control of the staff and in the process exacerbate tensions in the operating bureaus. Collegial decision making is not well-suited to the formulation of coherent policy, commission critics also state, since agreements are difficult to fashion when several policy makers must reach the same view before the course of action is set. Decisions tend to be inconsistent, depending as they do upon the support of shifting ad hoc majorities. Agreement is reached after lengthy bargaining sessions; long delays result in severe backlogs. Because a consensus on the substance of the issues before them is hard to achieve, so the argument proceeds, the commissioners concentrate on procedural solutions. Case evaluation thus focuses on form rather than substance.

In many contexts it may very well be the case that collegial bodies frustrate coherent policy making. However, the experience of the Federal Trade Commission indicates that the collegial form is not necessarily unworkable. Members of the Federal Trade Commission are held accountable for their actions: their votes are on the record. Vigorous congressional oversight and scrutiny of nominees could also increase the likelihood that the commissioners will act responsively. In drawing the attention of the media to agency activities, public interest groups make it difficult for the commissioners to act in secret.

Those who criticize the commission because collegial bodies are incapable of managing a bureaucracy seem not to realize that for all intents and purposes one individual—the chairman— exercises control over administrative and budgetary matters. As this chapter has described, the chairman has various means to influence the behavior of the staff. To be sure, when a collegial body is deeply divided about the course the agency should follow, then the setting of intellectually consistent policy becomes difficult. However, when there is some general consensus among the commissioners—as has been the case in the 1970s—collegial decision making does not seem to pose absolute barriers to the formulation of coherent policy. Certainly, compromises are made in the coalition-building process. But they are not limited to the Federal Trade Commission: in making judgments, single-headed administrators are often constrained by such forces as department heads, presidents, their own staffs, and Congress. If the setting of broad policy is a difficult task, it may not be so much because an agency is single- or multi-headed but because the issues that confront decision makers are complex and hard to resolve. While the existence of diverse interests may at times obstruct the formulation of policy, on other occasions, the input of different perspectives may improve the ultimate outcome.

Finally, in concentrating upon the differences between single-headed and collegial bodies, critics of the commission have inadequately considered the effects that the organizational arrangements and internal processes of the agency have on the quality of case-load decisions. In studying the Bureau of Economics and the Bureau of Competition, they might have concluded that the existence of two separate bureaus—one sometimes in competition with the other—increases the likelihood that the commissioners will have all relevant data in making judgments. Examination of bureau-level operations in the Federal Trade Commission would also reveal that collegial administration does not necessarily cause severe case backlogs. Through quality control mechanisms—the Evaluation Committee and the case-tracking system—the commission has virtually eliminated backlog difficulties.

Notes

1
64 Stat. 1264 (1950).

2
U.S., Congress, Senate, Committee on Expenditures in the Executive Departments, *Report No. 1562*, 81st Cong., 2nd sess., 1950, pp. 3–4.

3
U.S., Congress, House, Committee on Small Business, Ad Hoc Subcommittee on Antitrust, the Robinson-Patman Act and Related Matters, *Hearings on Recent Efforts to Amend or Repeal the Robinson-Patman Act,* part 3, 94th Cong., 2nd sess., 1976, p. 95.

On political statecraft in the bureaucracy, see Hugh Heclo, *A Government of Strangers: Executive Politics in Washington* (Washington, D.C.: Brookings, 1977), and Marver H. Bernstein, *The Job of the Federal Executive* (Washington, D.C.: Brookings, 1958).

4
Frederic M. Scherer, *Industrial Market Structure and Economic Performance* (Chicago: Rand-McNally, 1970).

5
All bureau directors returned to academia soon after concluding their stint with the commission, except Gaskins (1976–1977), who left the agency to become chief economist for the Civil Aeronautics Board (*National Journal,* 9 (6 August 1977), p. 1244).

6
In his efforts to secure acceptance for the structural case, for example, Engman, speaking before an ABA panel, invoked the name of Frederic Scherer, a leading industrial organization economist. See comment of Lewis Engman, "Interview with Lewis Engman," *Antitrust Law Journal,* 43 (1974): 449.

7
Immediately under the executive director's supervision are the assistant executive director for administration and the assistant executive director for regional operations.

8
Reorganization Plan No. 8 of 1950, 64 Stat. 1264.

9
Chairman Michael Pertschuk has apparently returned to the tradition of naming attorneys to the post of executive director. Margery Smith, McNamar's successor, has had a distinguished career with the commission; she served as assistant to Chairmen Engman and Collier and subsequently as acting head of the Bureau of Consumer Protection.

10
For a study of administrative feedback from "subordinates to leaders," see Herbert Kaufman, *Administrative Feedback: Monitoring Subordinates' Behavior* (Washington, D.C.: Brookings, 1973).

11
Antitrust and Trade Regulation Report, no. 750, 10 February 1976, p. A–25.

12
38 Stat. 717 (1914), as amended, 15 U.S.C. 46 (1976).

13
Paul Rand Dixon, "The Robinson-Patman Act is Not Dead, Merely Dormant" (Address delivered at the National Retail Merchants Association, 2 May 1975).

14
Perhaps there is no better example of a career attorney adviser than Charles Mueller. A populist, Mueller served several commissioners. He was at the forefront of efforts to bring economic analysis to bear in caseload determinations. While with the commission, Mueller often wrote under a pseudonym for the *Antitrust Law and Economics Review* and argued that the agency should prosecute the big case. He was one of the principal movers of the cereal case. Mueller left the commission in 1975, convinced that the agency's antitrust effort was floundering. In his last assignment Mueller was attorney adviser to Mayo Thompson. Mueller and Thompson were strange bedfellows. Both were concerned with consumer benefit as an objective on antitrust action. However, whereas Thompson would have placed greater reliance on the market, Mueller would have depended more on antitrust action.

15
By my calculations, the average tenure of a commissioner from 1961 to 1976 was 5.1 years, less than a single term. Of those commissioners sitting in 1972, only Paul Rand Dixon remains. Quite obviously, the inexperience of the commissioners is likely to contribute to the difficulties in making informed judgments about complex problems.

16
Statement of Commissioner Elizabeth Hanford Dole in U.S., Congress, House, Committee on Small Business, Ad Hoc Subcommittee on Antitrust, the Robinson-Patman Act and Related Matters, *Hearings on Recent Efforts to Amend or Repeal the Robinson-Patman Act,* part 3, 94th Cong., 2nd sess., 1976, p. 81.

17
See, for instance, The President's Advisory Council on Executive Organization, *A New Regulatory Framework: Report on Selected Regulatory Agencies* (Washington, D.C.: Government Printing Office, 1971).

The Ash Council, which criticized plural-headed administrations, argued that the antitrust responsibilities of the commission should be shifted to a Federal Antitrust Board. Why there should be two antitrust agencies within the executive (the Antitrust Division and the Federal Antitrust Board) is unclear. The Ash Council erred in distinguishing the FTC from the Antitrust Division by claiming that the former is more concerned with economic issues while the latter is more preoccupied with legal matters. For both agencies antitrust enforcement involves the interaction of law and economics. Moreover, in arguing that the antitrust functions of the commission should be divorced from its consumer protection activities, the council failed to grasp the ways in which antitrust law can be used in consumer cases (the cereal litigation, based in part on product differentiation, is illustrative of this point). Finally, although the council condemned the plural-headed agency, it recommended that the Federal Antitrust Board consist of three members—two economists and a chairman—who would have the responsibility of managing the bureaucracy. This proposal is hardly an improvement over the present arrangement. As has been noted, the chairman of the commission already is charged with managing the bureaucracy. The Ash Council proposal, by mandating that two economists be appointed to the Federal Antitrust Board, evidently envisioned an agency that would not be concerned with noneconomic objectives of antitrust policy, but rather with economic efficiency.

For a general examination of other areas covered by the Ash Council, see Roger G. Noll, *Reforming Regulation: An Evaluation of the Ash Council Proposals* (Washington, D.C.: Brookings, 1971).

8
Shaping Outcomes: The Uses and Limits of Reorganization, the Program Budget, and Quality Control Mechanisms

When executives try to effect major policy shifts, they often encounter opposition from those who perceive that change could threaten their interests. Recent bureau directors and chairmen have used reorganization and quality control devices in their efforts to overcome staff resistance and facilitate policy innovation and program implementation. Benefits have been immediate, but only limited in the long term. This chapter examines the ways in which commission chairmen and bureau officials have tried to affect the character of the case load and explains why the principal means for achieving their purposes have failed to eliminate the problems that plague the agency.

Affecting the Character of the Case Load through Reorganization

Reflecting upon various structural changes, Commissioner James Nicholson concluded that "the Commission's effectiveness is not materially related to its form or organization."[1] Certainly, well-designed structures may not be able to advance the purposes of an organization that lacks a talented staff. Where structural defects exist, superior personnel may be able to overcome them. However, it is important to recognize that organizational structures can constrain the decision maker as well as facilitate his exercise of control. Several government study groups, recognizing the importance of structural design, have viewed reorganization as a cure for various agency maladies.

The First Hoover Commission criticized the agency of the late forties for separating the bureau of investigation from the division of litigation.[2] The arrangement produced uncoordinated effort, and caused friction between investigators and litigators. The former resented the control that the latter, who determined whether to recommend the issuance of a complaint and assumed trial tasks, exercised over case-selection decisions. In its report the Hoover Commission recommended that the Federal Trade Commission organize according to a programmatic plan, reflecting the fundamental division of its responsibilities between deceptive practice cases and restraint of trade matters. This scheme was adopted but was operative for only a few short years.

Accepting the proposals of the Heller Committee, the commission in 1954 reinstituted an organizational plan according to functional responsibilities.[3] In an effort to avoid the problems of coordination and tension that plagued its operations when trial and investigative staffs were separated, the commission established a project attorney system: the investigative attorney and the trial lawyer were to work together from the outset of the case. However, the friction persisted as did the inefficiencies resulting from the separation of information-gathering and case-evaluation processes.

In 1960, the Landis Report condemned, as had the First Hoover Commission, the functional division of trial and investigative staffs.[4] Dean James Landis charged that this arrangement had "resulted in a fractionalization of the handling of cases before the Commission and has proved to be a failure."[5] With the advent of the new administration in 1961, the commission returned to programmatic divisions and established the Bureau of Restraint of Trade and the Bureau of Deceptive Practices as the agency's principal operating units.

In 1970, another administration reorganized the commission once again. The programmatic divisions were retained but were renamed. The Bureau of Restraint of Trade became the Bureau of Competition, and the Bureau of Deceptive Practices was retitled the Bureau of Consumer Protection. The changes that the incoming leadership sought to institute, however, were not merely cosmetic. Like previous administrations, the new regime viewed reorganization as a means to establish institutional arrangements that could facilitate the adoption of its policies and dissolve those structures that hindered the realization of its objectives.

By 1970, the Federal Trade Commission was an agency under siege; it was severely critized by the American Bar Association,[6] Ralph Nader and associates,[7] Congress, the Bureau of the Budget, and its own officials. In 1969, Commissioner James Nicholson wrote that much of the staff believed that the commission did not act "with any clearly and previously formulated purpose or objective."[8] Chairman Caspar Weinberger, whom President Nixon appointed and charged with revitalizing the agency, responded to Nicholson's statement:

If this is true (or even if the staff thinks this is true) then the Commission is not fulfilling its function. Major decisions are not being made by us but by the staff. . . .

Another undesirable situation is created by lack of central control and policy planning. If the staff believes its activities are not subject to central control and evaluation, a perfect opportunity is given them to delay or disregard vexing problems. This is especially true at the Division levels.[9]

The structural organization of the Bureau of Restraint of Trade contributed to the problems that concerned Nicholson and Weinberger. The bureau was divided into three divisions: the Division of Mergers, the Division of General Trade Restraints, and the Division of Discriminatory Practices. Each division was solely responsible for investigative and litigative tasks arising from particular types of violations. The Division of Mergers handled cases relating to corporate mergers, acquisitions, joint ventures, and interlocking directorates. The Division of Discriminatory Practices had jurisdiction over Robinson-Patman violations. The Division of General Trade Restraints was responsible for all cases having to do with trade and unfair methods of competition arising under section 5 of the Federal Trade Commission Act.

Because of the rigid division of labor among the various units within the Bureau of Restraint of Trade, most attorneys were skilled in pursuing only those violations that were part of their division's bailiwick. Experience in only a narrow area of antitrust law spawned parochial attitudes among the staff attorneys about the kinds of cases that merited resources. Having become familiar with a particular part of antitrust doctrine, the attorney was reluctant to become involved in areas in which his knowledge was limited.

The new leadership that assumed control of the commission in 1970 recognized that the organization of the Bureau of Restraint of Trade reinforced staff attitudes and behavior. Moreover, they believed that their efforts to change the nature of the case load— to bring innovative, economically oriented cases—would have little chance of succeeding if structural units, which posed obstacles to the realization of their plans, remained in place.

Within five months of assuming office, Chairman Caspar Weinberger (nicknamed "Cap the Knife" because of his reputation as a tough-minded manager when he was California's director of finance) presented to the commission a plan for internal reorganization of the agency.[10] Weinberger proposed that in the realm of antitrust the commission abolish the specialized divisions that comprised the Bureau of Restraint of Trade and replace them with general litigation units. Each unit (commonly referred to as a shop by commission attorneys) was to have investigative and litigative responsibilities, covering the entire range of the antitrust laws. Young recruits would be trained to handle all kinds of matters and would presumably develop a broad perspective of the ways in which the antitrust laws might be applied. They would not necessarily be under the direction of one assistant director. Every effort would be made to expose them to a number of supervisors with differing approaches to antitrust enforcement. The well-rounded attorney, the commission leadership reasoned, would be more receptive to innovative approaches to antitrust policy than would the lawyer who devoted all of his attention to a narrow area of the law. On 13 May 1970—one week after Weinberger presented his proposals—the full commission approved the reorganization plan.

Removing structural obstacles was not enough to upgrade the nature of the case load. If the commission chairman were to effect changes, then he would have to attract talented attorneys to serve at all levels of the agency. The general quality of commission lawyers in 1970 was not at all distinguished. In order to be able to persuade superior attorneys to join the commission, Chairman Weinberger had to find some means of ridding the agency of those lawyers who were not performing their tasks satisfactorily.[11] Promising attorneys would be unlikely to enter commission service if they perceived that their prospective colleagues did not meet adequate performance measures.

In devising a strategy to rid the agency of the great number of incompetent attorneys, the commission leadership determined the effect that the Civil Service rules would have on their efforts to change radically the composition of the staff. Because they are considered "excepted" personnel (according to schedule A of the Civil Service classification system), lawyers are not entitled to standard tenure rights.[12] They have appeal rights only through the federal courts. However, if an attorney has served in the military, then he is classified as "preference eligible," which means that an employer can take "adverse action" against him only "for such causes as will promote the efficiency of the service." In 1970, a number of commission attorneys were "preference eligibles."

In his efforts to root out incompetent attorneys, the chairman was aided by Reorganization Plan Number 8 of 1950 and Reorganization Plan Number 4 of 1961, which empowered him to eliminate any position pursuant to an overhaul.[13] By abolishing a position, the chairman can effectively pressure its occupant to leave the commission. All attorneys whose positions are eliminated receive thirty days' notice. Those categorized as "preference eligible" are reassigned or reclassified. Since the organization is not required to accommodate "preference eligible" lawyers when making transfer decisions, an attorney who is transferred to a location he deems undesirable has no means of forcing the agency to change its decision.

Armed with the means to remove attorneys, Weinberger still had to identify those persons whose services were no longer desired. For the purpose of determining the attorneys whose performance levels were unacceptable, the chairman (who knew few of the agency's personnel) appointed Basil Mezines as his executive assistant and later as the acting director of the Bureau of Competition. Mezines was not only a commission lawyer of some twenty years' experience but also one of the agency's few Republicans. For the nine months of his regime, Weinberger depended upon Mezines' knowledge of commission personnel, rules, and procedures. Miles Kirkpatrick, who became chairman in September of 1970, similarly relied upon Mezines, whom he designated as the executive director of the commission.

By the spring of 1971, eighteen of thirty-one top staff members left the agency because their positions had been eliminated through Weinberger's reorganization.[14] Approximately two hundred of the nearly six hundred middle- and lower-level staff attorneys (in both the Bureau of Competition and the Bureau of Consumer Protection) severed their association with the commission. Apart from the efforts of the commission leadership, many of these attorneys would have left the agency anyway: the turnover rate was generally high and the number of departing lawyers probably swelled as a natural consequence of the shift from a Democratic to a Republican administration. Still, the work of Mezines was not inconsiderable and probably had a snowballing effect throughout the agency. Mezines persuaded approximately sixty high-level attorneys to resign. He convinced several that retirement would be preferable to remaining with a revitalized commission, which, unlike its predecessor, would require much from its attorneys. Still others resign after Mezines indicated that he planned to transfer them to a regional office that they considered unattractive. Some agreed to leave the agency after Mezines suggested that he would do all that he could to help secure employment for them in other government organizations. Approximately one dozen attorneys were dismissed with thirty days' notice. At least ten other attorneys were transferred to the Cost of Living Council, which requested staff support from various government agencies.

With the cleansing of the agency, the commission leadership was ready to begin an aggressive recruitment effort to attract superior talent. The agency was successful in this campaign largely because of Chairman Kirkpatrick. A distinguished Philadelphia lawyer, who had been chairman of the ABA Section on Antitrust Law and had headed the bar association's investigation of the Federal Trade Commission, Kirkpatrick was widely regarded as a person of great integrity and competence. He was able to secure the services of three men of proven ability to head the operating bureaus. Alan Ward, who agreed to become the director of the Bureau of Competition, was a liberal Republican who had worked with Kirkpatrick on many ABA projects. The new director of the Bureau of Economics—H. Michael Mann— had served as special economics assistant at the Antitrust Division. Robert Pitofsky, who was professor of law at New York University Law School, and a former counsel to the ABA Commission to Study the FTC (and is currently a commissioner) assumed the post of director of the Bureau of Consumer Protection. They joined the FTC because of the challenge and with the confidence that the chairman seriously intended to revitalize the agency. With leadership of such high caliber, the commission was soon attracting graduates of the best law schools.

The Development of Evaluation and Control Processes within the Bureau of Competition

Restructuring the organization, eliminating incompetent personnel, and securing the services of superior talent were important elements of the agency's revitalization effort. However, these measures alone were not sufficient to achieve the commission's objective of upgrading the quality of the antitrust case load. If commission officials were to assume a significant role in determining the case load, launching major investigations, and prosecuting innovative cases, then they would have to create planning mechanisms and install monitoring devices to control staff behavior. They would have to institutionalize decision-making processes that would establish their authority to shape policy.

Under the Bureau of Restraint of Trade arrangement, the bureau hierarchy tended to ratify staff action rather than set policy. Bureau executives reviewed staff recommendations in a perfunctory manner; approval of staff suggestions was routine. There were no processes through which commission officials could impose their will on the staff. In the absence of efforts by their superiors to limit their discretion, the staff attorneys came to believe that they had a right to decide which matters should be investigated.

The consequences of the failure of the commission leadership to set the agency's course of action and of the de facto delegation of authority to the staff were predictable. Case-selection decisions were made on an ad hoc basis by individual attorneys. Each time a complaint was received, an attorney, usually at a rather low level, had to decide whether the matter was sufficiently important to justify an investigation. Because there were no agencywide standards available to enable him to compare the relative merit of the matter with some other activity within his division, the attorney had to make judgments based solely on his personal decision-making calculus, and he often exercised poor judgment. Most of the investigations were opened with apparently little thought as to whether the consumer could gain substantially if the case were prosecuted. (A vast number of man-hours were committed to the Robinson-Patman cases.) In general, attorneys opted for investigations that were simple, seemingly manageable, and easy to prosecute.

Few investigations led to case prosecutions primarily because the staff attorneys could not find sufficient evidence to justify the issuance of a complaint. Since the bureau hierarchy did not usually follow the daily development of cases and did not hold attorneys accountable for the investigations that they opened, the staff lawyers could waste resources on doubtful matters with impunity.

Most attorneys would not close investigations even after it became obvious that there was no reason to maintain an open file. Lawyers were loathe to recommend the termination of investigations, because they did not want to admit to the commission hierarchy that they had erred in originally opening the investigation. One veteran remarked with disgust: "The feeling among most of the guys was that the so-called division chiefs would never find out about an investigation that wasn't going well unless the attorneys on the case volunteered the information. So why should they draw attention to their shortcomings?" An attorney who concluded that he could not uncover evidence to prove his case would simply suspend work on the matter without formally asking the commission to close the investigation. As a result of the lax oversight procedures within the Bureau of Restraint of Trade, by 1969 there was a great proliferation in the number of unsupportable investigations—those inquiries which should have been closed but remained formally open. The problem had become so acute that in 1969 the commission created a Special Committee on Case Load Screening, consisting of bureau attorneys and attorney advisers. The committee—popularly known as the "Garbage Committee"—was charged with reviewing all of the agency's investigations to determine which should be closed. By 1970, the commission had accepted most of the recommendations of the Garbage Committee and terminated approximately 75 percent of the agency's investigations. On 1 December 1969 the commissioners authorized the closing of 700 of 1000 investigations.[15]

Bureau of Competition Director Alan Ward realized that the character of the commission case load would remain unchanged until means were found to prevent the attorneys from committing limited resources to worthless investigations and mechanisms were created to facilitate the rational allocation of bureau funds.[16] Institutional processes were needed to enable Ward and his staff to (1) review all existing investigations and ascertain whether they should be continued or terminated, (2) divest the staff attorneys of the authority to open investigations, (3) evaluate carefully all proposals for case investigations, (4) monitor closely the progress of inquiries, (5) set realistic time limits with respect to the duration of preliminary and formal investigations, and (6) decide in a timely fashion whether the commission should close its investigations. Ward and his staff—with the support of Chairman Kirkpatrick— were principally responsible for the development of quality control procedures in the Bureau of Competition. Basil Mezines, who deftly identified incompetent personnel, seemed to have only a limited interest in devising techniques that would upgrade case-evaluation efforts. A strong proponent of the Robinson-Patman cases, Mezines had little use for innovative cases.

The Reorganization Plan of 1970 called for a greater emphasis on case evaluation and created an assistant director for evaluation, who was charged with the tasks of developing and maintaining a new case-selection process. In staffing the position, Chairman Weinberger sought an individual who recognized the need for some evaluative mechanism, knew about bureau activities, but had no personal stake in the existing case load. Daniel Hanscom, who had served in the commission's Office of the General Counsel, which handles litigation in the federal courts, was appointed the first assistant director for evaluation. He described his task as "demanding" and "exciting." Reflecting upon his year as Assistant Director for Evaluation, Hanscom, who later became the commission's Chief Administrative Law Judge, commented: "The job description was incredible in that I was expected to do everything with very little assistance—from opening cases, to closing them, setting deadlines, monitoring progress. I felt as if I were the Bureau's nerve center, its quarterback."[17]

Hanscom spent much of his time determining which investigations should be closed. He usually terminated ones that had been dormant for several years. Initially, the assistant director for evaluation had primary responsibility for deciding whether to authorize a preliminary or formal investigation. It soon became apparent, however, that a single individual with limited staff support could not possibly shoulder all of the burdens associated with the evaluation process. Gradually, as the new Bureau of Competition leadership (the bureau director and the assistant directors for litigation) familiarized themselves with agency activities, they assumed a greater role in determining the case load. The tasks of the assistant director for evaluation shifted within one year (from 1971 to 1972) from supervising the opening and closing of cases to developing institutions and procedures for allocating resources rationally among cases.

Harry Garfield, who succeeded Hanscom in 1972, established procedures to facilitate the orderly screening of correspondence, the distribution of information to bureau executives, and the maintenance of accurate records. Soon the Evaluation Office became the principal support for the Evaluation Committee, created in 1972. The committee, which originally consisted exclusively of Bureau of Competition officials, was to be a centralized unit for the allocation of scarce resources to those cases that could substantially benefit the consumer. Later Ward and his successor James Halverson (bureau director from 1973 to 1975) invited representatives from the Bureau of Economics to participate at Evaluation Committee meetings.

A significant innovation, which strengthened the case-selection process within the Bureau of Competition, was a computerized case-tracking system—a precursor of the machinery subsequently introduced commissionwide by Executive Director Richard T. McNamar. Designed by Harry Garfield, the computerized system provided bureau executives with current and easily accessible data concerning profiles of the matters under investigation, the status of the investigations, the tentative schedule for the investigations, target dates for the processing of key events in the life of the matter, staff assignments, and the amount of resources committed to the cases. Such information is useful to the bureau executives in directing complex ongoing investigations and in planning new cases. Prior to the development of this information system, it would have been extremely difficult to undertake several industrywide investigations, simply because the bureau executives did not have readily available means of ascertaining the resources that could be allocated at any given moment.

Bureau executives and the chairman further tightened their grip on the decision-making process by controlling the budgetary process. As Wildavsky and others have noted, the budget is not merely a document that outlines expenditures, it is also a means of translating financial resources into specific purposes.[18] It can be a statement of what the government is doing or intends to accomplish. The budget is a record of the outcome of conflict among various interests. It reflects the choices and trade-offs that an agency has made among alternative programs. Thus, it is not surprising that commission officials took steps to assume the dominant role in the budgetary process. They recognized that if they could control how resources were allocated, then they could shape the direction of agency policy.

In the years before fiscal 1976, the focus of the budget was on the organizational units of the commission. More specifically, the budget was concerned with the requested personnel and funding level of these units and the object classes for which increases were sought. The budget request broadly outlined future activities and justified the need for increases. It also provided a description (mainly a compilation of existing cases and activities) of the previous year's base program. In the 1960s, when antitrust action was oriented toward cases that were often justified on non-economic grounds, the line-item budget seemed adequate. For the revitalized commission of the 1970s, however, the rational allocation of funds requires a budget that relates resources to objectives.

As an instrument of policy planning, the program budget seemed to offer promise.[19] The budget would aid the commissioners by (1) clearly defining the objectives of the organization, (2) describing how funds were spent and whether objectives were achieved, (3) arraying alternative policies, and (4) assembling as much data possible about the costs and benefits of each alternative. With this information about policy alternatives, the commissioners would decide which programs merited resources and then set funding levels for the various activities.

In connection with his administrative tasks, the chairman is intimately involved in formulating the budget. He communicates his instructions to the various operating units through the executive director who is charged with overseeing the preparation of the budget. Beginning in the late spring, the operating bureaus make their budget requests on a program by a program basis.[20] Next, the executive director and the commission's Office of Policy Planning and Evaluation (which reviews the work of the operating bureaus and proposes enforcement programs) study the requests of the bureaus. In July the executive director presents to the commission a draft budget, reflecting the chairman's policy preferences. At the same time the Office of Policy Planning and Evaluation undertakes an independent analysis of current commission programs, proposes new programs, and suggests appropriate fund levels for specific activities. The commissioners then review the draft budget, the proposals of the Office of Policy Planning and Evaluation, and the original bureau requests.

At a series of meetings at which the whole cast of commission officials participate, the commissioners are exposed to the full range of viewpoints and thus are better able, at least in theory, to make reasoned choices among various alternatives. Following these sessions (held over a period of five to seven days), the executive director drafts a proposed budget reflecting the commissioners' thinking and that of the bureau heads. The commissioners review, modify, and then vote upon the budget in September. The executive director conveys the results of the commission's deliberations to the staff and indicates those bureau programs that must be adjusted.

The approved budget is organized according to major *missions* —maintaining competition, consumer protection, and economic activities. Each mission section consists of a description of the individual programs that are part of it as well as the resource requirements of the various activities. The program summary outlines the problem each program is to address, states the goals of each program, and describes the resource requirements of the current and next fiscal years.

Several months after the commissioners have approved the budget, they conduct a midyear review of current programs. As is the case in the formulation of the budget, the Office of Policy Planning and Evaluation evaluates the work of the bureaus. As a result of their analyses of the data, the commissioners could alter the relative mix of resources among programs, add or eliminate programs, or decide that changes in resource allocation are unnecessary.

There are, it should be emphasized, limits to the utility of the program budget in antitrust decision making. The difficulty in predicting the effects of many kinds of enforcement actions constrains the applicability of cost/benefit analysis—the core of program budget making—to antitrust decision making.[21] As then Chairman Engman noted:

Although we can predict with some degree of certainty the probable cost of pursuing a particular investigation or case, it is extremely difficult in most cases to quantify with precision the probable impact of Commission successes in a given endeavor. It is difficult because of the paucity of hard economic data. And it is difficult because of imponderables such as the effect of deterrence.[22]

Costs are difficult to calculate, Chairman Engman's comments notwithstanding. An antitrust case can involve many parties, each of which can impose costs that could not or may not have been foreseen. If, for example, the companies involved in an investigation should unexpectedly withhold data, then the commission will have to divert resources from other cases to compel the release of the needed information. Not infrequently, the companies will exhaust all legal avenues before they will surrender data to the commission. At each juncture bureau attorneys will have to devote time (which would have been better spent on the investigation itself) to the preparation of legal arguments supporting their claims for the information. Contributing to the problem of forecasting costs is the complexity of many antitrust actions. Because such matters involve the interplay of many variables (legal, economic, and sometimes political), decision makers have great difficulty predicting a case's course before the final judgment is rendered.

The costs associated with high turnover rates—an acute problem of structural and industrywide cases—are also hard to measure. Yet the costs of staff instability are not even estimated in the program budget. Aside from the difficulty in determining such costs, the FTC may not want to draw attention to the problems of a high turnover rate for fear that Congress, which reviews the budget justification of the commission, might interpret the cost measures of attorney departures as evidence of agency shortcomings.

While it may have only limited applicability to antitrust decision making, the program budget has raised the quality of debate about how resources should be allocated. The program budget encourages the commissioners to think in terms of objectives, to ask questions about the costs and benefits of various courses of action, and to relate resources to objectives. Presumably, the process should enable the commissioners to set policy, if only in a general way. By setting funding levels for various programs, the commissioners and Bureau of Competition officials constrain what the staff can do with agency resources.

The Proactive Approach: Some Examples

Many examples illustrate the way in which the Bureau of Competition, through its evaluation procedures, has sought to shift from the reactive to proactive approach to case selection.[23] In examining the investigations of the petroleum and food industries, two representative proactive, or planned, efforts are presented.

The Petroleum Investigation
Until the *Exxon* case (D. 8934) of 1973, the commission, in its actions against oil companies, brought cases directed at three kinds of anticompetitive practices: price discrimination; vertical price-fixing; and overrides on tires, batteries, and accessories.

The case-by-case approach, Alan Ward believed, had been only partially successful in eliminating wasteful marketing practices, as well as dealer coercion. Moreover, these cases did not restore competition in the petroleum industry. In a 1973 staff report, the Bureau of Competition stated:

The staff did a thorough job in researching, developing and prosecuting the individual cases. . . . But the practice-by-practice approach to antitrust attack which sought to correct specific anti-competitive conduct at the marketing level, did not adequately address the industry's vertically integrated structure or its multi-level behavior. . . . To fashion a remedy for one level without considering the performance of a company, or the industry at the other levels, ignores the market structure association with vertical integration and limited competition.[24]

The commission's 1973 complaint against eight major oil companies marked a significant departure from the conduct-approach and signaled a new emphasis on structural imperfections in the petroleum industry. The commission charged the oil companies with having limited and weakened competition at all levels of the petroleum industry by monopolizing its refinery components in a large part of the United States. While the agency left open the question of relief, Bureau of Competition Director James Halverson made it clear that the remedy the staff would ultimately seek would be structural in nature and involve "significant divestiture at the refinery level, with connecting pipelines."[25] The *Exxon* case, which is currently in the postcomplaint, pretrial stage, is the "largest, most complex litigation" ever undertaken by the commission.[26]

The Food Investigations

The series of investigations in the food industries provide another example of the commission's attempts to deal programmatically with the competitive problems in those segments of the economy that are highly sensitive to inflationary trends. The commission had always been involved in the food area. At the time of the creation of a food program, the Bureau of Competition had sixteen nonpublic investigations underway and six cases in litigation. By 1974, Bureau Director James Halverson commented:

Our initiatives suffered from an *ad hoc* approach to the food industries. . . . Accordingly, we decided to review the larger picture on food so that we would be in a position to evaluate market conditions, locate problem areas and decide what the Commission would be able to do to correct any such problems.[27]

The food program was begun in 1974 at a time when food prices had skyrocketed. Congressional committees and various interest groups demanded that the commission attempt to determine the factors that lead to the higher prices. Prodded to action, Chairman Lewis Engman stated that the agency had created a food program. As the commission had not yet undertaken such a program, Chairman Engman's announcement necessitated its almost immediate creation. One assistant director, who was very much involved in the evaluation process, remembers the bureau director (James Halverson) approaching him one day with a command: "Get me a food program by tomorrow."

Because of the haste in which it was formulated, the original food program was really nothing more than an inventory of existing cases, attractively packaged for public consumption. Since fiscal year 1975, however, the Bureau of Competition has devoted much time to the development of a program to eliminate anticompetitive abuses in the food industry. In attacking abuses, the bureau has attempted to organize its work according to the five broad categories that reflect the principal segments of the food economy: the grower-producer, the manufacturer-processor, the distribution and marketing, and the food retailing and commodities levels. At each level attorneys and economists analyze market structure as well as industrial performance and then undertake investigations designed to uncover abuses.

Summary and Conclusion

In its efforts to change the character of the case load (and devote more attention to structural and industrywide investigations and less to simple conduct matters), the commission leadership of the 1970s proceeded in three major stages. First, decision makers redesigned the agency's structure to increase the leadership's control of the operating bureaus and eliminate organizational barriers that reinforced parochial attitudes held by many attorneys. Second, they removed incompetent attorneys and replaced them with persons of proven ability or promise. Third,

Bureau of Competition officials developed an evaluation process to facilitate the fashioning of a coherent antitrust policy, closed many cases unworthy of agency resources, and took away the staff attorneys' authority to open cases.[28]

With the aid of a case-tracking system, bureau officials could monitor the progress of all matters. The executive director also sought to improve the commissioners' (principally the chairman's) capacity to affect bureau activities: the program budget and the case-tracking systems are examples of that effort. In selecting cases at the bureau level, the director of the Bureau of Competition invited the participation of the Bureau of Economics. Within time the economists routinely passed upon the recommendations of the Bureau of Competition at Evaluation Committee meetings. Significant investigations were soon launched. In recent years, the commission has allocated much of its resources to activities that the agency believes could have "far reaching economic and consumer significance."[29] Indicative of the commission's increasing emphasis on cases that could benefit the consumer is the substantial allocation of resources to structural matters and industrywide investigations: in fiscal year 1978, the agency budgeted 32 percent of its antitrust resources on energy, 10.8 percent on food investigations, 7 percent on health matters, and 5.2 percent on transportation programs.[30] Less than 10 percent of its resources were allocated to Robinson-Patman Act cases—the staple of the commission of the 1960s.[31]

Several factors account for the commission leadership's ability to restructure the agency. The political climate was conducive to the making of sweeping changes. There existed a consensus across the political spectrum (ranging from President Richard Nixon to Ralph Nader) that held that the commission was performing poorly and should be revitalized. The new leadership was given a clear mandate to alter existing arrangements. It is unlikely that the commission leadership would have been able to move so swiftly in reorganizing and purging the agency of personnel without such widespread support.

The commitment of Chairmen Caspar Weinberger and Miles Kirkpatrick to the tasks before them was also important to the apparent success of the reorganization effort. Both chairmen were able to instill a sense of purpose throughout the commission and to attract persons of high quality to agency service. In their efforts to rid the agency of incompetent personnel, they were aided by a career attorney, Basil Mezines, whose accumulated knowledge was invaluable to a leadership generally unfamiliar with agency personnel and practices. Subsequent chairmen and executives were no less assiduous in their attempts to improve the quality of agency work.

Having examined the efforts to change the case load by restructuring the agency, it is important to emphasize that there are limits to what reorganization can accomplish.[32] To be sure, if the commission intended to launch complex and innovative cases, then it was necessary that the agency first restructure institutional processes and create control mechanisms. However, the installation of such arrangements, as the agency's continuing difficulties show, is generally not sufficient to achieve the agency's objective of successfully prosecuting proactive matters. No matter how well the organization is designed, the commission will be beset with severe problems in prosecuting big cases if the turnover rate of its staff is so high that the agency has great difficulty sustaining cooperative activity for the duration of the processes of investigation and litigation. The lack of expertise and the cumbersome nature of antitrust proceedings also raise questions about the ability of the commission to triumph in the end. In short, until some means are found to induce attorneys with expertise to remain with the agency for longer periods of time, the commission will have difficulty realizing the policy objectives that reorganization sought to accomplish.

Notes

1
Memorandum of James M. Nicholson to the commission, 11 August 1969, p. 6; memorandum made available courtesy of Commissioner Nicholson.
2
Commission on Organization of the Executive Branch of the Government, *Task Force Report on Regulatory Commissions* 125 (1949).

3
Robert Heller and Associates, *Federal Trade Commission Management Survey, Report of Robert Heller and Associates, Inc.* (1954).

4
U.S., Congress, Senate, Committee on the Judiciary, *Report on Regulatory Agencies to the President-Elect* (Committee Print), 86th Cong., 2nd sess., 1960.

5
Ibid., p. 48.

6
Report of the American Bar Association Commission to Study the Federal Commission (1969); more generally, see Harrison Wellford, "How Ralph Nader, Tricia Nixon, the ABA and Jamie Whitten Helped Turn the FTC Around," *Washington Monthly,* 4, no. 8 (October 1972), pp. 5–13.

7
Edward Cox, R. Fellmeth, and J. Schulz, *The Consumer and the Federal Trade Commission* (New York: Richard W. Baron Publishing Company, 1969).

8
Quoted by Caspar Weinberger in "Proposed Internal Reorganization of the Federal Trade Commission," 7 May 1970, p. 3.

9
Ibid., p. 4.

10
In devising his plans, Weinberger requested and received a critical evaluation of agency performance from the Bureau of the Budget. See Bureau of the Budget, "Management Review of the Federal Trade Commission," January 1970.

11
A few studies have been done concerning the housecleaning of the commission. See U.S., Congress, Senate, Committee on Government Operations, *Study on Federal Regulation: The Regulatory Appointments Process,* vol. 1, 95th Cong., 1st sess., 1977, pp. 205–222; and Kennedy School of Government Case Publication Series, *The Federal Trade Commission,* no. C94-75-080 (Cambridge, Mass.: Harvard University, 1973).

12
U.S., Congress, Senate, Committee on Post Office and Civil Service, *Statutory Exceptions to the Competitive Service* (Committee Print), 93rd Cong., 1st sess., 1973.

13
Moreover, the plans provided that the chairman could impose *reduction in force procedures* (an across-the-board cut in the number of persons

employed in the agency). When commission officials invoke reduction in force proceedings, the first attorneys to be discharged are those who were the last to join the agency. As a means of ridding the agency of incompetent personnel, reduction in force methods have been of limited utility, because the agency generally wants to dismiss lawyers who have been with the commission for several years. Elimination of employees through reorganization is a more effective way in which to reach incompetent attorneys who serve in high-level positions. If their positions are abolished through reorganization, then the attorneys have no jobs and are usually forced to leave the commission. Reduction in force procedures were not applied to lawyers, although they were used to force the departure of some doctors who worked in a specialized unit (the Division of Scientific Opinion). See the memorandum of Richard E. Neustadt to Public Policy 240 students, "Re: February 19—the Mezines Case," 14 February 1974. The memorandum was part of instructional materials on the Federal Trade Commission (Kennedy School Case Publication Series); see n. 11.

14
Statistics made available by the FTC's Office of Executive Director.

15
Information secured through a Freedom of Information Act request.

16
The problems associated with the absence of standards in case-load determinations have plagued the commission throughout its history. See, for example, Gerard Henderson, *The Federal Trade Commission* (New Haven: Yale University Press, 1924), and Bureau of the Budget, Executive Office of the President, *Federal Trade Commission Study 4*, no. CF-60-124 (1960), p. 12.

17
Hanscom's interview was for attribution.

18
See Aaron Wildavsky, *The Politics of the Budgetary Process*, 2nd ed. (Boston: Little, Brown and Company, 1974).

19
For a typical commission budget see budget justification of the FTC for fiscal year 1977 in U.S., Congress, Senate, Committee on Appropriations, *Hearings on Departments of State, Justice, Commerce, the Judiciary and Related Agencies, Appropriations, F.Y. 1977, Justifications*, part 3, 94th Cong., 2nd sess., 1976, pp. 2579-2732 (hereafter *1977 Appropriations Hearings*).

20
Federal Trade Commission, "Overview of Operational Review Process."

21
Compare the utility of program-budgeting antitrust decision making with that of the planning-programming-budgeting-system in defense matters; see Alain C. Enthoven and K. Wayne Smith, *How Much is Enough? Shaping the Defense Program 1961–1969* (New York: Harper and Row, 1971).

22
Address by Lewis Engman, reprinted in U.S., Congress, Senate, Committee on Government Operations, *Hearings on Regulatory Reform* part 1, 93rd Cong., 2nd sess., 1974, p. 549.

23
Two early cases involving the breakfast foods and office copier industries are noteworthy because of their structural focus. In the former, *Kellogg Company, et al.* (D.8883)—popularly known as the cereal case—the Commission charged that four major manufacturers of "ready-to-eat" (RTE) breakfast foods had maintained a shared monopoly and noncompetitive market structure through the use of restrictive retail shelf-space tactics, the proliferation of brands and trademark promotion, the artificial differentiation of products, the unfair promotion and advertising of products, and the acquisition of companies. Although the commission issued·its complaint in 1972, the cereal case, which largely relies on an innovative "shared monopoly" theory, has yet to be resolved.

In the office copiers case, *Xerox* (D. 8909), the commission attacked the monopoly power exercised by the leading corporation in the industry. The matter was withdrawn from adjudication and settled through a consent order in 1975. Commission officials believe that the consent agreement could result in the restructuring of the office copier industry.

24
"Preliminary Federal Trade Commission Staff Report on Its Investigation of the Petroleum Industry," in *Antitrust and Trade Regulation Report,* no. 622, 17 July 1973, p. E–2.

25
Antitrust and Trade Regulation Report, no. 623, 24 July 1973, p. A–1.

26
1977 Appropriations Hearings, p. 2593.

27
James T. Halverson, "FTC and the Food Industries—1974's Major Antitrust Emphasis," (Paper delivered at the Eighth Annual Antitrust Institute of the Ohio State Bar Association, Antitrust Law Section, Columbus, Ohio, 18 October 1974).

28
The sharp decrease in the number of open, formal investigations is indicative of the dramatic consequences of taking away the staff at-

torneys' authority to open and close investigations. As a result of review procedures, the Bureau of Competition had less than 130 open investigations at the end of fiscal year 1975. At one point in fiscal year 1969 the antitrust bureau was thought to have several hundred investigations open. (Records are so poor that exact figures are unavailable.) See *1977 Appropriations Hearings*, p. 2689.

29
Ibid.

30
U.S., Congress, House, Committee on Appropriations, *Hearings on Departments of State, Justice, Commerce, the Judiciary and Related Agencies, Appropriations, F.Y. 1978*, part 7, 95th Cong., 1st sess., 1977, p. 8.

31
Ibid.

32
On this point, see Herbert Kaufman, "Reflections on Administrative Reorganization," in Frederick S. Lane, ed., *Current Issues in Public Administration* (New York: St. Martin's Press, 1978), pp. 214–233.

9
Outside Actors and Case-Selection Decisions

Perhaps case outcomes cannot be understood simply by focusing upon the internal processes of an organization. A public bureaucracy does not exist in a vacuum; it operates in a political environment. What the commission does affects others. Those who are touched by commission action or who are obligated by law to interact with it might be keenly interested in agency activities. Several such actors might attempt to influence commission policies: the president, who is charged with appointing the commissioners; the Office of Management and Budget of the Executive Office of the President, which reviews the budgetary requests of the agency; congressional committees, which judge the qualifications of the commissioners, appropriate funds, authorize legislation, and oversee the performance of the FTC; public interest groups, which support antitrust policies that could aid the consumer; and private attorneys who are anxious to secure favorable results for their clients. What follows is an effort to examine the relationships that existed through 1977 between the commission and these various elements for the purpose of determining the effect external actors have on the antitrust caseload decisions of the agency.

The Presidency

The Appointment of Commissioners
Apart from the impact that he could have (at least in theory) on commission affairs through his review of the budget, the president could conceivably shape policy through the exercise of his authority to appoint the commissioners with the advice and consent of the Senate. The only "constraint" on the chief executive holds that he cannot choose a member of his party to fill a vacancy if a majority of the commission already shares the political affiliation of the nominee.[1] In practice, presidents have been able to circumvent the spirit of the restriction, which allows only a bare majority of the commissioners to be of the same political party, by nominating members of the other major party and independents who are sympathetic to the administration's viewpoint.[2] In short, the president is virtually free to use his appointive powers to further his own policies by nominating

persons whom he believes are likely to pursue programs that are in accord with the objectives of his administration.

Somewhat surprisingly, therefore, recent administrations have not used systematic procedures for the identification, investigation, evaluation, and nomination of candidates.[3] Usually the White House does not actively search for qualified individuals but reacts to campaigns waged by candidates or their sponsors. A candidate aids his cause considerably when he secures the support of those who have access to administration officials involved in the selection process. Key congressmen and public interest groups, for example, often bring candidates to the attention of the White House. (Because the Federal Trade Commission does not regulate a particular industry, the White House is not pressured by business interests to nominate selected candidates.) When White House aides trust the judgment of the commission chairman, they will carefully consider his views about possible nominees. Occasionally administration officials compose their own lists of candidates and include persons drawn from their own ranks.

The cast of White House aides and other officials involved in identifying candidates is not fixed. Usually a president designates one of his assistants to review candidates for regulatory vacancies and present recommendations. Often, the White House personnel director, the attorney general, or a close friend of the president can be instrumental in securing a nomination for a particular candidate. (During the Kennedy years, for example, the president relied upon the advice of Robert Kennedy, who was both a confidante and attorney general.)

White House aides usually take vacancies for the chairmanship quite seriously. Because the commission head, more than any other agency official, has the authority to affect policy, the administration generally seeks an individual of high quality whose philosophy and policy objectives are consonant with those of the president. The White House is less likely to be concerned about the qualifications of candidates for regular commission seats. A number of factors could affect the recommendations of the president's White House aides for these commissioners. The identity of the candidate's political backer is important. If the president owes a favor to the political sponsors of the candidate, then the likelihood that the office seeker will receive White House support is increased. The endorsement of an influential politician or public interest group may weigh more heavily than the fitness of the candidate for the job. Not infrequently, administration officials have difficulty judging candidates on the basis of their attitudes toward antitrust and consumer protection enforcement, partly because the leading nominees are often unfamiliar with the work of the commission. Moreover, the problem of evaluating candidates in terms of their policy views is not always simple, since White House staff members may have little knowledge of the commission.[4] Still, staff members usually make some effort to predict the performance of the candidates and consider their professional backgrounds and political affiliations. How the Senate is likely to react to the candidate is another factor in the White House's calculations. The administration will probably be reluctant to nominate a candidate whose controversial views are certain to meet with strong Senate opposition.

The White House staff also screens candidates for eight non-career executive positions (excepted service jobs that are not subject to merit staffing procedures): executive director, director of Policy Planning and Evaluation, director of the Bureau of Consumer Protection, director of the Bureau of Competition, director of the Bureau of Economics, secretary of the Federal Trade Commission, general counsel, and assistant to the chairman. The commission refers candidates to the Civil Service Commission, which "apparently checks ... with the White House."[5] White House review of the candidates is perfunctory. From 1970 to 1977, the commission filled these positions without any White House objections.

With respect to possible commission nominees, presidents have tended to accept the recommendations of their staffs. With the exception of Johnson, they have seldom been deeply involved in selecting commission members. Whether the president personally meets with his nominees before his name is sent to the Senate is a matter of individual style. Johnson almost always met with his nominees, while Nixon seldom visited with his candidates. Presidents rarely appoint persons for the purpose of executing a specific policy. A striking exception involved the appointment of

Caspar Weinberger in 1969. Nixon personally asked Weinberger to assume the chairmanship and "revitalize" the agency. "Go in there and clean it up and you won't have any trouble from me,"[6] the president is reported to have told Weinberger. Nixon, however, did not have a clear conception as to what should be done besides reorganization.

The general lack of presidential involvement in agency affairs is understandable. A chief executive simply does not have the time to immerse himself in the appointment process. The Federal Trade Commission has a small budget. Quite naturally, the president is more likely to devote his attention to the appointment of department and cabinet heads, who are charged with managing huge programs, which could have a far greater effect on the economy than could the activities of the Federal Trade Commission. Because the president is held accountable for the performance of the executive branch, he tends to be more involved in appointing individuals to cabinet and subcabinet positions than he is in choosing members of independent regulatory commissions, for whose performance he is not generally held responsible.

The Office of Management and Budget's Review of Commission Activities

It might be thought that the executive would not be in a position to affect the budgetary requests or programs of the commission. After all, the commission is not part of the executive branch but is an independent government agency. However, the Federal Trade Commission (as well as all other independent commissions) must submit budget requests to the Office of Management and Budget (OMB) prior to transmitting them to Congress. The funding levels in the budget justification that the commission sends to Congress are, at least in theory, determined by OMB (and sometimes by the president, when the commission appeals OMB's decision). The commission has, or so it would seem, no choice but to submit a request that reflects the executive's view of how the agency should allocate its resources.

The commission is required to submit its budget estimates by 15 September to the Office of Management and Budget for the consideration of the president.[7] Very shortly thereafter, an OMB examiner studies the estimates and compares them with the scheduled expenditures of the current fiscal year. If they deem personal meetings desirable, the examiner and the officials of the commission (usually the executive director and the bureau heads) will discuss the budget request in October hearings. Such hearings give the commission the opportunity to answer any questions the examiners might have about particular programs. Moreover, they enable the Office of Management and Budget to secure a more sophisticated understanding of the policies and problems of the commission. Subsequently the examiner revises the commission's budget request and readies his own estimates for the consideration of his director. In late November or early December, following the director's review of the estimates, the Federal Trade Commission receives its first mark: OMB's determination of the funding levels for the agency. Should the commission leadership find the mark unacceptable, it can appeal OMB's decision to the director and then, if necessary, to the president. By the middle of December, the appeals process is exhausted. Once the president has considered the estimates and made a judgment, the commission is informed of his decision. The totals of the budget justification that the commission submits to Congress must conform to the levels set in the presidential budget. Moreover, the commission is prohibited from disclosing information about the president's proposals concerning the agency until the chief executive transmits the budget to Congress.

In dealing with the Office of Management and Budget, the chairman and the executive director employ strategies designed to ensure that the president's budget will reflect what they believe are the needs of the commission. First, when formulating the requests, they attempt to anticipate the reactions of the OMB examiner. Because they realize that the examiner will, as a matter of course, cut some of their funding requests, the executive director and the chairman deliberately propose a budget that exceeds the actual operating requirements of the commission. After the examiner cuts the budget, the commission officials expect that the revised funding levels will satisfy most of the needs of the agency. Second, commission personnel, who are involved in the budget-making process, seek to educate OMB officials about the policies of the agency in the belief that an informed examiner is more likely to render a judicious judgment than one who knows little about commission affairs. An examiner who perceives that the commission is cooperating with him may be inclined to look favorably upon the agency's requests. Knowledgeable OMB officials, moreover, could become advocates of particular programs at internal staff meetings where commission personnel are absent.

The approach that the commission has adopted in its dealings with the Office of Management and Budget has undoubtedly contributed to the uncomplicated relationship these agencies share.[8] For their part, commission officials seem satisfied with the treatment they have received. Stated one such official in 1976: "On the whole, we've got nothing to complain about. . . . Rapid increases in funding are difficult to absorb and lead to waste. . . . If we received too much, too quickly, then we would have very difficult quality control problems."

While under no constraint to deal with the agency on legislative matters, commission officials believe that OMB performs a useful role as a federal agency clearinghouse. The commission noted in response to a congressional inquiry that OMB

affords the Commission the opportunity to comment upon legislation, or proposed legislative reports prepared by other agencies, dealing with matters in which the Commission has an interest. It is also helpful for the Commission to have a chance to consider relevant facts and opinions of other interested parts of the Federal Government prior to submitting its views to Congress on a particular matter.[9]

OMB is not generally concerned with the merits of a particular case but with determining whether the direction of the commission (for example, an emphasis on antitrust rather than consumer protection matters) is in accord with the president's program. Specific questions are not likely to focus upon investigations but upon housekeeping expenditures (for example, whether a commission request for an increase in personnel is justified).

There are several reasons for the lack of attention the OMB gives to commission policies. First, the budget examiners tend to devote little energy to the task of evaluating the commission's requests, because most of their time is spent reviewing the activities of agencies with larger budgets. Commented the examiner charged with analyzing the commission's budget:

Even if you spent months studying the way the 32 million dollars in antitrust funds is spent, you would probably recommend, at most a cut of a few million from the request for increases. With Treasury, on the other hand, you would be dealing with a budget that is many times that of the Commission. You can make a real dent in the Treasury budget.

Second, because the administration has repeatedly supported vigorous antitrust efforts, the examiners have looked favorably upon commission requests for increased funding. In the last few years the OMB has consistently approved commission requests for increases in its budget authority.

Third, the budget examiners are convinced that the executive director and the commissioners are genuinely committed to improving the agency's management systems. Commented one OMB official: "The FTC is a model agency. We don't have to prod them to institute management techniques which will increase efficiency." For their part management specialists in the commission regard the OMB as a useful ally in instituting organizational changes that are designed to centralize control and are opposed by the bureau heads. Commented one commission staffer who worked closely with the executive director:

We know the bureau heads don't like procedures which enable the chairman and the other commissioners to get a better idea about what the troops are doing. So, we tell them it's not just a question of what the chairman or the other commissioners want. The Office of Management and Budget, which could make trouble for us, will react unsympathetically to requests for more attorneys if we don't accommodate them by tightening up our management systems.

Congress

The Senate Confirmation Process

The president's nominee for commissioner cannot assume office without the advice and consent of the Senate.[10] One might expect that the Senate would use its power of confirmation or rejection to shape the character of antitrust enforcement in the Federal Trade Commission. In practice, however, the Senate has tended to play a passive role in the appointment process and routinely approves the nominees of the president.

The Commerce Committee, which judges the qualification of the nominees and recommends confirmation or rejection of the candidates to the whole Senate, performs its tasks in a perfunctory fashion. Committee clearance of the nomination has been tantamount to confirmation: since the Truman administration, no FTC nominee has been rejected on the floor of the Senate. Moreover, Senate debate on an FTC nomination has occurred but once since 1949.[11] Since 1950, only one nominee has not been confirmed.[12] It may be, as James M. Graham and Victor Kramer suggest in their study of regulatory appointments, that the Senate has been docile because the White House has already cleared the nominee with the FBI, key senators on the Commerce Committee, and the Senate leadership. (In recent times, the practice of senatorial courtesy has not been followed as a matter of course; certainly, if the candidate's homestate senator is influential and indicates his intention to oppose the prospective appointment, then the would-be office holder might ultimately not be nominated.)

In addition, the absence of a formal role in the designation of agency chairmen may generate Senate indifference to the process by which commissioners are confirmed. If the president designates as chairman a sitting commissioner whose term is not about to expire, then his appointee is not subject to a Senate vote. It is only when the chairman-designee is not a sitting commissioner or when his appointment is coincidental with a new seven-year term that the senators will vote to confirm or reject him. But if the Senate carefully reviewed each nomination, then the absence of a formal role in the appointment would not reduce its ability to influence antitrust policy through the confirmation process. Under such conditions the Commerce Committee will have previously judged the fitness of the chairman-designee, who served as a commissioner immediately prior to his ascension, at that time when he was first nominated to fill a vacancy. In practice, however, the Commerce Committee seldom reviews the qualifications of would-be commissioners with care.

Apart from consensus politics and the lack of a formal role in the selection of agency chairmen, an explanation for the Senate's apathy to the confirmation process may lie, as James Graham and Victor Kramer have written, in its failure to distinguish between executive departments and independent commissions. There has been a time-honored custom that the Senate should routinely confirm presidential nominees (unless they are clearly incompetent) to executive department positions on the grounds that the chief executive should be free to work with those persons with whom he is comfortable. It may very well be that the Senate has not appreciated that the independent agencies are not executive departments but are more nearly creatures of the Congress. Closer Senate scrutiny of the appointees to regulatory commissions would, therefore, be appropriate.

There are various ways in which the Senate could exercise a more vigorous role in the confirmation process. The hearings could be used as a tool to flesh out the views of the nominees, to determine whether they have the substantive knowledge their prospective office requires. Too often the hearings are merely ten- or fifteen-minute meetings in which discussions of important issues (for example, Commission priorities) are superficially examined. Attendance at such hearings has been strikingly low.[13] Chairman Magnuson declared that the Commerce Committee, despite its attendance records,

has progressively tightened and made more substantive the confirmation process. . . . [The] Committee . . . instituted the practice of submitting detailed written interrogatories covering the broad range of major policy decisions facing the agency to each regulatory nominee, requiring that these be answered in writing at least 48 hours prior to the scheduled hearing date.[14]

Quite obviously, committee members, who do not attend the hearings, cannot ask in-depth questions based on the questionnaires. The nominee's written responses to the interrogatories tend to be evasive. Typical answers include such phrases as "I have not had the opportunity to research the question in depth"; "I am reluctant to categorically endorse the view"; "at the same time, I recognize"; and "Government policy should prohibit monopoly or undue industrial concentration resulting from acquisitions. . . . However, I am chary of a policy that would prohibit enterprises from growing internally by lawful means or entering new fields of commercial activity."[15]

As a matter of courtesy, most nominees do arrange meetings with committee members in advance of the hearings. These sessions, however, tend to last for a very few minutes and usually consist of nothing more than an exchange of pleasantries.

Because most senators devote little attention to the confirmation process, the Commerce Committee staff (at least through the Magnuson chairmanship, which ended in 1977) has done the bulk of the preparation. The committee assigned to the staff the tasks of reviewing financial statements, compiling background information on the nominees, preparing questions to be asked of the candidates, and of identifying potential conflicts of interests or other disqualifying material. In order to secure the necessary data, the staff requests that the nominees supply responses to questions listed in a standard financial disclosure form, and asks those candidates whose law firms deal with regulated industries to submit the names of their clients. The staff counsel oversees the work of the Commerce Committee. Because then chairman Magnuson (Dem.; Wash.) relied so heavily on his judgment, chief staff counsel Michael Pertschuk (who became the FTC chairman in 1977) was considered to be a powerful figure on Capitol Hill. (Undoubtedly, Pertschuk, who enjoyed a very distinguished career in the legislative branch, benefited from his affiliation with the Commerce Committee in his quest for the commission chairmanship.)

While the committee (or perhaps more accurately the staff) has seldom attempted to block the approval of a presidential nominee, it has occasionally intervened actively in the appointment process. Recent instances involved the nominations of Mayo Thompson, Thomas Sowell, and David Clanton. Before acting on the nomination of Mayo Thompson, a man whose self-affixed conservative label did not endear him to the Democratic majority, Chairman Magnuson "sought and received informal assurances from the White House" that the next vacancy would be filled "by a nominee with a background in consumer affairs, committed to the support of the vigorous use of the Commission's power to protect consumers."[16] With that pledge, the Senate approved Thompson in 1973. When the next seat became vacant, the White House nominated Elizabeth Hanford, an expert in consumer affairs.

The committee staff responded vigorously once again when President Ford announced his intention on 6 April 1976 to name Thomas Sowell, a black economics professor from UCLA, to fill the unexpired term—ending on 27 September 1976—of Lewis Engman, who had resigned in December 1975.[17] A conservative, Sowell's philosophy was unacceptable to the Commerce Committee staff.[18] The staff indicated to Sowell and to the White House that the committee would probably vote to allow the nominee to serve the remaining six months of the Engman term but would not confirm him for a full seven years once the term to which he was first nominated had expired. If the Democrats captured the White House that November, then the new chief executive would select his own candidates. Thus, there was no reason for the Democrats to approve a Ford nominee if they found the candidate unacceptable.

Sowell sought from the White House a guarantee that President Ford would renominate him to a full seven-year term once he had served the six remaining months of the Engman term. The White House, however, refused to offer Sowell such an assurance, apparently because it did not want to risk nominating an individual whose possible Senate rejection a few months before the presidential election could embarrass Gerald Ford. Charging that the White House had "misled" him by not informing him of "certain things they could not have avoided knowing," Sowell asked the administration to withdraw his nomination.[19] Commenting upon his conversation with the Commerce Committee staff, Sowell stated, "I was given the impresson that if this year hadn't been divisible by four, there would have been no problem."[20]

Apparently, the staff then indicated to the White House that the committee would recommend the confirmation of a Republican to both the short six-month and full seven-year terms if the nominee were David Clanton. The minority counsel of the committee from

1971 to 1976, Clanton was thought to be in agreement on most issues with his Democratic counterparts. In his quest for the nomination, he had the support of the senator he was then serving, minority whip Robert Griffin (Rep.; Mich.). The White House nominated Clanton in July. He was easily confirmed to both the unexpired and succeeding terms.[21]

The Appropriations Process
An appropriations committee could use a variety of techniques to control policy and administration. It could set funding levels for specific programs, specify the purposes for which money is to be spent, and attach statutory provisos. Moreover, the committee could use various nonstatutory means—a committee report, for example, could strongly urge the commission to pursue a particular course of action—to affect the policies and processes of the agency.[22] Thus, the appropriations subcommittee might be expected to attempt to exercise tight control over the antitrust activities of the Federal Trade Commission. In fact, the subcommittee in the period studied (through 1977) generally did not take full advantage of its control devices: it played a passive role.

In evaluating the performance of the commission and in recommending how much money should be appropriated, the Subcommittee on State, Justice, Commerce, the Judiciary and Related Agencies of the House Committee on Appropriations focuses upon the agency's budget justification.[23] A subcommitee hearing typically begins with a presentation by the commission chairman, describing the events of the past year and explaining the need for increases in funding levels. In the main, subcommittee members tend to be concerned with general matters rather than with specific cases. First, in assessing the performance of the agency, the subcommittee determines whether it has been responsive to the will of the Congress (that is, the subcommittee). Criticizing the commission in its 1974 report, the Subcommittee on Agriculture, Environmental and Consumer Protection, which then had jurisdiction over FTC appropriations, stated that the agency "has . . . been very tardy in its responses to the needs of the committee and the needs of members of Congress."[24] Clearly setting forth to then Chairman Lewis Engman the consequences of failing to make timely reports to the Congress, subcommittee Chairman Jamie Whitten commented: "We study everything you send us, *but if we do not have the facts in time, we lean on the safe side and hold you down tighter. So I do not think it is your interest to let us have this information too late.*"[25]

A second yardstick that the subcommittee uses in judging how well the commission is performing has to do with case-load statistics. The subcommittee is very much interested in the number of investigations that the commission opens and closes. A decrease in the number of investigations from one year to the next and/or a high percentage of case closings raises questions about commission performance.[26] Another case-load statistic that presumably indicates whether the commission is operating efficiently is the investigation backlog.[27] The subcommittee also seeks case-load data having to do with the won/lost record of the commission in the courts.[28] These data may reflect upon the adjudicative competence of the commissioners. If the commission loses a high percentage of cases in the courts, then there may be reason to believe that its members have failed to interpret the law expertly. It is noteworthy that the subcommittee does not request won/lost antitrust data specifically and is satisfied with information that includes both antitrust and consumer protection statistics. Quite obviously, the subcommittee cannot make meaningful judgments about the commission's adjudicative record in antitrust matters if it does not distinguish antitrust from consumer protection matters.

A third measure of commission performance is the turnover rate of agency personnel. A high rate suggests to the subcommittee that the commission suffers from low morale and mismanagement. Similarly, a large number of vacancies also raises questions among subcommittee members about commission performance.[29]

To conclude upon examination of its hearings and reports that the appropriations subcommittee did not concentrate upon the substantive programs of the Bureau of Competition and the Bureau of Economics is not to suggest that this congressional body was not at all concerned with antitrust decision making in the Federal Trade Commission. The subcommittee did probe into some of the more important programs and cases of the commission. For example, in a hearing, subcommittee members questioned the commissioners about the status and cost of the *Exxon* case, which consumes more of the agency's resources than any other matter.[30] The subcommittee also routinely inquired about the progress the commission has made in completing congressionally mandated studies and investigations. It was largely because of the inititative of the appropriations subcommittee that Congress required the commission to undertake a study of the energy industry for the purposes of reporting on the structure, practices, and performance of that sector and with the objective of evaluating the impact of government regulation on energy exploration, production, and utilization.[31]

Members of the Subcommittee on Agriculture, Environmental and Consumer Protection were very interested in the progress of the food program, which was created in response to their demands. Convinced that major antitrust investigations are quickly completed, Congressman Mark Andrews (Rep.; N.D.) impatiently asked Chairman Engman during the 1975 hearings: "What is the status of FTC's food-pricing investigation. . . . We were pretty direct in urging you to get with it. . . . What are you finding out, if anything? It has already been two years, since we initally brought this up with the FTC."[32]

The Subcommittee on Agriculture, Environmental and Consumer Protection also seemed quite concerned about the commission's line of business program (although the subcommittee's successor has not exhibited the same interest).[33]

With the exception of these matters, the appropriations subcommittee did not probe deeply into the antitrust activities of the Federal Trade Commission. Its reports generally did not discuss the status of particular cases or urge the commission to alter its antitrust policies. The committee has quite consistently recommended that the agency's appropriations be increased from one year to the next (although, with the exception of fiscal 1976, its recommendations have been less than what the commission has requested).[34]

Several reasons could explain why the subcommittee on appropriations did not use the various tools at its disposal to exercise tight control over the antitrust policies of the commission. It may be, as one appropriations subcommittee staffer claimed, "that the subcommittee [did] not believe it should make policy—that's a responsibility which belongs to the authorization committees." While plausible, this explanation does not account for various subcommittee attempts to influence commission policy in the consumer protection area. Another possible explanation for the subcommittee's behavior is the reluctance of the congressmen and staff to imperil ongoing cases and investigations. As then Chairman Whitten once commented to Lewis Engman: "I want to repeat again, this committee, and I am sure I reflect the views of all the members, does not wish to jeopardize anything."[35]

More fundamentally, the subcommittee did not use the budget axe—its principal instrument for affecting policies of a bureaucracy—because it felt that the FTC was performing well. Clearly, slashing the budget by large amounts hardly makes sense when the subcommittee approves of an agency's behavior or at worst faults it for not doing more. That the FTC will be forever free of the subcommittee's budget axe is unlikely. Indeed, at this writing (September 1979) it appears that the tranquil relationship between the agency and the appropriations body is about to change. The subcommittee, unhappy with the Pertschuk administration, has threatened to recommend that the full committee and House cut the agency's budget deeply and adopt appropriations measures that would effectively halt the FTC's investigations of the petroleum and car manufacturing industries.

On the Senate side, the Subcommittee on State, Justice, Commerce, the Judiciary and Related Agencies examined the antitrust activities of the Federal Trade Commission in an even more cursory fashion than does its appropriations counterpart in the House. Indicative of the passive role of the Senate appropriations subcommittee was the poor attendance of its members at hearings. At a typical meeting, only two of twelve committee members were present. The Senate appropriations subcommittee has traditionally functioned as an appeals forum for executive agencies, dissatisfied with the judgment of the House of Representatives. Subcommittee hearings have tended to focus on particular issues raised by senators (who are usually, but not necessarily, members of the subcommittee) and upon the zone of dispute between the agency and the House of Representatives.[36] The staffer, who is charged with reviewing the commission budget, claimed that a thorough review of the agency's activities would be wasteful of the subcommittee's time:

We have accesss to reports and hearings of the substantive committees of both Houses and of the appropriations subcommittee of the House of Representatives. We welcome letters and suggestions from all senators. So, if there is anything that needs looking into, we'll find out about it.

Oversight and Investigations

Congressional opportunities to influence the antitrust policy of the Federal Trade Commission are not limited to the confirmation and appropriations processes. Through its legislative committees, Congress can oversee the activities of the agency and use various means (hearings, legislation, investigations) to effect changes in the policies and processes of the commission. The act that created the commission states that the agency "shall . . . have power . . . upon the direction of the President or either House of Congress to investigate and report the facts relating to any alleged violations of the antitrust Acts by any corporation."[37] Congressional oversight would presumably ensure that the commission was responsive to the legislature and fulfilled its responsibilties under the FTC Act. Very likely, the public debate about the efficiency of various forms of regulation would also stimulate congressional interest in commission activities.

In examining the relationship between the commission and the legislative committees of Congress, the focus will be on those congressional bodies that have interacted with the agency on antitrust matters: the House Subcommittee on Oversight and Investigations of the Committee on Interstate and Foreign Commerce, the Subcommittee on Commodities and Services of the House Committee on Small Business, the Ad Hoc Subcommittee of the Robinson-Patman Act, Antitrust and Related Matters of the House Committee on Small Business, the Subcommittee on

Monopolies and Commercial Law of the House Judiciary Committee, the Subcommittee on Antitrust and Monopoly of the Senate Judiciary Committee, and the Senate Committee on Interior and Insular Affairs.

Of all the congressional bodies that have sought to influence the policies and processes of the commission, the Subcommittee on Oversight and Investigations of the House Committee on Interstate and Foreign Commerce has been the most aggressive. In theory, the subcommittee is to "coordinate its work with the other standing subcommittees" and is to "maintain regular communication with the standing subcommittees in order to obtain advice on subjects for investigation."[38] In practice, however, the Subcommittee on Oversight and Investigations and its chairman, while open to suggestions from other subcommittees, determine and often conceive of the matters that warrant examination. Two instances of commission-subcommittee interaction deserve attention because each illustrates the clash of differing interests; one involved an investigation of the agency's natural gas case, the other a "comprehensive" inquiry into the policies and procedures of the commission.

Then Chairman John Moss's (Dem.; Cal.) concern about energy matters sparked the subcommittee's examination of the status of the commission's natural gas investigation.[39] Convinced that the gas producing industry had contrived a shortage in order to secure higher wellhead prices, Moss was determined to hold hearings to expose evidence of deliberate underreporting of gas reserves. By showing that no gas shortage existed, he believed that he would strengthen those forces that opposed natural gas deregulation. Moss knew of the commission's investigation of the natural gas reserves, which had been underway for four and one-half years by the time of the subcommittee hearings in 1975. Moreover, it was common knowledge that attorneys in the commission were preparing a recommendation urging the agency to issue a complaint against the American Gas Association. In order to substantiate their conviction that the natural gas industry had behaved in a way that was tantamount to collusive price rigging, Chairman Moss and his staff decided to secure testimony from those commission attorneys who supported their claim. The subcommittee staff believed that the expected public outcry resulting from disclosure of the findings of the commission attorneys would induce the commissioners to issue a complaint.

For the Bureau of Competition attorneys, congressional exposure of the commission's natural gas reserve investigation was risky for several reasons. First, the American Gas Association and many of the gas producers under investigation had given their records to the commission with the understanding that the documents would remain confidential. By surrendering these records to the subcommittee, commission attorneys feared that their ability to collect data in the natural gas investigation and in future inquiries would be impaired simply because the companies under investigation could not be certain that the agency would adhere to its pledge of confidentiality. These companies might choose to balk at agency requests for data. Second, the hearings, many attorneys thought, would expose the conflict between the Bureau of Competition and the Bureau of Economics (which hotly opposed the issuance of a complaint against the natural gas producers). Disclosure of the Bureau of Economics memoranda could invaluably aid the representatives of the gas producers in charting a strategy designed to forestall the issuance of a complaint. Third, the Bureau of Competition attorneys believed that the commission would try to minimize the controversy, which would be magnified by the publicity surrounding the hearings. The commissioners are usually reluctant to undertake a major initiative when there is division between the agency's bureaus. The exposure of the internal split, the attorneys felt, would make it more likely that the commissioners would avoid making a final decision.

Given the commission's aversion to public scrutiny of internal division, officials of the Bureau of Competition were surprised and disappointed when then Chairman Engman did not vigorously resist Moss's demands for memoranda on the investigation. A frequently advanced explanation holds that the commission chairman believed that Moss would have secured the information eventually and that he, therefore, did not want to antagonize the subcommittee chairman over an argument that he would ultimately lose.

The staff attorneys assigned to the case did not testify willingly. They feared the committee's hearings could jeopardize their case and told the subcommittee staff that they would respond to questions only if the inquiries were made pursuant to a subpoena. In order to discredit the position of the attorneys, the Republican minority on the subcommittee asked the economists of the Bureau of Economics to present their arguments.

Just as the attorneys predicted, the committee hearings exposed the deep division within the commission. Shortly after the hearing, counsel for the American Gas Association met with then Chairman Engman and other key officials and contended, according to an agency memorandum, that "a formal complaint proceeding . . . would publicly pit the Bureau of Competition against the Bureau of Economics which would not be in the best interest of the public or the Federal Trade Commission."[40] On 29 July 1975, several weeks after the Congressional hearings and the meeting with the American Gas Association, the commission voted 4 to 0 against issuing a complaint. In a letter to Representative Moss and Senator Philip Hart (the man who had requested the commission inquiry), then-Chairman Engman explained that the FTC "had determined that it should have the internal reserve data of the seven natural gas companies which have resisted . . . subpoenas before concluding an investigation."[41]

While it officially returned the matter to the staff for further investigation, the commission intended to quash action for the foreseeable future. Kenneth Anderson, who supervised the Bureau of Competition inquiry, termed the commission decision "tragic."[42]

In their evaluations of the effect the Subcommittee on Oversight and Investigations had on the commission decision, bureau attorneys expressed different opinions. Some hold the subcommittee responsible for the outcome. In their memoranda and in their congressional testimony, the attorneys had purposely sought to separate the charges of underreporting of reserves from the natural gas decontrol issue because they felt that the commissioners might issue a complaint if it were not tied to the deregulation controversy. Chairman Moss, however, inextricably bound the two together. Moreover, by exposing the sharp differences between the lawyers and economists, he created an emotionally charged atmosphere, which inhibited commission action.

A few attorneys, it should be noted, believe that the subcommittee hearings had little effect on the commission's ultimate decision. This minority is convinced that the commissioners may have reached their judgment because they really thought it would be rash to issue a complaint without data from seven natural gas companies. Some lawyers also argued that Chairman Engman, whose political ambitions were hardly concealed, was reluctant to act because he did not want to risk the disfavor of President Ford, who strongly supported the deregulation of natural gas prices. Prosecution of the American Gas Association and the gas producers might have strengthened the argument of those forces that opposed deregulation.

The commission and the Subcommittee on Oversight and Investigations tangled once again over the latter's survey of regulatory agencies. In connection with its study of regulatory reform, the subcommittee examined various agencies, including the Federal Trade Commission.[43] The agencies were asked to provide data within thirty days about their operations. The questions in the survey did not deal specifically with commission cases or programs.[44] According to a subcommittee staffer, "we didn't know enough about each commission to ask pointed questions." He noted that the staff hoped to compose more specific queries on the basis of the answers to the questions and ask them at future hearings. For their part, commission officials resented having to devote so much of their attention to the subcommittee questionnaire. Many charged that they had to divert their time from important commission matters in order to work on it.

Another source of contention was Chairman Moss's subpoena demanding that the commission and seven other agencies give the subcommittee all copies of their responses to the questionnaire as well as all working papers prepared in conjunction with the answers to the survey.[45] Moss claimed that the subcommittee intended to release the documents after a careful staff review. Two publications, which sought the commission's responses to the questionnaire, asked a federal court judge to overturn the subpoena.[46] A U.S. District Court judge did issue a restraining order, barring the regulatory agencies from complying with the congressional subpoena. Federal Trade Commission Chairman Engman stated that Representative Moss's efforts to circumvent the Freedom of Information Act were "deeply disturbing."[47] Moreover, he claimed that "for the Commission to surrender all copies of the responses which have already been provided to you [Moss] will render it virtually impossible to prepare in a meaningful way for oversight hearings held pursuant to your investigation."[48]

It is interesting to note that the questionnaire was of little aid in identifying the issues that ultimately concerned the subcommittee at the hearings.[49] The subcommittee was concerned with the *Exxon* case, the line of business program, the natural gas investigation, and the rules of clearance to practice before the commission —areas that were not covered in the survey.

Just as the House Subcommittee on Oversight and Investigations of the Committee on Interstate and Foreign Commerce attempted to influence the course of the natural gas case, so the Subcommittee on Commodities and Services of the House Committee on Small Business sought to prod the agency into opening an investigation dealing with the home canning-lid shortage. Consumer advocate Ralph Nader and several congressmen charged that the manufacturers of the canning lids had contrived the shortage and that antitrust action was, therefore, in order.[50] At hearings held in 1975 to dramatize the problem, Acting Director Robert Liedquist of the Bureau of Competition stated that preliminary investigations, conducted earlier in the year, had not uncovered evidence of collusive behavior between lid manufacturers and food processors to withhold lids from the marketplace.[51] Despite the commission's conviction that further inquiry would not yield different results, the agency, spurred by pressure from the committee and consumer groups, began a priority investigation of the canning-lid shortage. The Bureau of Competition invested five weeks in a comprehensive examination and concluded that the shortage was due to an unprecedented demand that the industry was unprepared to meet despite substantial increases in jar-lid production.[52] Because no evidence existed of collusion between lid manufacturers and food processors to create a shortage, the commission decided that antitrust action would be inappropriate.

A committee seems to be able to exert pressure on the commission to pursue a specific policy or investigation when the agency is subject to its jurisdiction or when the matter in which it is interested enjoys widespread congressional support. If the agency does not have to answer to the committee in authorization or appropriations proceedings and if the policy for which the committee is pressing does not have the support of the whole Congress (or the authorization or appropriations committees, which deal with the FTC), then the commission need not be too mindful of the consequences of not following the suggested course of action.

An illustrative case in point involved the efforts of the Ad Hoc Subcommittee on Antitrust, the Robinson-Patman Act and Related Matters of the House Committee on Small Business to encourage the commission to prosecute more Robinson-Patman Act matters. The subcommittee was created in September 1975 at the prompting of those who were concerned about the commission's de-emphasis of Robinson-Patman actions. Speculation that the act might be repealed also provided an impetus for the establishment of a special subcommittee. Especially eager for the creation of such a subcommittee were representatives of small business and members of the private bar, whose incomes were at least partly dependent upon litigating Robinson-Patman cases. The subcommittee held hearings on several days and questioned commission officials on their views about Robinson-Patman enforcement.[53]

While the hearings exposed the differing views within the commission about the appropriate level of Robinson-Patman Act enforcement, the agency did not change its policy in the aftermath of the subcommittee proceedings. Apart from the subcommittee's lack of jurisdiction and control over commission activities, the agency's unresponsiveness reflects the absence of strong sentiment within Congress in favor of an increase in Robinson-Patman prosecutions. The commission has persuaded those legislative and appropriations subcommittees to which it must be responsive that consumer-oriented cases are of greater value than are Robinson-Patman Act matters. The Ad Hoc Subcommittee on Antitrust, the Robinson-Patman Act and Related Matters seems to have realized that commission policy would not change unless the committees to which the agency had to answer exerted control. At the confirmation hearings of Calvin Collier, subcommittee Chairman Henry Gonzalez (Dem.; Tex.) told the Senate Commerce Committee: "I recommend that the Committee obtain a clear idea of the views any nominee to the FTC holds, with regard to the firm enforcement of the Robinson-Patman Act and the protection of small business in general."[54]

Finally, with respect to House legislative bodies, it should be noted that the Subcommittee on Monopolies and Commercial Law of the Judiciary Committee has not been concerned with the ongoing activities of the commission but has concentrated on efforts to strengthen the antitrust statutes.

On the Senate side, the Commerce Committee, which reviews all commission appointments, has generally not sought to monitor the antitrust activities of the agency. The committee has preferred to focus its attention on the consumer protection aspects of the commission's work, leaving study of antitrust matters to the Subcommittee on Antitrust and Monopoly of the Judiciary Committee.

While it was extremely aggressive in studying antitrust problems,[55] the Subcommittee on Antitrust and Monopoly, under the direction of Philip Hart, did not devote much attention to reviewing the policies and administrative processes of the Federal Trade Commission.[56] The subcommittee staff held the view that the commission was performing well. The agency initiated a number of important structural cases that met with the approval of the subcommittee. Subcommittee scrutiny of those cases was thus unnecessary and could have been harmful. That is, committee hearings could have drawn attention to these cases and provided a forum for opponents of the structural cases to defend their position. Moreover, because committee staff members were convinced that litigation is often a cumbersome means of resolving antitrust problems, they chose not to focus upon commission cases, but to concentrate upon devising a legislative approach that would accomplish the objectives of courtroom trials.

This is not to suggest that the Hart Subcommittee on Antitrust and Monopoly was not concerned at all with the cases and investigations of the commission. The commission undertook the natural gas investigation, for instance, at the request of Senator Hart. The subcommittee, under the chairmanship of Senator Edward Kennedy (Dem.; Mass.) from 1977 to 1979, and now Senator Howard Metzenbaum (Dem.; Ohio), has probed more deeply into the ways in which the commission discharges its responsibilities. The subcommittee, for example, held hearings on transferring the commission's antitrust enforcement duties to the Antitrust Division.

Interestingly, it was not the Commerce Committee or the Subcommittee on Antitrust and Monopoly but the Senate Interior Committee that pressed for commission action in the *Exxon* investigation—the costliest antitrust matter in agency history. Interior Committee Chairman Henry Jackson (Dem.; Wash.), who was delving into the causes of the projected energy shortage, knew of the commission's two-year investigation of allegedly anticompetitive activities of the major petroleum companies and was concerned that the agency might not act upon its findings, which purportedly indicated that the antitrust laws may have been violated. In an effort to expedite commission action, he requested in June 1973 that the agency submit to him within thirty days a report detailing the results of its investigation. Then Chairman Lewis Engman replied that his staff would provide Jackson with a report by July 1.[57] Shortly thereafter, however, the commission's general counsel informed the Interior Committee chairman that the agency would not supply him with much of the raw data on energy resources. The release of information about individual companies, he said, "might impede further progress of the investigation" because firms under inquiry would refuse to cooperate with the FTC if they believed that their data might be sent to Congress.[58] In addition, the general counsel stated that disclosure of data "might jeopardize the staff's strategies."[59]

In response to the commission position, Senator Jackson charged that:

The Federal Trade Commission, the agency of the executive branch looking into this subject, is not equipped to move quickly and effectively. . . . Undoubtedly, the FTC is being spoon-fed the information the industry wishes it to get. This drawn-out process has gone on long enough.[60]

He announced that his own Permanent Subcommittee on Investigations would use its subpoena power, if necessary, to secure the petroleum information that the commission declined to reveal and that hearings on the energy problem would consist of sworn testimony.[61]

In a move to ease the pressure placed on the commission to act more quickly, Commission Chairman Engman did provide Jackson with a report, discussing the two-year investigation of the Bureau of Competition and the Bureau of Economics. In a covering letter, Engman warned Senator Jackson that "unnecessary publicity" relating to the staff report could jeopardize future enforcement steps. Despite the objections of the FTC chairman, Senator Jackson released the study to the press.[62] His objective was to draw attention to the commission document and to generate pressure that would force the commissioners to issue a complaint against the major oil producers. In summarizing the report's findings, Jackson termed the study "historic" in that it revealed that federal policies had inflicted hardships "on the average American and the independent small businessman."[63] However, he remarked that the "report has shortcomings" and lacked "hard-hitting and specific recommendations for corrective action."[64] Jackson ordered his staff to examine the investigative files of the commission to determine whether evidence existed indicating that the major producers had contrived the gasoline shortage.

Within weeks of the Jackson committee's campaign to pressure the commission to prosecute the major vertically-integrated petroleum companies, the commissioners voted to issue a complaint against eight oil firms.[65] Most within the agency believe that the Jackson subcommittee can take much of the credit for the commissioners' decision. Commented an attorney who was involved in the investigation:

If it weren't for the Jackson people, the Commission might never have voted to prosecute. The attorneys and even the economists wanted the commissioners to prosecute, but they didn't want to become embroiled in controversy. Jackson tightened the screws —he brought everything out in the open. The press, the interest groups—the Nader people—were all clamoring for a case. If the Commission had not followed with a case, its credibility with the public would have been destroyed.

It should be noted that the commissioners who issued the complaint deny that they succumbed to congressional pressure. However, former Commissioner Mary Gardiner Jones admitted that commission action "may have been accelerated a little."[66]

Individual Intervention
Collective congressional control may not be the only means that congressmen have to affect the character of the commission case load. Conceivably, congressmen could attempt to influence commission affairs by intervening individually. An elected official might involve himself covertly in case-selection matters, especially when intervention is of questionable propriety. It is possible that a representative or senator might contact a commission member or employee at the behest of a prospective respondent in order to forestall agency action. Some commission observers and participants in the decision-making process believe that at least a few congressmen have made such attempts. However, because solid evidence substantiating allegations of wrongdoing did not surface during the course of research, further discussion of the efforts of individual congressmen to interfere with agency proceedings would be nothing more than idle speculation. It might be fruitful, however, to examine how effective individual congressmen have been in persuading the commission to undertake particular investigations. Because reliable information exists about attempts by congressmen to encourage commission action, some judgment can be made as to how successful the senators and representatives have been in achieving their objectives.

One might expect that the commission would react favorably to requests for action made by the elected officials on Capitol Hill— especially those who sit on the legislative and authorization committees that have jurisdiction over agency matters. To be sure, commission officials will give prompt and careful consideration to communications from individual congressmen. It is probably true that the commission is likely to be particularly attentive to those congressmen who are in a position to affect the fortunes of the agency. However, the commission does not usually automatically grant requests for investigations, which congressmen make on behalf of their constituents.

Illustrative of the way in which the commission handles such requests is the case of Congressman Bill Alexander (Dem.; Ark.), a member of the Appropriations Subcommittee on the Departments of State, Justice, Commerce, the Judiciary, and Related Agencies. Prompted by a constituent's letter, Alexander wrote Chairman Engman to request an investigation of the causes of a serious shortage of petrochemical fertilizers used in agricultural production.[67] Charles Tobin, then secretary of the commission, in acknowledging Representative Alexander's letter (within six days time), stated that the commission would furnish him "with a report as promptly as possible."[68] The matter was forwarded to the Bureau of Competition and its Evaluation Committee concluded that the commission should not commit resources to an investigation. In his reply to Congressman Alexander, The Bureau of Competition's assistant director for evaluation stated:

We are deeply concerned with your constituent's plight and with the survival of small independent firms whose sources of supply have been or are likely to be cut off. . . . At this time, however, I am constrained to advise that no affirmative investigative or enforcement action on this complaint is presently contemplated.[69]

Many of the congressmen who call for action, several Bureau of Competition officials claimed, realize that the agency will not respond favorably to their requests. A principal objective of these elected officials is to meet the expectations of their constituents, to show them that they are responsive to their needs. Recounted a former bureau director:

What happens is that Congressman X has a meeting in his office with constituents who have come all the way from their home-towns to discuss their beef. . . . He picks up the telephone, calls me up and chews me out for not opening an investigation. I know he damn well understands why we wouldn't do anything. . . . I may never hear from him again about the matter after he hangs up. . . . In any event, he can say to his constituents: "You see, it's not my fault, but the Commission's."

The Impact of Nongovernmental Actors on the Case Load

Certainly, it would be reasonable to assume that there are others, besides governmental actors, who might attempt to affect the course of antitrust policy. Public interest groups, with their concern for consumer affairs, could be expected to become involved in commission matters. Trade associations of small businessmen and large corporations undoubtedly have an interest in the way in which the commission interprets its responsibilities. Attorneys in the private bar—not a few of whom were once employed in the government—are attentive observers of the commission because knowledge of agency affairs is essential if they are to represent their clients successfully.

Agency decision makers have hailed the participation of nongovernmental actors. As then Chairman Calvin Collier stated: "By increased public participation and awareness, openness in Government can lead to improved decision-making, to greater accountability, and to a restoration of public confidence."[70]

It is not at all clear, however, how the public can affect outcomes. Nor is it obvious that facilitating the participation of parties not in the service of the commission would necessarily increase public trust in the organization. One could conceive of situations in which providing nongovernmental parties (for example, representatives of corporations or members of the private bar) easy access to the commission might raise doubts rather than restore confidence among the public about the integrity of the agency. The commissioners, moreover, could ignore the recommendations of the public. Clearly, before drawing conclusions about the impact of outside parties on the character of the commission case load, an inquiry must be made into the agency's openness policy, the nature of the involvement of the nongovernmental parties, and the safeguards (if any) that are designed to prevent these actors from intervening improperly in commission affairs.

The Openness Policy

The openness policy announced by the commission in 1974 is supposed to make more information available to the public. In explaining the policy, then-Chairman Engman stated that he believed that it struck "a reasonable balance between conflicting interests—the American people's inherent right to know what their government is doing on the one hand and legitimate rights of privacy, as well as the need for some degree of confidentiality if the commission is to carry out effectively its law enforcement mission on the other hand."[71] The policy consists of six features: (1) the commission will issue news releases at the outset of an investigation involving an entire industry or practices that pose substantial risks to the public health or safety; (2) the agency will reveal when investigations of individual firms have been terminated by placing on the public record the closing letter sent to the party under investigation; (3) upon request the commission will make available to the public an analysis of provisionally accepted consent orders so that the public will have a better understanding of the terms of decree; (4) the period for public comment on proposed settlements was extended from thirty to sixty days; (5) the commission will ordinarily disclose internal staff memoranda to the public after a file has been closed for three years and will release all internal documents after a file has been inactive for ten years, unless some specific reason makes disclosure contrary to the public interest; and (6) the agency imposed restrictions on ex parte communications.

On other occasions the agency broadened its policy of disclosing commission votes to include the issuance of complaints, the acceptance of consent orders, the closing of investigations, and the promulgation of final orders. All motions to quash compulsory process as well as commission responses to such maneuvers are now part of the public record. The commission has also decided to disclose to the public not only their advisory opinions but also all staff advisory opinions. Moreover, the agency has determined that all meetings between the commission and outside groups should be open to the public unless a majority of the commissioners vote to close the session. Usually the commission places an announcement in the *Federal Register* thirty days in advance of the meeting. The notice includes a brief description of the intended topic, identification of the participants, and for

closed meetings, an explanation for prohibiting public attendance.

In compliance with the Government in Sunshine Act (Public
Law 94–409), which became effective on 12, March 1977, the
commission reaffirmed its commitment to an openness policy.[72]
The commission opened discussions of advisory opinions, economic reports, surveys, rule-making deliberations, and congressional and other liaison matters to the public. However, the
agency has the authority to close meetings if it deems such action
advisable. Proceedings having to do with ongoing investigations,
cases, and subpoenas will generally be closed to the public. When
the commission votes to close a meeting in accordance with one
of the exemptions provided in the Government in the Sunshine
statute, it must keep detailed minutes or a complete transcript of
the session. An edited version is made available to the public for
the cost of transcription or duplication. Within a day of the action
to close a meeting, the commission provides a written explanation
of its decision and a list specifying the names and affiliations of all
persons expected to attend the nonpublic session.

Public Interest Groups, the Openness Policy, and the Case Load
Undoubtedly, the openness policy is a commission response to
the demands of public interest groups, which have argued that
the citizenry have a right to know about the activities of government and that the state agencies are more likely to act in the
public interest if they make policy in the sunshine.[73] The openness
policy does enable the public interest group to learn more about
commission activities and to evaluate the performance of the
agency.[74] Public interest group participation has been most evi-
dent in rule-making deliberations having to do with consumer
protection matters. While the openness policy facilitates the
monitoring of commission activities by public interest groups, it
does not involve them in the antitrust selection process. The
commission generally closes its meeting to the public when
deliberating about antitrust cases and investigations. Thus, public
interest groups do not have a direct role in determining whether
a complaint should issue or in allocating resources among different kinds of enforcement action. However, on the basis of their

assessment of commission performance, they do make recommendations (through the media, in testimony before congressional committees, and in communications to the commissioners) about the ways in which the agency should exercise its discretion.

Typically, a public interest group will argue that a particular program merits a greater percentage of commission resources. When there appeared to be a serious shortage of canning lids, for instance, Ralph Nader criticized the FTC and the White House for being slow to initiate an investigation and spurred the House Committee on Small Business to question commission officials about antitrust violations.[75] In another instance of public interest group activity, the Corporate Accountability Research Group (CARG) announced that it had uncovered "eight apparently illegal interlocking directorates" and requested a commission investigation. Mark Green, then CARG director, declared that both the Federal Trade Commission and the Justice Department had "established a very poor record" in the enforcement of interlocking directorate cases.[76] Forewarned about the Nader group's accusation, the commission responded by undertaking an investigation of two of the eight interlocks.

In general, public interest groups have not had much of an effect on the agency's case load. Their involvement in antitrust proceedings has been irregular. Rarely do the public interest groups identify possible violations that the commission has not already uncovered. The public interest groups have tended to focus their energies on Congress. More specifically, they have lobbied actively in support of measures to legislate the deconcentration of major industries that are dominated by a few firms.

Indicative, perhaps, of the low level of public interest group activity with respect to particular antitrust matters is the fact that consumer organizations accounted for a mere 4.2 percent of initial requests filed under the Freedom of Information Act in 1975 and only 3.8 percent of all appeals.[77] It is indeed ironic that the Freedom of Information Act, which was largely intended to serve the interests of the consuming public, has mostly benefited the corporations challenged by the commission and the legal counsel that represents them. These corporations and law firms account for 67 percent of all initial Freedom of Information Act requests and 63 percent of all appeals.[78]

The Influence of the Private Bar and Business Interests on Case-Load Decisions

That the corporations and the lawyers who represent them should file a majority of the Freedom of Information Act requests is hardly surprising. Because commission action could affect their interests, these parties attempt to secure staff memoranda that might aid them in charting strategy.[79] Firms that are subjects of commission inquiries believe that they are at a disadvantage in defending their interests, partly because of the agency's sweeping investigatory powers and their exclusion from formal pre-complaint proceedings. At the meetings in which the commissioners determine whether a complaint should issue, only the staff attorneys and economists are present and able to argue their case. In order to compensate somewhat for their felt disadvantages, corporate executives will retain sophisticated counsel who are familiar with commission practices and who enjoy personal friendships with key commission officials. In many instances, these attorneys secured knowledge of agency decision-making processes and formed friendships while serving in the commission either as staff lawyers or commissioners. Their personal relationships with former colleagues, who presently hold important commission positions, provide them with an informal channel to the decision-making process. The value of these attorneys to their clients lies largely in their ability to influence the thinking of those involved in the decision-making process, to communicate effectively to agency officials the concerns of the parties that they represent.

On occasion, private attorneys, whose clients may face commission action, argue their cases directly before individual commissioners in private, precomplaint meetings. While such meetings are held for only a small percentage of the matters that the commission considers, those gatherings often involve discussion of a major investigation (for example, the natural gas case). These meetings, which are permissible under FTC rules, are indicative of the open door policy of the commissioners. In describing this unofficial policy, Commissioner Paul Rand Dixon explained:

If a Commissioner gets all of his information filtered through the staff, it could be good information, but it could be so-called bias by people. So, I have always welcomed anyone coming into my office on any matter up until the time a matter enters adjudication. After that, any communications must be made on the record. . . . I sometimes find proposed respondents more knowledgeable about such matters than I am individually. How they find things out, I don't know, but I find they sometimes follow well what is going on inside the Commission.[80]

Some commissioners invite bureau staff and an attorney adviser to the conferences with representatives of the prospective respondents. "It's a good idea to get both sides together at the same time," stated one commissioner, "because the arguments become so much clearer when each party has to respond to the points made by the other." Moreover, he claimed that "each side is less likely to shade the truth in its favor if the other side is in the same room." The presence of staff, another commissioner argued, may reduce public distrust in the process by which decisions are reached:

If I meet the private counsel by myself and subsequently vote in a way that is favorable to the clients of private counsel, then somebody from a Nader Group, the media or Congress will say that the vote was bought in a closed meeting in my office. When Bureau of Competition attorneys are at the meeting with respondent's counsel, the aura of public suspicion dissipates.

Still another commissioner remarked that he did not believe it was necessary to invite the staff to conferences with private counsel: "I'm an honest man with a good reputation. I don't need Commission witnesses to attest to my honesty. We live in an era of gossip and innuendo—it's disgusting."

In order to shield themselves from the charge that they seek to avoid public scrutiny of their relationships with private counsel, the commissioners maintain a log of all outside contacts connected with pending investigations or cases. They are not required, however, to keep detailed accounts of their meetings in the log books. A Common Cause study revealed that some commissioners have detailed diaries, while others record very little information about the content of their meetings with private attorneys.[81]

Logs of appointments with outside counsel notwithstanding, the threat to the integrity of the case-selection process would seem to be particularly acute when the private attorneys participating in proceedings before the commission acquired knowledge of the case at hand while serving in the agency. If an attorney, seeking to represent a party in a commission hearing, had access to staff memoranda describing tactical and substantive issues in a proposed complaint, was exposed to candid internal discussion of these issues, or could capitalize on his friendship with former colleagues, then he could hold an undue advantage.

In its rules of practice the commission recognizes the dangers of improper intervention and attempts to confront them.[82] A former staff member or commissioner is prohibited from participating in a case that was pending during his employment with the agency. However, he may petition for a clearance to practice in which he explains the nature of his involvement in the matter when he was a commission employee. More specifically, he must discuss the extent of his access to nonpublic documents. The commission will grant clearance unless it finds that any one of the following three circumstances exist: (1) the former commissioner or employee "participated personally and substantially in the proceedings or investigation" during his service with the commission, (2) the petitioner who filed the application for clearance within one year after leaving the commission was "officially responsible" for the case "within a period of one year prior to the termination of his service," and (3) an "actual or apparent impropriety" will occur if the commission authorizes participation.[83]

What constitutes an "actual or apparent impropriety" is not defined in the rules. Quite obviously, the problem confronting each commissioner lies in determining whose perception of impropriety must be taken into account. A commissioner might consider the views of a number of persons and organizations: the private bar, public interest organizations, Congress, current commission employees, and the commissioners themselves. The rub, of course, is that these persons and organizations may differ with one another as to what constitutes "actual or apparent impropriety." What is proper to some is improper to others.

A case in which the commission decided by a 3 to 2 vote to grant clearance to a former executive director who, when an agency official, had access to relevant nonpublic documents, highlights the difficulties in reaching a definitive standard by which to determine impropriety.[84] Writing for the majority, then-Commissioner Stephen Nye stated:

Although presumably Congress could enact such a law [prohibiting former agency employees from ever practicing before the commission] and we could so provide by rule, there is little question that the result would be to foreclose large numbers of attorneys from a practice they well understand and at which they are most competent. . . . Such a result, we are convinced, would be highly detrimental to the public interest.[85]

In his dissent then-Chairman Engman argued that the majority weighed too heavily the effect that a strict standard of conduct might have on the ability of the commission to recruit superior attorneys and the hardships that such a rule might place on former commission employees. Urging the commission to adopt a strict standard, he declared: "The Commission has a duty to the public not only to *assure* it of absolute scrupulousness, but to *convince* it of that fact. In effect, the majority is asking the public to believe the Commission on blind faith. . . . This is not very convincing to me."[86] He was aware, he continued, "that a strict standard could impede the Commission's efforts to recruit highly qualified persons, especially for management positions. . . . I would hope that a standard such as the one I propose would deter no one. But I place even greater importance on the preservation of public trust in our proceedings."[87] The argument of then-Chairman Engman notwithstanding, the commission has chosen not to abandon the amorphous "apparent impropriety" standard, but has decided to deal with "clearance to practice" matters on a case-by-case basis.[88]

Outside parties may attempt to influence case outcomes improperly, not only through their dealings with the commissioners but also through their discussions with staff attorneys. While exchanges between staff attorneys and counsels to the firms under investigation are to be expected, communications between bureau lawyers and persons with whom contact would not normally be made in the routine handling of an investigation could threaten the integrity of the case-selection process. These "non-involved persons," according to a commission directive, include, but are not limited to, a member of Congress or his staff, an official of another government agency or of the executive branch, and any other person in public or private life, not directly involved in the matter.[89]

The Federal Trade Commission has sought to discourage communication between its staff and noninvolved persons (commonly known as "influence peddlers") by requiring that every agency employee make a record of all oral exchanges (transmitted by telephone, delivered in person, or otherwise) between the outside contacts and commission personnel. This record is to include the identity of the pending commission investigation or case, the file number or docket number, the name and position of the outside party who made the contact, the name and position of the commission employee who was contacted, the date and time of the communication, and a brief discussion of the subject of the conversation.

The extent to which representatives of the private bar or of business groups have improperly influenced decisions made by the commissioners or other agency employees is difficult to gauge. While there is no evidence that inappropriate transactions have occurred, most commission participants and observers believe that on occasion representatives of private interests have improperly affected the outcome of agency deliberations. However, most also think that such instances are rare.

Notes

1
38 Stat. 717 (1914), as amended, 15 U.S.C. 41 (1973).

2
In the 1955 confirmation hearings of William Kahn, a self-described Democrat who was sympathetic to the views of his Republican sponsors, Senator Herbert Lehman (Dem., N.Y.) argued that the FTCA meant to "insure minority representation . . . not minority representation in

theory, but minority representation in fact." It is not enough for the nominee to be a "registered member of the minority party, or even if he simply asserts, beyond power of contradiction that he is a member of the minority party." Minority members "should be dedicated to the social and economic viewpoint of the minority party." (U.S., Congress, Senate, Committee on Interstate and Foreign Commerce, *Kern Hearings,* 84th Cong., 1st sess., 1955, p. 2.) Needless to say, neither Democratic nor Republican administrations have found it in their interest to heed Lehman's interpretation of the FTCA.

3

For a thorough discussion of the White House appointment process with respect to the Federal Trade Commission, see James M. Graham and Victor H. Kramer, *Appointments to the Regulatory Agencies,* printed for the use of U.S., Congress, Senate, Committee on Commerce, 94th Cong., 2nd sess., 1976.

4

Richard Cohen, "Making a Point on Appointments," *National Journal* 9 (19 February 1977), p. 291.

5

See "Response of Federal Trade Commission to Questionnaire For Federal Regulatory Agencies of House Subcommittee on Oversight and Investigations of the Committee on Interstate and Foreign Commerce" (hereafter referred to as "Response to Moss Questionnaire"), July 1975 (available under Freedom of Information Act), response to question 67.

6

New Republic 165 (2 October 1971), p. 14.

7

Executive Office of the President, Office of Management and Budget, *Preparation and Submission of Budget Estimates,* no. A–11, June 1975, p. 5.

8

Indicative of that relationship is the fact that the OMB has consistently authorized the commission to request that Congress raise its funding levels. See "Response to Moss Questionnaire," response to question 79.

9

U.S., Congress, House, Committee on Interstate and Foreign Commerce, Subcommittee on Oversight and Investigations, *Hearings on Regulatory Reform,* vol. 4, 94th Cong., 2nd sess., 1976, p. 647.

On the origins of the role of the Bureau of the Budget in legislative clearance, see Richard E. Neustadt, "Presidency and Legislation: The Growth of Central Clearance," *American Political Science Review* 48 (1954): 641.

10
38 Stat. 717.

11
In 1949, John Carson, a liberal independent who was chosen to fill a Republican seat, stirred opposition not only from Republicans but also from industrial interests. Carson survived a difficult committee fight and was subsequently confirmed. Graham and Kramer, *Appointments to the Regulatory Agencies,* p. 405.

12
That nominee was rejected because of the objection of the powerful Virginia senator, Harry Byrd, who invoked the doctrine of senatorial courtesy. Ibid., p. 404.

13
At the 1976 confirmation hearings of Calvin Collier, whom President Ford nominated to be chairman, only Senators Frank Moss (Dem.; Utah) and James B. Pearson (Rep.; Kan.) were present. U.S., Congress, Senate, Committee on Commerce, *Hearings on the Nomination of Calvin Collier to Be Chairman, Federal Trade Commission,* 94th Cong., 2nd sess., 1976, p. 83. Similarly, Stephen Nye had to confront only two senators at his confirmation hearings: Senator Moss and John Tunney (Dem.; Calif.), Nye's homestate senator. (U.S., Congress, Senate, Committee on Commerce, *Hearings on the Nomination of Stephen Nye to be Commissioner, Federal Trade Commission,* 93rd Cong., 2nd sess., 1974, p. 108).

14
See Magnuson's preface to Graham and Kramer, *Appointments to the Regulatory Agencies,* p. vi.

15
See responses of Calvin Collier to questions posed by the Commerce Committee, *Antitrust and Trade Regulation Report,* no. 755, 16 March 1977, p. D–1 (hereafter *ATRR*).

16
Letter from Magnuson to Paul Scanlon, associate editor of *Antitrust Law and Economics Review,* reprinted in Graham and Kramer, *Appointments to the Regulatory Agencies,* p. 355.

17
ATRR, no. 758, 6 April 1977, p. AA–2.

18
ATRR, no. 765, 25 March 1976, p. A–30.

19
Ibid., p. A–31.

20
Ibid., p. A-30.

21
ATRR, no. 775, 3 August 1976, p. A-5.

22
Arthur Maass develops this point in his lecture course on government (130) at Harvard University.

23
A number of House appropriations subcommittees have successively had jurisdiction over commission matters: the Subcommittee on Independent Offices and the Department of Housing and Urban Development; Subcommittee on Agriculture, Environmental and Consumer Protection; and the Subcommittee on State, Justice, Commerce, the Judiciary and Related Agencies. Of these, only the Subcommittee on Agriculture, Environmental and Consumer Protection, chaired by Jamie Whitten (Dem.; Miss.), actively monitored the antitrust affairs of the commission. Whether a subcommittee is active tends to depend upon the interests and style of the chairman.

24
U.S., Congress, House, Committee on Appropriations, *Report on Agriculture-Environmental and Consumer Protection Appropriations Bill,* (93-1120), 93rd Cong., 2nd sess., 1974, p. 86. Although reports are issued by the entire Appropriations Committee, the parts dealing with the commission are clearly the work of the subcommittee with jurisdiction over it.

25
U.S., Congress, House, Committee on Appropriations, *Hearings on Agriculture, Environmental and Consumer Protection Appropriations,* part 6, 93rd Cong., 2nd sess., 1974, p. 667 (italics mine).

26
Ibid., p. 665.

27
The following exchange between Congressman Joe Evins (Dem.; Tenn.) and Chairman Engman illustrates a typical line of questioning on investigational backlogs (Ibid., p. 760):
Mr. Evins: What is your backlog now and what was your backlog this time last year?
Mr. Engman: It is roughly 125 cases.
Mr. Evins: How does that compare with your backlog this time last year?
Mr. Engman: It was approximately 200 more than a year ago.

28
Ibid., p. 719.

29
In its 1973 report for example, the appropriations committee stated that it was

concerned that many of the additional personnel provided for in 1973 were not hired. . . . The Committee attributed this inability to fill positions to the Commission's excessive reliance on too narrow a recruiting base, and advised the Commission to explore ways to hire other than inexperienced employees directly out of law schools or graduate school. Since the Commission has not yet had time to comply with this directive, and in view of the Commission's inability to fill positions added last year, the Committee had deleted $417,000 and 40 new positions requested in 1974. (U.S., Congress, House, Committee on Appropriations, Subcommittee on Agriculture, Environmental and Consumer Protection, *Report 93–275*, 93rd Cong., 1st sess., 1973, p. 92).

30
See, for example, U.S., Congress, House, Committee on Appropriations, *Hearings on Departments of State, Justice, Commerce, the Judiciary and Related Agencies, Appropriations*, F.Y. 1976, part 7, 94th Cong., 1st sess., 1975, p. 336.

31
U.S., Congress, House, Committee on Appropriations, *Hearings on Departments of State, Justice, Commerce, the Judiciary and Related Agencies, Appropriations*, F.Y. 1975, 93rd Cong., 2nd sess., 1974, p. 658.

32
U.S., Congress, House, Committee on Appropriations, *Hearings on Departments of State, Justice, Commerce, the Judiciary and Related Agencies, Appropriations*, F.Y. 1976, 94th Cong., 1st sess., 1975, p. 185.

33
At the outset of the program, the committee restricted the initial data-collection effort to 250 firms rather than 500 firms (as the commission had proposed) "in order to assure that the new venture should begin at a manageable level." In addition the committee directed "that the 250 firms be selected at random rather than concentrating exclusively on the largest firms. Uses of this random approach will assure that the report is more objective and more diverse in its coverage." At the root of this directive was the committee's concern that the commission's proposal to limit its collection to the largest firm seemed "to imply a pre-judgment that bigness is suspect *per se*." *Report 93–1120*, p. 88.

34
For fiscal year 1976, the committee requested that the commission receive $278,000 more than it sought. See U.S. Congress, House, Committee on Appropriations, *Report 94–318*, 94th Cong., 1st sess., 1975. For fiscal 1978, the committee recommended the appropriation of $59,500,000 for consumer protection and antitrust activities—$43,000 below the commission's budget estimate, but $4,820,000 above appropriations for fiscal

1977. U.S., Congress, House, Committee on Appropriations, *Report No. 95–382*, 95th Cong., 1st sess., 1977, pp. 39–40.

35
Hearings on F.Y. 1975, p. 667.

36
The narrow range of matters that concern the subcommittee is illustrated by its debate on the protection and security of data collected by the commission. On a point of order in its action on the appropriation bill, the House had deleted language that prohibited commission employees from disseminating information collected under the line of business program. Senator Roman Hruska (Rep.; Neb.), the ranking minority member of the subcommittee, was concerned that commission employees might disclose such data, even though the corporations had supplied information about their operations in the belief that it would be kept confidential. In order to safeguard that data, Hruska insisted that appropriations bills include language that would prohibit the commission from paying the salaries of any officials who violated the understanding of confidentiality; Hruska's recommendation was adopted. U.S., Congress, Senate, Committee on Appropriations, *Hearings on Departments of State, Justice, Commerce, the Judiciary and Related Agencies, Appropriations, F.Y. 1977,* 94th Cong., 2nd sess., 1976, pp. 26–41.

37
15 U.S.C. 46 (1976).

38
U.S., Congress, House, Committee on Interstate and Foreign Commerce, Subcommittee on Oversight and Investigations, "Rules for the Committee on Interstate and Foreign Commerce," 94th Cong., 1st sess., 1975, rule 11, p.8.

39
See generally U.S., Congress, House, Committee on Interstate and Foreign Commerce, Subcommittee on Oversight and Investigations, *Hearings on Natural Gas Supplies,* vol. 1, part 1, 94th Cong., 1st sess., 1975.

40
U.S., Congress, House, Committee on Interstate and Foreign Commerce, Subcommittee on Oversight and Investigations, *Hearings on Regulatory Reform,* vol. 4, 94th Cong., 2nd sess., 1976, pp. 573–575.

41
ATRR, no. 725, 5 August 1975, p. A–4.

42
Ibid.

43
ATRR, no. 721, 7 July 1975, p. A-1.

44
The questionnaire was divided into sections on the history and goals of the organization; the "prior and subsequent" employment records of the commissioners; the procedures for conducting meetings, casting votes, and publicizing decisions; regulatory process problems such as delays; internal management systems (for example, auditing, budgeting, and case-tracking devices); planning; personnel evaluations; studies of the social and economic effect of agency policies and the actions taken when such studies contributed to the decision; and contracts awarded to consultants.

45
ATRR, no. 726, 12 August 1975, p. A-1.

46
Ibid.

47
Ibid., p. A-12.

48
Ibid.

49
Hearings on Regulatory Reform, pp. 543–636.

50
ATRR, no. 724, 29 July 1975, p. A-5.

51
Ibid.

52
Statement of Robert E. Liedquist, acting director, Bureau of Competition, FTC, Before the Subcommittee on Commodities and Services of the House Committee on Small Business, mimeographed, (10 September 1975).

53
See statement of vice-chairman James M. Hanley (Dem.; N.Y.). U.S., Congress, House, Committee on Small Business, Ad Hoc Subcommittee on Antitrust, the Robinson-Patman Act and Related Matters, *Hearings on Recent Efforts to Amend or Repeal the Robinson-Patman Act,* part 2, 94th Cong., 1st sess., 1975, p. 131.

54
Ibid., part 3, pp. 357–358.

55
The subcommittee has produced several volumes having to do with deconcentration.

56
When acting on legislation mainly concerning the Antitrust Division, the Senate Subcommittee on Antitrust and Monopoly and the House Judiciary Subcommittee on Monopolies and Commercial Law will occasionally affect the operations of the FTC. One such example is the Antitrust Improvements Act of 1976 (90 Stat. 1383), which required, in part, that the commission and the Antitrust Division formulate rules and forms for premerger notification. See *National Journal* 8, no. 39 (25 September 1976), pp. 1353–1355.

57
ATRR, no. 617, 12 June 1973, pp. A–4, A–5.

58
ATRR, no. 618, 19 June 1973, p. A–8.

59
Ibid.

60
Ibid., p. A–7.

61
Ibid.

62
ATRR, no. 621, 10 July 1973, p. A–12.

63
Ibid.

64
Ibid.

65
ATRR, no. 623, p. A–1.

66
New York Times, 17 July 1977, section 3, pp. 1, 3.

67
Hearings on Appropriations, F.Y. 1976, pp. 409–410.

68
Ibid., p. 411.

69
Ibid., p. 417.

70
Hearings on Regulatory Reform, p. 551.

71
FTC News, "Commission Announces Increased Openness," 13 March 1974.

72
ATRR, no. 805, 15 March 1977, pp. A–19, A–20.

73

See Mark Green, Beverly C. Moore, and Bruce Wasserstein, *The Closed Enterprise System: Ralph Nader's Study Group on Antitrust Enforcement* (New York: Grossman Publishers, 1972).

74

In May 1977 in response to a petition from the Institute for Public Interest Representation of the Georgetown University Law Center, the commission voted 3 to 2 to routinely disclose information supplied by respondents during consent order negotiations and to release such data during the sixty-day period when the agency is open to public comments on the proposed consent order. The staff attorneys opposed this action. See *ATRR,* no. 814, 19 May 1977, pp. A-13, A-14.

75

ATRR, no. 724, 29 July 1975, p. A-5.

76

ATRR, no. 725, 5 August 1975, pp. A-16, A-17.

77

Hearings on Regulatory Reform, p. 553.

78

Ibid.

79

This section focuses on the efforts of attorneys and business interests to influence the commission directly, although they do not limit their efforts to the commission to affect antitrust policy. For example, the private bar sought to pressure the commission to increase its Robinson-Patman case load by working with a specially created Ad Hoc Subcommittee of the House Small Business Committee. In another instance, the *Business Roundtable*—an umbrella for leading corporate organizations—lobbied vigorously, but unsuccessfully, against the Antitrust Improvements Act of 1976. Sometimes a business interest that believes that the commission is hostile to its interests will attempt to pull an end run around the agency. For example, the soft drink industry promoted a bill in Congress that was intended to exempt from antitrust prosecutions those soft drink manufacturers who allocate exclusive sale territories among their bottlers. The bill's purpose was the rescission of antitrust actions brought by the commission in 1971 against seven major companies, which annually sell $8 billion of soft drinks. See *National Journal* 8 (28 August 1976), p. 1223.

80

Hearings on Regulatory Reform, pp. 575–576. Commissioner Stephen Nye supported Dixon's statements when he commented:

We aren't just a grand jury, we are also a prosecutor, and as such we have an obligation to get both sides and to make sure the case we have is sufficient and sound. . . . Some firms and some lawyers make [meetings with Commissioners] more of a habit than others. Some lawyers think it's

a waste of time, and I suppose if you look at our record—their presenta-
tions usually aren't successful—you might agree. But I think it's a great
deal of help to the Commissioners. (*ATRR*, no. 764, 18 May 1976, p. A-17).

81
Commissioner Elizabeth Hanford Dole, for example, maintained a log of
meetings with outsiders and a brief summary of conversations with
private counsel. Commissioner Stephen Nye's log consisted of three large
spiral notebooks, hundreds of pages long, with descriptions of every
office meeting and phone call with private counsel. At the other extreme
is Commissioner Dixon, who makes note of appointments on his desk
calendar, often without describing the subject of the meetings. Ibid., pp.
A–16, A–17.

82
Federal Trade Commission, *Organization, Procedure and Rules of Practice,* section 4.1(b).

83
Ibid.

84
The case involved Basil Mezines, whose twenty-four years (1949–1973) of
service in the commission included two years and eight months (November 1970 to June 1973) as executive director. Upon his departure from the
commission, Mezines entered private law practice in Washington, D.C.
On 13 April 1974, he applied to the commission for permission to appear
as an attorney in three actions—Lustre Chevrolet, Peacock Buick, Inc.,
and Rosenthal Chevrolet Company. In performing his tasks as executive
director, Mezines acknowledged that he probably saw three intra-agency
memoranda dealing with the particular cases in which he was currently
involved, and that he may very well have attended the meetings of the
commission at which it issued complaints against the three automobile
dealers. See *Hearings on Regulatory Reform,* pp. 584–586.

85
Ibid., p. 588.

86
Ibid., p. 591.

87
Ibid.

88
There is every indication that Chairman Michael Pertschuk agrees with
Engman's position regarding clearance. In a matter in which Chairman
Miles Kirkpatrick and his assistant Caswell Hobbs were granted clearance,
Pertschuk stated, "I share Engman's view that public trust and confidence
in the integrity of our substantive decision-making cannot be achieved
unless the public is convinced that no former member or employee who

practices before this agency possesses an improper advantage." *ATRR,*
no. 812, 5 May 1977, pp. A–22, A–23.

89
FTC News, "Commission Announces Increased Openness," 13 March
1974.

10
Conclusion: The Federal Trade Commission, Antitrust, and Public Policy

The Case-Selection Process in the Federal Trade Commission: A Review

In the absence of clearly defined statutory objectives, the Federal Trade Commission apparently has wide discretion in determining the goal (or goals) that it should pursue. Antitrust policy may have any of several, sometimes conflicting, objectives: (1) fostering competitive processes in the market, (2) securing desirable economic performance by individual firms and ultimately by the whole economy, (3) limiting the power of "big business", and (4) maintaining fair standard of business conduct.[1]

Within the commission, debate about the ends of antitrust policy and the means to achieve those objectives has centered upon two different conceptions of antitrust policy: the reactive perspective and the proactive approach. The former holds that the Bureau of Competition should rely upon the letters of complaint as the sources of its investigations. Proponents of this approach tend to be skeptical about big structural cases. They point to the problems associated with prosecuting such matters (the lack of qualified staff, the high turnover rate, the technical complexity of the cases, the uncertainty of success in the courts). Rather than prosecute cases that they believe are unlikely to yield positive results, supporters of the reactive approach argue that the commission should pursue those conduct matters that are relatively simple to investigate and try in the courtroom.

Proponents of the proactive approach are convinced that the commission should use its scarce resources selectively to combat abuses in those sectors of the economy that most affect the consumer. They argue that with the aid of planning mechanisms, the commission should be able to establish priorities and to weigh the costs and benefits of possible enforcement actions. The cereal, *Exxon,* and various industrywide investigations are examples of the agency's effort to prosecute matters that could yield substantial consumer benefits.

Although there has been an increasing emphasis on the proactive approach, commission decision-makers still allocate resources to those conduct cases of the reactive kind that are unlikely to yield much consumer benefit in order to establish an important precedent in the law, to deter businesses that might be tempted to violate sections of the law, and to show Congress that it intends to enforce all laws. To satisfy Congress, the FTC issues some complaints rooted in the Robinson-Patman Act; the general lack of congressional enthusiasm for Robinson-Patman matters, however, has allowed the commission in recent years to reduce considerably the percentage of resources allocated to such cases.

Perhaps more importantly, the director of the Bureau of Competition, regardless of his desire to satisfy the Bureau of Economics or of his preference for structural cases and industrywide investigations, will authorize the opening of a number of easily prosecuted conduct cases because considerations of organizational maintenance virtually require him to do so. Prosecution of such cases may be necessary to meet the career expectations of attorneys, who value trial experience. Such cases lessen (if only temporarily) the dissatisfaction among those attorneys who are assigned to the large, structural investigations.

Explaining Organizational Outcomes:
A Critique of Some Theories

The findings presented in this book raise serious doubts about the correctness of the approach taken by economists who believe that they can explain the factors that govern case selection by focusing upon the industry economic characteristics of the agency's prosecutions.[2] Industry economic characteristics do not by themselves explain the prosecutions the commission has undertaken. Economists err when they ignore other variables such as professional values and goals; certainly, one cannot explain the FTC's case load without reference to the interaction between lawyers and economists—professionals whose differing goals, norms, and training led to disagreements about agency policy. Legal precedent, the need to satisfy the professional objectives of staff attorneys, the availability of requisite expertise, and the occasional influence of outside actors affect the decision-making calculus of commission officials. Even when agency decision makers choose to pursue a big structural case, they are likely to consider not simply economic variables, but the other factors just mentioned as well. Finally, the prescriptions of the economists regarding antitrust policy are often limited in value because they are divorced from evaluations of the capacity of the agency to prosecute the suggested menu of cases.

A political scientist, Alan Stone, writes in a very thoughtful book that the antitrust case load promotes both competition and stability because the Clayton Act and the Federal Trade Commission Act enshrines these contradictory impulses.[3] However, his work does not fully explain the criteria governing case-selection decisions because it does not describe how institutional arrangements affect outcomes; his account does not discuss the multiplicity of organizational factors bearing upon case-selection decisions. Moreover, simply by focusing upon the FTC's statutory authorities, Stone cannot explain how the commission allocates resources among cases or why the mix of cases has changed over time.

The analysis of commission decision making, as presented in this book, is also not consonant with the judgment of those scholars, ranging from conservative economist George Stigler to radical historian Gabriel Kolko, who contend that government generally serves the very economic interests that it is supposed to regulate. Professor Stigler, a leading authority on antitrust matters, states that "as a rule, regulation is acquired by the industry and is designed and operated primarily for its benefit."[4] In support of the "capture" theory, Kolko argues in several works that the purpose and effect of government regulation is to entrench the dominant economic class' control of wealth.[5] Samuel Huntington also believes that the regulator will almost certainly succumb to pressure from corporate interests.[6] Using a life-cycle image, Marver Bernstein maintains that public agencies, which at first seek to further the public interest, eventually sacrifice fidelity to the rule of law in favor of the businesses that they are supposed to regulate.[7] That government generally responds positively to corporate elements has been a basic assumption of leaders of public interest groups. For example, in his introduction to the Closed Enterprise System, an interesting study dealing with the operations of antitrust enforcement agencies, Ralph Nader writes, "this is a report on crime in the suites"[8]—an allusion to what Nader perceives to be the unholy relationship between government and business.

To be sure, there have undoubtedly been instances in which various regulatory bodies have not acted in the public interest. However, sweeping generalizations about agency capture or the causes and effects of regulatory legislation are suspect. As James Q. Wilson has noted, "Regulatory laws can have a variety of political causes and . . . it is necessary, in order to understand why regulation occurs, to specify the circumstances under which one or another cause will be operative."[9] With respect to the Federal Trade Commission, the evidence does not support the assumption that the agency was created to serve industry or was later captured by it. Rather, the legislation creating the FTC secured support from diverse elements—consumers, small businessmen, large corporations—with differing and sometimes opposing views of the law's purposes.[10] As this book has attempted to show, moreover, it certainly cannot be stated categorically that the disproportionate possession of resources by various economic interests necessarily results in an inordinate exercise of political power. Clearly, an agency dominated by corporate interests would be unlikely to launch major actions against segments of the petroleum, cereal, or business copying industries. Even Richard Posner, a proponent of the economic theory of regulation, which conceives of regulation as a service supplied to effective political interest groups, admits that his view cannot account for the recent activism of the Federal Trade Commission.[11]

The findings of this book also challenge those theorists who argue that bureaucracies are simply rational actors that attempt to respond to their environment so as to maximize organizational self-interest. For example, in *Bureaucracy and Representative Government* William Niskanen, Jr., an economist, writes that bureaucracies seek to maximize the size of their budgets.[12] The behavior of the bureaucrat, he assumes, is best explained by his desire to maximize his budget because desired rewards—salary, prestige, power, or patronage—are generally a function of such maximization. Similarly, George Stigler's theory of regulation assumes that regulators seek to retain their jobs and secure greater appropriations for their agency as a means of increasing personal power (and frequently compensation as well).[13]

It is clear, however, that commission officials are not fundamentally motivated by a desire to maximize budgets. While they do seek increases in funding, most expressed concern that a rapid influx of money and attorneys could undermine the agency's efforts to maintain control of case-load decisions—bureau executives might sometimes have to authorize investigations of dubious value, simply to provide work for the new attorneys. Moreover, a rapid influx of funds and lawyers could magnify the problems of attorney training and supervision. Finally, most staff attorneys and officials view government service as a stint; they join the commission with the expectation of departing within a few years. Increasing salaries is not likely to induce many to remain with the agency.

Richard Posner argues that the fact that most commissioners do not pursue careers in public service and thus may not be motivated by a desire to increase their government salaries does not invalidate the assumption that they will not do anything in office that could jeopardize future earnings—as members of the private bar. More specifically, he contends:

A commissioner concerned with his future success at the bar will have no greater incentive to promote the consumer interest fearlessly and impartially than one whose guiding principles are job retention and agency aggrandizement. He will receive no bonus upon entry (or reentry) into private practice for the vigorous championing of the consumer interest. . . . On the other hand, the enmity of the organized economic interests, the trade associations and trade unions, that a zealous pursuit of consumer interests would engender may do him some later harm, while making his tenure with the Commission more tense and demanding than would otherwise be the case. Exceptional people may rise to the challenge but they are unlikely ever to constitute a sizable fraction of the commissioners.[14]

Certainly, recent agency history has failed to confirm Posner's 1969 forecast about the course that the commissioners were likely to follow.

Perhaps the commission may be properly understood as an organization that does not proceed in any obvious, maximizing way. Its behavior is not simply that of a rational self-interested actor, seeking to maximize its budget, power, or convenience. Rather, the commission is an agency that has struggled in the last several years to pursue actions in what it perceives to be the public interest, although it has not always been certain as to which policy course would most serve that interest. In choosing the case load, agency policy makers are constrained by staff attorneys, whose felt professional objectives must be satisfied to some degree if the organization is to be maintained. The agency operates in a political environment—it must, therefore, not be unmindful of the actors (for example, Congress, the executive) that might attempt to influence antitrust policy. But the agency, while respectful of these elements, does not act as their servant.

The Problem of the Big Structural Case

The shift in emphasis from the reactive to the proactive approach to antitrust enforcement was engineered by a new commission leadership, consisting of dedicated chairmen and bureau executives, who felt strongly that the agency should devote resources to investigations that could benefit the consumer. Commission officials sought to create conditions that would facilitate change. Yet, while the commission leadership has surely shown its commitment to undertake major actions, it is clear that merely allocating resources to such ambitious efforts does not ensure that such cases can be prosecuted easily. Indeed, it is somewhat doubtful whether allocating an increasing percentage of resources to such matters or taking steps designed to lessen the level of dissatisfaction among the lawyers assigned to the complex structural investigations will enable the agency to prosecute such cases successfully. The problems that opponents of the proactive approach are quick to emphasize do exist. The high turnover rate —90 percent of all attorneys who joined the commission between 1972 and 1975 expected in July of 1976 to leave within two years— makes prosecution difficult.[15] As then-Director of the Bureau of Competition Owen Johnson recently noted:

A lot can be lost, in substance and strategy, each time a new group of attorneys takes over the prosecution of an oligopoly case such as *Cereal* or *Exxon*. We are becoming reconciled to the inevitability of substantial turnover in such litigation. We have noticed that when the case is in its early stages—fighting off motions to dismiss and other "legal" or "jurisdictional" motions—staff morale is usually high and turnover low. Attorneys like these skirmishes. When the case moves into document discovery and depositions, morale drops and staff suffers attrition. *Exxon* is presently in that stage.[16]

As Johnson suggests, the high turnover rate is costly in several respects. Every time a qualified attorney leaves the agency, the commission loses an investment. The Bureau of Competition must devote resources to training new recruits who have replaced those lawyers who have left the FTC. The brief tenure of most attorneys means that few lawyers have the expertise or experience needed to prosecute complex cases. Those who do acquire the requisite skills do not remain with the FTC for long. The agency can expect to have severe problems in prosecuting mammoth cases if the staff attorneys leave the commission shortly after they secure knowledge that makes them valuable to both the government and private law firms.

Although there is evidence that the morale and turnover problems lessen once the case reaches trial,[17] the rub is that years often pass before the matter moves to the courtroom.[18] Most attorneys enter government service with the intention of leaving after gaining trial experience that would make them attractive to corporations or lucrative firms of the private bar. By the time the case enters the courtroom (if it does at all), the original team of attorneys (and most probably several other sets of later teams) will almost certainly have left the agency.

The persistent problems in prosecuting complex cases point to the difficulty of accurately predicting the effects of institutional reform. For those who wrote the ABA Commission's study of the FTC,[19] as well as for Ralph Nader and his associates whose report called attention to the agency's ills,[20] it seemed clear in 1969 that a concerted effort to upgrade the recruitment system would have to be made. They also recognized the need to create policy-planning mechanisms and to install devices to control case-load decisions. To be sure, they correctly understood that the commission could not hope to prosecute complex matters without attorneys of high caliber; most staff attorneys in 1969 did not have the skills to pursue complex structural cases, and many did not have the inclination to investigate anything but the simple conduct cases.

Yet while the commission of recent years has attracted graduates of the best law schools, the difficulties in prosecuting structural matters remain, largely because of the high turnover rate among its most promising attorneys. Nearly all of those who criticized the commission of the sixties and offered prescriptions assumed wrongly that the consumer movement would produce enough talented young attorneys in the years ahead to work on the challenging structural cases. Most analysts neglected to consider that the public interest fervor of the late sixties would not continue indefinitely or that the staff lawyer might be concerned not so much with the social or economic benefits of structural litigation as he would be with securing trial experience that would make him attractive to the private bar.[21] At the time commission critics (from inside and outside the agency) did not foresee that by the mid-seventies, the typical young recruit would not join because of a commitment to public service and that he would have every incentive to resist assignment to the complex investigations, which offered little prospect of immediate courtroom exposure. In short, they did not consider how the goals of the personnel with the agency might constrain an organization in the pursuit of objectives, however worthwhile.

An Analysis of Proposals to Resolve Problems in Antitrust Enforcement

Indicative of the seriousness of the commission's difficulties in prosecuting complex structural cases are the many measures that have been proposed to upgrade the quality of antitrust enforcement. Generally, these suggestions either seek to affect changes within the existing commission framework or argue that the antitrust responsibilities of the commission be shifted to another organization. Among the former kind are those that call for (1) procedural reform, (2) contracting for the services of private attorneys, and (3) greater use of rule-making authority to resolve antitrust problems. Among the latter type are those that recommend that (1) the Antitrust Division of the Department of Justice assume sole jurisdiction over major prosecutions or that (2) a Trade Court assume the adjudicative functions of the commission. In the next section I will attempt to evaluate the merits of the proposals.

Internal Reforms

Procedural Reform   Many observers of the commission contend that the agency could expedite the resolution of antitrust cases if it instituted procedural reforms. Owen Johnson has urged that the commission revise its discovery rules and allow interrogatories that would enable the attorneys to reduce the time needed to determine those areas upon which they should concentrate in subsequent document and deposition discovery.[22] Moreover, he suggested that the agency eliminate the requirement that the Bureau of Competition undertake voluntary interviews before resorting to depositions of respondents. Delays could be shortened, many experts believe, if the commission had full contempt and penalty power. Currently, commission attorneys must expend considerable energies in federal court if they want to force respondents to comply with subpoenas. Johnson noted that "multiple levels of review are built into Commission discovery and thus effectively invite respondents not to cooperate."[23]

Litigation might proceed more quickly if the administrative law judges, who have jurisdiction over cases once a complaint is issued, assumed a greater role in sharpening issues to be adjudicated. In 1977, Robert Pitofsky (who became a commissioner in 1978) stated:

Many of these administrative judges had little or no antitrust experience prior to appointment and no special knowledge or training in economics. . . . I suspect that this lack of experience in antitrust . . . leads to the most critical failure in the trial of complicated antitrust cases—that is, the failure at an early point to take control of formulation of the issues away from the parties. It is essential in these mammoth cases that the issues at trial be reduced in number and sharpened to manageable proportions.[24]

While these important proposals would almost certainly expedite the pace of antitrust prosecutions, they are unlikely to solve the problems associated with large structural cases. The complex nature of such cases means that they will still involve lengthy proceedings, even if the proposals are adopted. The difficulties in retaining staff will remain. The proposals, which focus upon the postcomplaint stages, do not address the turnover problems that affect the commission in the period between the beginning of an investigation and the issuance of a complaint.

Contracting for the Services of Attorneys in the Private Bar   Since the commission's difficulties in prosecuting structural cases stem to a large extent from the lack of experienced staff and there seems to be no way to induce the more promising attorneys to work for the government for more than a few years, some have suggested that the agency might find it practical to contract with seasoned lawyers of the private bar who would be willing to handle the complex matters for their duration. Commissioner Paul Rand Dixon, former Executive Director Richard T. McNamar, and former Attorney General Nicholas Katzenbach have expressed their interest in the idea of the government's contracting for the services of attorneys of the private bar.[25] Presumably, the hiring of qualified private lawyers would eliminate the costs associated with high turnover—the constant investment of resources needed to train new recruits, the loss in terms of substance, strategy, and momentum.

While the proposal that the commission hire private attorneys is superficially attractive, it has severe drawbacks. The arrangement between private firms and the commission could create conflict of interest problems. The entanglement of the commission with the private bar could preclude the agency's decision makers from maintaining a proper distance from the law firms. Suspicion about the commissioners' ability to act fairly would be heightened if the firms with which the agency contracts also represented companies under FTC investigation. In addition, the danger exists that private attorneys, while working for the commission, could learn of Bureau of Competition strategies regarding other cases in which their firms are opposing agency action.

The incentives for young talent to join the commission would probably diminish greatly if the services of private attorneys were sought. Law school graduates on the job market would assume that the commission contracted for the services of private attorneys because its own staff was of poor quality. Promising young lawyers are unlikely to join the commission if they believe that their reputations would be tainted because of their association with the agency. Moreover, should the private attorneys who work for the government receive higher salaries than agency employees, then there is certain to be an exodus of commission attorneys, who might resent earning less than their temporary colleagues for performing comparable tasks. Even if the commission reimbursed lawyers in private practice at the standard civil service pay rates, the firms that employed them would probably supplement their salaries to meet the wage levels of their colleagues in the private bar.

Rule Making   As a means of reducing costs some observers have urged the commission to more seriously consider rule making as an alternative to adjudication. Presumably, a rule would cover a large number of matters and would make case-by-case adjudication unnecessary. Chairman Michael Pertschuk recently stated that antitrust trade regulation rules "could establish bright-line standards of prohibited conduct, allowing the development of antitrust policy by a fair and effective procedure on an industrywide (or even broader) basis."[26] Professor Kenneth Culp Davis has long held that "antitrust law, involving both criminal prosecutions and suits in equity" is "an outstanding example of the need for confinement of prosecutor's discretion through rule-making."[27] Despite these pronouncements it is unclear whether rule making has much utility in antitrust law. The limits of rule making are due to the nature of antitrust and the staff attorney's opposition to its widespread application.

Rule making might be of value when the violations in question have to do with specific areas of conduct where circumstances are not likely to vary from case to case. Complex structural cases, however, do not lend themselves to resolution by rule. Given the numerous factual situations, the changes of industrial organization, the shifts in the economy and in notions of utility, it is doubtful whether rule making can replace adjudication in resolving complex structural cases. Where fact patterns do not often recur and conditions are subject to change, the commission might find, as King Rex of Lon Fuller's allegory eventually learned, that rule making can be quite a complex assignment.[28]

Bureaucratic resistance decreases the likelihood that the commission will use rule-making procedures extensively, even when applicable. Then-Director of the Bureau of Competition Owen Johnson commented that "there's a managerial fear of biting off more than you can chew."[29] Moreover, attorneys who are convinced that trial experience is central to their career prospects are not likely to look favorably upon rule making, since it may reduce litigative activity with respect to conduct cases—precisely those vehicles that lawyers believe will help them secure their professional objectives. In addition, many lawyers might conceivably interpret the use of rule-making as an attack on their competence as litigators. In Johnson's view: "It's a little hard to convince them they won't lose their masculinity if they get into rule-making."[30]

Transferring the Commission's Antitrust Responsibilities to Another Organization

Shifting Responsibility to the Antitrust Division of the Justice Department
Some antitrust experts maintain that the Federal Trade Commission is beyond institutional reform: the agency, in their view, is and always will be incapable of discharging its antitrust responsibilities. Their solution is drastic: the Federal Trade Commission should transfer its duties in antitrust enforcement to the Antitrust Division of the Department of Justice. The notion that the Antitrust Division should have sole jurisdiction over antitrust cases (with perhaps the exception of Robinson-Patman matters) is not new. In 1960, for example, Dean James Landis made such a recommendation to President-elect Kennedy.[31]

In the wake of the commission's difficulties in prosecuting oligopoly cases, several witnesses, testifying at oversight hearings held in May 1977 before the Subcommittee on Antitrust and Monopoly of the Senate Judiciary Committee, addressed themselves to the question of whether the Federal Trade Commission should be stripped of its antitrust enforcement functions. Different views were expressed. Former Commission Chairman Miles Kirkpatrick argued that "the present dual enforcement of the antitrust laws have strengths which should be preserved."[32] Echoing this judgment was Robert Pitofsky, former director of the Bureau of Consumer Protection and presently a commission member. However, Dean Ernest Gellhorn of the Arizona State University Law School concluded otherwise.[33]

Those who support transference of the Federal Trade Commission's antitrust duties contend that (1) the decision-making apparatus of the Antitrust Division is superior to that of the commission; (2) the Antitrust Division, being part of the executive branch, is more likely to make prosecutorial decisions based on the merits of the case than is the commission, which must be sensitive to the political needs of Congress; and (3) the Antitrust Division's staff is of higher quality than that of the commission and therefore the Department of Justice is more likely to prosecute complex cases successfully. Before considering each of these arguments, it might be useful to examine the relationship between the Federal Trade Commission and the Antitrust Division to determine how the two agencies divide the work.[34]

The FTC-Antitrust Division liaison. Although the Antitrust Division and the Federal Trade Commission share responsibilities under some statutes, there are other antitrust laws that each enforces alone. The former has sole jurisdiction over criminal matters arising under the Sherman Act and has left enforcement of section 2 of the Clayton Act, as amended by the Robinson-Patman Act, to the latter. The commission enforces section 5 of the Federal Trade Commission Act, which is broader in its reach than the antitrust laws. Otherwise, both agencies share enforcement for sections 2, 3, 7, and 8 of the Clayton Act. Moreover, the courts have held that conduct violative of the Sherman Act may also be considered illegal under section 5 of the Federal Trade Commission Act, thereby conferring authority on the commission to prosecute matters that might ordinarily be thought to be in the bailiwick of the Antitrust Division.

In theory, it is conceivable that both agencies would concentrate on the same enforcement areas. In exercising discretion—

especially when what the law mandates is uncertain—each might independently choose to allocate resources in the same way. The sharing of enforcement responsibilities could result in a duplication of effort. Alternatively, it is possible that each could have different conceptions of the antitrust policies that the government should pursue. In that case, the Antitrust Division and the Federal Trade Commission might oppose each other in court.

However, the two agencies have in reality generally avoided major confrontations. The Federal Trade Commission and the Antitrust Division meet regularly to discuss possible investigations. Pursuant to an agreement entered into in 1948, the two agencies established a liaison system designed to prevent one organization from duplicating the work of the other.[35] The commission charges its liaison officer, who is attached to the Evaluation Office of the Bureau of Competition, with the task of communicating on a routine basis with his counterpart in the Antitrust Division. Each officer maintains a file system listing requests for clearance by their agencies to conduct investigations.[36] For its part, the Bureau of Competition does not seek clearance from the Antitrust Division until the bureau director has determined whether the agency should commit resources to an investigation. Until the clearance process has run its course each organization is bound not to approach a potential respondent or to disclose the plans for an investigation.

Usually, one agency will automatically grant clearance to the other to pursue an investigation, unless the contemplated action duplicates or interferes with a case that it is already conducting. In theory, an agency could refuse to authorize clearance and perhaps argue that it has greater expertise in the area under inquiry. In practice, however, disputes that might arise if work were allocated on the basis of expertise have been avoided because the agencies have divided responsibility according to industry. For example, they have agreed that the commission will prosecute matters having to do with supermarkets and department stores, while the Antitrust Division will pursue investigations having to do with the steel industry. Should the agencies disagree as to which organization should have clearance to prosecute, the liaison officers will attempt to resolve the dispute. If they are unable to settle the dispute, then the assistant director for evaluation of the Bureau of Competition and the director or deputy director of the Office of Operations of the Antitrust Division will meet and almost always resolve the differences between their agencies. Only rarely must the bureau director or the chairman negotiate with the assistant attorney general over which agency should have clearance to prosecute.

The clearance process has prevented a wasteful duplication of effort. There have been no instances in recent memory of both agencies committing resources to the same investigation.[37] Moreover, the liaison process has operated swiftly. Requests for clearance are generally handled within five days. If either agency believes that the matter should be dealt with expeditiously, then the clearance process may run its course within twenty-four hours.

While commission officjals maintain that the system has generally worked well, the agencies could improve the process. The Antitrust Division and the Federal Trade Commission, as Miles Kirkpatrick suggests, might use the process as a means to upgrade policy-planning efforts.[38] An agency could take responsibility for a particular investigation not only because its attorneys are interested in the matter or the agency has traditionally prosecuted such violations; before clearance is granted, the agencies could make a more serious attempt to detemine which organization's administrative processes are better suited to the case at hand. It is, however, unlikely that the Antitrust Division and the Federal Trade Commission will allocate work in this manner. Bureaucracies, protective of their autonomy, cannot be expected to accept any arrangement that could threaten their spheres of dominance in antitrust law.

Whether the decision-making processes of the Antitrust Division are superior to those of the FTC. In arguing that the Justice Department should have sole responsibility for pursuing infractions of the antitrust laws, several experts have stated that the single-headed administration of the Antitrust Division (led by an assistant attorney general) is superior to the FTC's collegial form of governance. However, the commission-style of administration is not necessarily unworkable. As the FTC's recent history has shown, collegiality need not lead to irresponsibility; commissioners cast their votes on the record and their actions are subject to congressional, media, and public interest group scrutiny. Moreover, the internal arrangements of the commission —the competition between the Bureau of Economics and the Bureau of Competition, the existence of quality control devices— are designed to facilitate reaching informed decisions, monitoring ongoing activity, and reducing administrative inefficiency.

The claim that the Antitrust Division operates more effectively than the FTC because it is governed by a single administrator who does not have to compete with other persons for control of the staff, ignores the fact that the commission's bureaucracy can be effectively controlled by the chairman. Furthermore, just because the Antitrust Division is single-headed does not mean that the staff is easily controlled. Suzanne Weaver has written that attorneys in the Antitrust Division are jealous of their autonomy, and executives therefore often have great difficulty imposing changes on the staff.[39] The assertion that the Antitrust Division is better able to set coherent policy than the Federal Trade Commission (because the Antitrust Division head does not have to make compromises with other decision makers) fails to recognize that in making decisions, the assistant attorney general for antitrust is not unconstrained; he must consider the views of the attorney general, the president, and his own staff of lawyers.

Whether the Commission is less likely than the Antitrust Division to undertake innovative action because it is independent of the executive. For some time, several observers of antitrust decision making have argued that the commission is less likely than the Antitrust Division to undertake innovative actions because it is independent of the executive branch. As early as 1935, E. Pendleton Herring stated that "the control of business remains too controversial and too vital a political issue to be relegated successfully to a Commission independent of close control by the policy-formulating agencies of government."[40] Thirty-five years later, outgoing Commissioner Philip Elman echoed Herring's thoughts, stating that independence "tends to discourage creative and courageous regulation in the public interest. Independence means that an agency lacks a constituency, a power base and the backing of the President."[41]

The attorney general, commented Richard Posner, "is more independent than the Commission of another powerful source of political pressure, the Congress, whose committee chairmen have over the years exerted a strong and on the whole baleful influence over the FTC's activities."[42] Others have stated that the quality of commission decisions is likely to be poor since the president, who is not responsible for the work of the independent agencies, tends to use his appointing prerogatives to reward the politically faithful, though they might be unqualified.

Contrary to the aforementioned assertions, the independence of the Federal Trade Commission from the executive branch has not prevented the agency from pursuing controversial and/or innovative cases. The commission in recent years has sponsored several major actions: such matters as *Exxon, Xerox,* cereal, the food investigations, and the natural gas case are certainly bold efforts. To be sure, the commission may at times be sensitive to the demands of influential congressmen or interest groups. On those relatively few occasions in recent years when congressional committees or legislators have intervened in the case-selection process, however, they have not thwarted the commission but have prodded the agency to act swiftly. Congressional involvement in the *Exxon* matter and the natural gas investigations are cases in point.

It need not be the case that the quality of the commissioners will be low because the president is not accountable for the work of the independent agencies. Even in its darkest days the commission had able commissioners. Certainly, not all appointees have had the requisite skills needed to be effective. There is, however, no reason why less than qualified individuals should secure nomination and confirmation to commissionerships. A president committed to appointing talented persons and a Senate Committee on Commerce, Science and Transportation prepared to reject unqualified nominees could easily assure that the five members of the commission are individuals of high competence.

Finally, it is not all clear that the Federal Trade Commission would have undertaken some of its major initiatives if the agency had been directly responsible to the president. The Antitrust Division may generally be free of political pressures, and the support of the president may help legitimate controversial decisions. However, there have undoubtedly been instances in which the White House thwarted Department of Justice actions for reasons not based upon considerations of public policy. One such case allegedly involved the proposed merger in 1970 of the Warner-Lambert Pharmaceutical Company and the Parke-Davis and Company.[43] Then-Assistant Attorney General Richard McClaren of the Antitrust Division reportedly favored action to prevent the merger. Attorney General Mitchell had to remove himself from the case because his former law firm (and President Nixon's as well) represented Warner-Lambert. Deputy Attorney General Richard Kleindienst overruled McClaren's judgment, arguing that the merger should not be blocked because Parke-Davis was failing. (In this assertion he was mistaken.) According to Mark Green many observers hold that the Justice Department's decision reflected the administration's unwillingness to block action, opposed by Warner-Lambert's honorary chairman, Elmer Bobst—a close friend of Nixon and a general campaign contributor.[44] In the wake of the publicity surrounding the Justice Department's determination not to challenge the merger, the matter was referred to the Federal Trade Commission. Ultimately, the commission decided to contest the merger. Thus, the existence of another antitrust agency increased the probability that the government would prosecute.

Whether the staff of the Antitrust Division is better equipped than the FTC to prosecute structural cases. Those who argue that the Justice Department should have exclusive jurisdiction over antitrust cases maintain that the Antitrust Division is better able to prosecute structural matters than the Federal Trade Commission because its staff is of higher quality. It is true that until the commission's revitalization the Antitrust Division had far greater success in attracting able attorneys. As Suzanne Weaver has noted in her enlightening study, many talented individuals, either by accident or design, spent their careers in the Justice Department.[45] The commission—without the leadership of a Thurman Arnold or a reputation for professionalism—had difficulty securing the talents of the lawyers of the caliber found in the Department of Justice. Today, however, the commission is able to compete with the Antitrust Division for promising recruits.

Notwithstanding the ability of the FTC to attract superior talent, the Bureau of Competition has had much difficulty in prosecuting big cases. The situation in the Antitrust Division is much the same. Like the Federal Trade Commission, the Antitrust Division has a serious problem of staff turnover. Young attorneys leave within a few years after joining the Antitrust Division. The small cadre of experienced attorneys who have staffed the agency for twenty-five or thirty years is retiring; there is not a comparable core group of younger attorneys who can train the new recruits and guide them through the complexities of a structural case. As then-Assistant Attorney General Donald Baker recently stated:

The simple fact is that our best senior trial lawyers are very good indeed—but we do not have enough of them to meet our needs at a time when our litigation burden is substantially increasing. . . . [T]he private sector successfully bids away a substantial portion of our best people after they have gained their basic experience (approximately half of our turnover involves people having 3–5 years experience). Secondly, many of the best who remain—those who give up money and "perks" for the satisfaction of public service—end up being appointed as supervisors and are thus often lost to the courtroom for most purposes.[46]

The promotion system compounds the assistant attorney general's burdens.[47] A trial attorney cannot be promoted beyond the GS–15 level; only if he relinquishes his litigating responsibilities and assumes supervisory tasks can he move into supergrade positions (GS–16, GS–17, GS–18). The pressure to relieve financial problems often prompts the experienced litigator to become a supervisor. Consequently, the Antitrust Division loses the trial expertise of the relatively few persons who are both seasoned and capable of prosecuting complex cases. It may be that the Antitrust Division could retain such individuals in trial positions if they were able to move into supergrade slots without having to assume supervisory tasks. But even if grade levels or salaries were raised, Baker admitted:

It is simply folly to pretend that you can hire, train and retain for ten or fifteen years someone with a salary ceiling of $45,000 or

$50,000, when he or she could draw two to five times that amount in private practice. The simple fact is—and will continue to be—that the Division must rely for the bulk of its litigating strength on bright, hard-working but relatively inexperienced young attorneys.[48]

In sum, it is doubtful whether shifting the antitrust responsibilities of the commission to the Antitrust Division would substantially upgrade the quality of enforcement. The problems that hinder the commission in pursuing structural cases also plague the Antitrust Division. The existence of two agencies in the antitrust arena may have some value. The likelihood that the government will initiate antitrust action may be greater because of the presence of two organizations that share responsibility. To be sure, there may be instances where the decision of one agency to proceed after the other has chosen to act otherwise may be ill-advised from a legal or policy perspective. But it is also the case that if one agency does not proceed because of political considerations, then there is still a chance that the other may pursue the investigation.

Trade Court Another proposal designed to solve some of the problems associated with prosecution of complex cases holds that the forum for the adjudication of issues should shift from the commission to a Trade Court, consisting of judges who would be chosen because of their expertise in economics and antitrust law.[49] Having judges who are knowledgeable about complex structural cases could eliminate delays in the postcomplaint stage. The judges could attempt to ensure that issues are narrowly drawn in the early stages of the adjudicative process so as to make the case more manageable in scope. However, the Trade Court proposal does nothing to solve the crucial problems of staff turnover and attorney inexperience that hamper enforcement efforts in the precomplaint and postcomplaint stages. Moreover, there may be some danger in having a court with limited areas of jurisdiction (antitrust law and economics); it may lose touch with the real world.

The Fitness of Legal Processes to Resolve Economic Problems

The difficulties that the Federal Trade Commission and the Antitrust Division have in prosecuting structural cases raise questions about the capacity of legal processes (both judicial and administrative) to resolve matters that hinge upon economic analysis. The legal process moves slowly. The market conditions that gave rise to the structural prosecution may change so dramatically from the case's beginning to its resolution that the remedies originally sought may no longer be appropriate. Lon Fuller, in arguing that tasks of economic allocation cannot be effectively performed within the limits set by the internal morality of the law (that is, through adjudicative forms) because there is a mismatch between the procedure adopted and the problem to be solved, stated:

To act wisely, the economic manager must take into account every circumstance relevant to his decision and must himself assume the initiative in discovering what circumstances are relevant. His decisions must be subject to reversal or change as conditions alter. The judge, on the other hand, acts upon those facts that are in advance deemed relevant under declared principles of decision. His decision does not simply direct resources and energies; it declares rights and rights to be meaningful must in some measure stand firm through changing circumstances.[50]

Perhaps, at first glance, economics might seem to be the handmaiden of the law. The court of law provides an institutional setting where practices judged to be anticompetitive are halted, where actions that may tend to substantially lessen competition are prohibited; economics furnishes the technology on which to base the decisions. The reality is not so simple.

Law is rooted in the past—precedent, custom, and tradition. Legal reasoning, as Edward Levi has documented, is reasoning by example—from case to case.[51] Described by the notion of precedent, legal reasoning is essentially a three-step process: "Similarity is seen between cases; next the rule of law inherent in the first case is announced; then the rule of law is made applicable to the second case."[52] Thus, in fashioning a legal opinion, a judge usually heeds the state of the law, seldom moving more than a few steps away from the current doctrine. Similarly, the lawyers on both sides of a case appeal to precedent to support their claims. In building a case, devising strategies, and writing opinions, precedent is uppermost in the minds of lawyer and judge. For the attorney the assertion of economic arguments, no matter how sound, will prove to be of little benefit if they are inconsistent with legal precedent (no matter how ill-grounded in economic sense).

It has often been remarked that the body of judicial opinions in antitrust cases seldom meets the rigorous tests of the microeconomist. A number of reasons may explain why this should be true. The lawyer, as has just been noted, is not primarily concerned with economics but with legal precedent. Quite obviously, lawyers and not economists argue cases and write opinions. Moreover, courts have interpreted antitrust statutes as serving ends, which are not necessarily consonant with the objective of economic efficiency. The Robinson-Patman Act is a striking illustration of a statute that is principally concerned with the protection of competitors rather than with promoting competition. Writing about the Warren Court, Thomas Kauper commented that it often "seemed less concerned with economically necessary levels of rivalry within the market than with what may be described as the rights of the individual firms which comprise the market."[53]

The economist, unlike the lawyer, is guided not by legal precedent but by the theoretical models of his discipline. Whether a particular merger satisfies the requirements of *Brown Shoe* is irrelevant to the microeconomist. Whether the merger will promote efficiency or a proper allocation of resources is important. The role of the economist, Robert Dorfman has written, "is to describe the way the world operates and if possible to describe it so well and so profoundly that he can infer how the world would operate if conditions were somewhat altered, that is, so he can predict the consequences of following different policies."[54]

Some scholars believe that law and economics need not conflict, that economic principles should be applied to the resolution of legal problems.[55] In their view the judicial system should seek to facilitate economic efficiency. They assume that legislators enacted the antitrust laws to maximize consumer welfare and assert that the courts have veered from congressional intent in interpreting the antitrust laws.

In fact, it is highly questionable whether the purpose of the laws was simply to maximize the welfare of the consumer; legislators often spoke in terms of political and social values that conflict with economic efficiency. If the maximization of consumer welfare is to be the criterion in decision making, then perhaps that standard should first be promulgated in the political rather than the judicial arena. Until legislators have determined that the antitrust laws should have as their end the promotion of economic efficiency, it may not be advisable for the court to disregard accepted non-economic values. Were jurists to ignore such ideals, absent legislative directives, then the authority of the courts could be damaged. For the judge might then be viewed not as a value-free medium through which the fundamental law is revealed, but as an unelected legislator who invokes extralegal criteria to further his policy preferences. (Certainly, judges do make policy. Their actions, however, have at least some legitimacy when based on precedent and an accepted conception of the judicial role.)

The Role of the FTC as a Protector of Competition: The Years Ahead

Quite clearly, the measures for alleviating the problems entailed in prosecuting mammoth cases are not likely to resolve these difficulties, despite the FTC's dedicated efforts. Perhaps, the commission should consider placing its much improved decision-making apparatus at the service of activities better suited to the organization's institutional capacities.

If history is a guide, then the leadership that assumed office in April 1977 will undoubtedly alter various internal arrangements to fit its style and perceptions of the agency's needs. At this writing (January 1979), the extent to which the direction of antitrust policy will change is unclear. Chairman Michael Pertschuk, who thus far has shown particular interest in consumer protection affairs, has indicated that the FTC should give greater attention to goals other than allocative efficiency.[56] Perhaps signaling a lesser role for the Bureau of Economics in case-selection matters in the years ahead,

Pertschuk has criticized conservative economists and stressed the importance of promoting political and social objectives.[57]

Allocating resources to cases with noneconomic objectives could lead to a greater emphasis on conduct matters and a reassessment of big cases. Certainly, in prosecuting conduct cases the commission has served ends that, though not necessarily economic in nature, are nonetheless worthwhile. Whatever support antitrust has derived from the public has not been as dependent upon its economic value as it has been upon the political and moral principles it seems to represent.[58] Simply by attacking conduct violations, the agency deters others who, had they acted illegally, might have threatened such a cherished value as fairness in the marketplace. The commission can maintain public support precisely because its effectiveness in preserving those values—by deterring wrongdoing, for instance—is not easily quantified. As Richard Hofstadter noted:

It is . . . one of the strengths of antitrust that neither its effectiveness nor its ineffectiveness can be precisely documented; its consequences rest on events of unknown number and significance that have *not* happened—on proposed mergers that may have died in the offices of corporation counsel, on collusive agreements that have never been consummated, on unfair practices contemplated but never carried out.[59]

Unlike the conduct vehicle, the big case poses risks for the commission because it promises tangible and substantial economic results, which will certainly not be realized if the agency is not prepared to prosecute the matter to its end.

To state that the commission might consider revising its objectives is not to say that the agency should abandon the big case. Rather, it is to suggest that before embarking on ambitious enforcement actions, the agency should determine what is required in terms of resources, contributive effort, and manpower to prosecute the case to its conclusion and then ascertain whether it has the means to pursue the matter.[60] Moreover, even if the commission placed less emphasis on the big case, it still could maintain its efforts to examine how government can pursue policies that increase consumer benefit. As it has in the past, the commission could perform an important service by gathering data on industrial organization.

Its studies could help resolve the current public-policy debates about the role of antitrust in economic policy. Intense disagreement rages among economists about the efficacy of antitrust enforcement with respect to a wide range of economic matters—inflation, the rate of economic growth, the distribution of income, and technological innovation.[61] Some economists maintain that even if FTC attorneys scored legal victories in pursuing the big structural case, the consuming public might not realize expected consumer gains. They are not as sanguine, as are many politicians, about the effectiveness of vigorous antitrust action as a weapon against inflation. These scholars believe that concentrated industries actually moderate inflationary trends; their findings indicate that price increases are higher in less-concentrated industries and lower in the more-concentrated industries. Hence, they argue that antitrust activity directed against concentrated sectors makes no economic sense.[62] Contesting this view are economists who contend that the high profits associated with high market concentration stimulate large wage increases; for these scholars market concentration is a cause of inflation and should be attacked through antitrust action.[63]

At the heart of these disputes concerning the impact of antitrust on a host of economic matters are disagreements about the effects of market concentration: whether or not market concentration generally results from realization of economies of scale;[64] whether advertising stifles competition and new entry or is in fact a basis for new entry, yielding high volume, low price, and good quality;[65] whether the profit level of an industry should be viewed as a measure of departure of competition or as an indicator of health (the performance paradigm versus the structure-conduct-performance pattern);[66] or whether concentration and large firm size retards or facilitates innovation.[67]

More work needs to be done about the effects of market concentration; there is a paucity of information about the impact of antitrust action on various economic indices. To be sure, statistical and analytical problems, compounded by imperfect economic data, impede the undertaking of impact studies.[68]

Moreover, the commission may be reluctant to measure the effects of its actions, especially if the possibility exists that results might show that the impact on inflation or other economic factors is limited. However, without studies indicating whether antitrust policy is technologically capable of achieving various economic goals, government is vulnerable to the charge that antitrust is a charade or a lightning rod that absorbs the frustrations of those who might otherwise push for greater state intervention in the economy.[69]

Conceivably, the commission might determine that market concentration is indeed the cause of many economic ills.[70] But, if it is indeed true that concentrated industries are not the source of such economic problems as inflation, then the consumer benefit justification for the big structural case could lose much of its force. In that event, and assuming that the FTC's interest in concentrated industries stems from economic considerations, then an agency decision to attach less importance to mammoth cases would perhaps be appropriate in terms of both policy objectives and organizational maintenance needs.

Congress and the executive have had great difficulty fixing the role of antitrust enforcement in economic policy largely because the state of knowledge about the relationship between industrial concentration and various economic indices is inconclusive.[71] Quite predictably, the mixed nature of the findings has resulted in the propagation of seemingly countless proposals about government's approach toward and policies with respect to antitrust enforcement.[72] Some of these proposals—for example, those calling for the restructuring of leading firms in industries in which the four-firm concentration ratio reached a high percentage—could have profound consequences for public policy.[73] In the end, congressional decisions about the deconcentration of certain industries may hinge only partly on economic findings. Legislative choices may also reflect political and social judgments about the desirability of preserving the Jeffersonian ideal of small institutions, the nexus between the private accumulation of wealth and the exercise of political power, and the relationship between competition and the development of character, as well as the fostering of creativity. However, to the extent that economics is part of the decision-making calculus—and it will almost certainly be an important factor—the commission, with its broad investigative powers, could continue to contribute to the public-policy discourse by undertaking thorough studies of the structure, performance, and conduct of suspect industries. In so doing, the commission could retain a significant role as a protector of competition.

Notes

1
See Kenneth G. Elzinga, Lawrence A. Sullivan, and Gray Dorsey, "Antitrust Jurisprudence: A Symposium on the Economic, Political and Social Goals of Antitrust Policy," *University of Pennsylvania Law Review* 125, no. 6 (1977): 1182.

2
See William F. Long, Richard Schramm, and Robert Tollison, "The Economic Determinants of Antitrust Activity," *Journal of Law and Economics* 16 (1973): 351; John J. Siegfried, "The Determinants and Effects of Antitrust Activity," *Journal of Law and Economics* 18 (1975): 559.

3
Alan Stone, *Economic Regulation and the Public Interest: The Trade Commission in Theory and Practice* (Ithaca: Cornell University Press, 1977). Stone argues that the public ownership model should be used because other modes of business control—free market, atomistic restructuring of industry, restructuring of industry at a lower level of oligopoly, full-scale public utility—are not viable. He does not, however, adequately explain what the distinctive merits of the public ownership model actually are.

4
George Stigler, "The Theory of Economic Regulation," *Bell Journal of Economics and Management Science* 2 (1971): 3; and George Stigler, "The Process of Economic Regulation," *The Antitrust Bulletin* 17 (1972): 207.

5
Gabriel Kolko, *Railroads and Regulation 1877–1916* (Princeton: Princeton University Press, 1966); and Gabriel Kolko, *The Triumph of Conservatism* (New York: Free Press, 1962).

6
Samuel Huntington, "The Marasmus of the ICC: The Commission, the Railroads and the Public Interest," *Yale Law Journal* 61 (1952): 467.

7
Marver Bernstein, *Regulating Business by Independent Commission* (Princeton: Princeton University Press, 1955).

8
See Ralph Nader's introduction to Mark J. Green, Beverly C. Moore, Jr., and Bruce Wasserstein, *The Closed Enterprise System: Ralph Nader's Study Group on Antitrust Enforcement* (New York: Grossman Publishers, 1972), p. viii.

9
James Q. Wilson, "The Politics of the Regulatory Process," in James McKie, ed., *Social Responsibility and the Business Predicament* (Washington, D.C.: Brookings, 1974), pp. 138–139; see generally, Paul H. Weaver, "Regulation, Social Policy, and Class Conflict," *The Public Interest*, no. 50 (Winter 1978): 45–63.

10
The conclusion that the FTC Act and the Clayton Act resulted from a diverse coalition of groups and persons is in contrast both to those who contend that the laws were enacted to bolster large corporations eager to extinguish competition or that the legislation was designed to defeat those large business interests seeking to increase their power. For the latter perspective, see, for example, Harold U. Faulkner, *The Decline of Laissez-Faire* (New York: Holt, Rinehart & Winston, 1951); for the revisionist view, see, for example, Gabriel Kolko, *The Triumph of Conservatism*. The legislative debates surrounding the acts can be found in *Congressional Record*, vol. LI (63rd Cong., 2d sess., 1914). For a fine summary of the events, see Alan Stone, *Economic Regulation and the Public Interest: The Federal Trade Commission in Theory and Practice*, pp. 26–51.

11
Richard A. Posner, "Theories of Economic Regulation," *The Bell Journal of Economics and Management Science* 5 (1974): 353.

12
William A. Niskanen, Jr., *Bureaucracy and Representative Government* (Chicago: Aldine Press, 1971).

13
Stigler, "The Process of Economic Regulation," pp. 230–232. Professor Posner views Stigler's assumptions as reasonable with regard to careerists and commissioners seeking reappointment; see Richard A. Posner, "The Federal Trade Commission," *University of Chicago Law Review* 39 (1969): 85.

14
Posner, "The Federal Trade Commission," p. 86.

15
Meredith Associates, Inc., *Report to the Chairman, Federal Trade Commission, Attorney and Attorney Manager, Recruitment, Selection and Retention* (15 July 1976), pp. 12–14.

16
U.S., Congress, Senate, Committee on the Judiciary, Subcommittee on Antitrust and Monopoly, *Hearings on Oversight of Antitrust Enforcement*, 95th Cong., 1st sess., 1977, p. 359 (hereafter *Oversight Hearings*).

17
Ibid.

18
Such has been the fate of *Exxon* and cereal. See *National Journal* 9 (9 January 1977), pp. 1071–1075.

19
Report of the ABA Commission to Study the Federal Trade Commission (Chicago, 1969).

20
Edward Cox, R. Fellmuth, and John E. Schulz, *The Consumer and the Federal Trade Commission* (New York: Richard W. Baron Publishing Company, 1969). pp. 172–173.

21
Richard Posner correctly perceived that the staff attorneys would seek trial experience above all else. He was, as has been stated, wrong in believing that the commissioners would not bring actions against major economic interests (Posner, "Federal Trade Commission," pp. 85–87).

22
Johnson, *Oversight Hearings,* pp. 359–361.

23
Ibid., p. 360.

24
Statement of Robert Pitofsky, *Oversight Hearings,* pp. 616–617.

25
See *Antitrust and Trade Regulation Report,* no. 757, 3 March 1976, p. A–17 (hereafter *ATRR*), and *ATRR,* no. 318, 12 May 1977, p. A–12.

26
Testimony of Michael Pertschuk, *Oversight Hearings,* p. 27.

27
Kenneth Culp Davis, *Discretionary Justice: A Preliminary Inquiry* (Urbana: University of Illinois Press, 1969), p. 198.

28
Lon Fuller, *The Morality of Law* (New Haven: Yale University Press, 1969), p. 38. Similarly, the commission is likely to find it difficult to devise *Policy Protocols,* a new attempt by the agency to rationalize the decision-making process. Protocols are to consist of questions whose answers, supplied by the bureaus, are to serve the commission as decisional guides in different classes of cases.

29
ATRR, no. 793, 14 December 1976, p. A–23.

30
Ibid. For similar reasons, staff attorneys are likely to prove hostile to *Policy Protocols,* which could lead to issuance of rules.

31
U.S., Congress, Senate, Committee on the Judiciary, *Report on Regulatory Agencies to the President-Elect* (Committee print), 86th Cong., 2nd sess., 1960, pp. 51–52.

32
Statement of Miles Kirkpatrick, *Oversight Hearings,* p. 609.

33
Statement of Dean Ernest Gellhorn, *Oversight Hearings,* p. 627.

Attorney General Griffin B. Bell is also keenly interested in examining the relationship between the FTC and the Justice Department. He directed the Antitrust Division to prepare a report on a possible merger with the Bureau of Competition (*ATRR,* no. 809, 14 April 1977, p. A–19).

34
There is a need for comparative analyses of organizations in order to determine the effect of structures on the way in which discretion is exercised. Only through a comparative analysis of at least two organization with different structural characteristics, but charged with performing the same tasks, can such a finding be attempted. Without such comparisons it is virtually impossible to reach judgments, however tentative, about the effect which differences in organizations have on the behavior of executives, managers, and operators or on outcomes.

35
The substance of the 1948 agreement found in Memorandum; Re: Details of Proposed liaison arrangement of Federal Trade Commission with Antitrust Division of the Department of Justice, 30 June 1948. The Hart-Scott-Rodino Antitrust Improvements Act of 1976 institutionalizes the liaison relationship that has existed since 1948.

36
See Johnson, *Oversight Hearings,* pp. 357–358.

37
Pitofsky, *Oversight Hearings,* p. 614.

38
Kirkpatrick, *Oversight Hearings,* p. 609.

39
Suzanne Weaver, *Decision to Prosecute: Organization and Public Policy in the Antitrust Division* (Cambridge, Mass.: MIT Press, 1977), pp. 133–156.

40
E. Pendleton Herring, "Politics, Personalities and the Federal Trade Commission," *American Political Science Review* 28 (1934): 1016.

41
Philip Elman, "A Modest Proposal for Radical Reform," *American Bar Association Journal* 56 (1970): 1047.

42
Richard Posner, "Separate Statement of Richard Posner," *Report of the ABA Commission to Study the Federal Trade Commission* (Chicago, 1969), p. 98.

43
The story is recounted in Green, Moore, and Wasserstein, *The Closed Enterprise System,* pp. 45–47.

44
Ibid.

45
Weaver, *Decision to Prosecute,* pp. 36–55.

46
Donald Baker, "Testimony . . . Before Senate Judiciary Antitrust Subcommittee on 'Oversight of Antitrust Enforcement,'" *ATRR,* no. 813, 12 May 1977, p. E–8.

47
Ibid.

48
Ibid.

49
Pitofsky has lent support to the Trade Court concept; the Trade Court was embodied in the late Senator Philip Hart's various legislative deconcentration proposals.

50
Fuller, *Morality of Law,* p. 172.

51
Edward Levi, *An Introduction to Legal Reasoning* (Chicago: University of Chicago Press, 1949).

52
Ibid., pp. 1–2.

53
Thomas Kauper, "The 'Warren Court' and Antitrust Laws: Of Economics, Populism and Cynicism," *Michigan Law Review* 67 (1968): 288. Writing about the pre-Warren Court era, Joel B. Dirlam and A.E. Kahn made a similar observation about the absence of economic reasoning in many judicial decisions. See their *Fair Competition* (Ithaca: Cornell University Press, 1954).

54
Robert Dorfman, "The Economics of Products Liability: A Reaction to McKean," *University of Chicago Law Review* 38 (1970): 92.

55
An influential book arguing that the antitrust laws were meant to maximize consumer welfare is Robert H. Bork's *The Antitrust Paradox: A Policy at War with Itself* (New York: Basic Books, Inc., 1978). Also, see Richard Posner's *Economic Analysis of Law* (Boston: Little, Brown and Company, 1973) and *Antitrust Law: An Economic Perspective* (Chicago: University of Chicago Press, 1976). Posner's views have stirred much comment. Of particular interest, because it is written by a former Bureau of Economics director, is "The Posnerian Harvest: Separating Wheat from Chaff," by Frederic M. Scherer, in *Yale Law Journal* 86, no. 5 (1977): 974.

56
ATRR, no. 832, 29 September 1977, pp. F–1 to F–3.

57
Remarks of Michael Pertschuk, in U.S., Congress, House, Committee on Appropriations, *Hearings on the Departments of State, Justice, and Commerce, the Judiciary, and Related Agencies, Appropriations, F.Y. 1979*, 95th Cong., 2nd sess., 1978, pp. 1018–1037; Statement of Michael Pertschuk before U.S., Congress, House, Committee on Small Business, Subcommittee on Antitrust, Consumers and Employment, 95th Cong., 2nd sess., 26 July 1978.
   The dilution of the economists' influence may be signaled by the expansion of the Evaluation Committee in 1978; the committee now includes, for example, representatives of the Office of Policy Planning.

58
On the role of symbols in American society, see Murray Edelman, *The Symbolic Uses of Politics* (Urbana: University of Illinois Press, 1964).

59
Richard Hofstadter, "What Happened to the Antitrust Movement," in *The Paranoid Style in American Politics and Other Essays* (New York: Vintage Books, 1965), p. 234.

60
Herbert A. Simon, *Administrative Behavior,* 2nd ed. (New York: Macmillan, 1959), p. 61.

61
See Harvey J. Goldschmid, H. Michael Mann, and J. Fred Weston, eds., *Industrial Concentration: The New Learning* (Boston: Little, Brown and Company, 1974).

62
J. Fred Weston and Steven Lustgarten, "Concentration and Wage-Price Charge," in ibid., pp. 307–332.

63
Willard Mueller, "Industrial Concentration: An Important Inflationary Force," in ibid., pp. 280–307.

64
Compare Frederic M. Scherer, "Economies of Scale in Industrial Concentration," with John S. McGee, "Efficiency and Economies of Size," in ibid., pp. 15–122.

65
Compare Yale Brozen, "Entry Barriers: Advertising and Product Differentiation," with H. Michael Mann, "Advertising, Concentration and Profitability: The State of Knowledge and Directions for Public Policy," in ibid., pp. 114–161.

66
Compare Harold Demsetz, "Two Systems of Belief About Monopoly," with Leonard Weiss, "The Concentration-Profits Relationship and Antitrust," in ibid., pp. 162–245.

67
Jesse Markham, "Concentration: A Stimulus or Retardant to Innovation?" in ibid., pp. 247–277.

68
James A. Dalton and David W. Penn, *The Quality of Data as a Factor in Analyses of Structure—Performance Relationships* (Washington, D.C.: Government Printing Office, 1971); on the information gap, see Testimony of F.M. Scherer, *Oversight Hearings,* pp. 634–640.

69
A representative view in support of the charade theory of antitrust law can be found in John Kenneth Galbraith, *Economics and the Public Purpose* (New York: Houghton-Mifflin, 1973), p. 121.

70
For a view maintaining that market concentration is a serious problem and that the big cases are effective means of restoring competition and lowering prices, see Don. E. Waldman, *Antitrust Action and Market Structure* (Lexington, Mass.: Lexington Books, 1978).

71
Congress and the White House is attempting to remedy that difficulty through the creation of a fifteen-member National Commission for the Review of Antitrust Laws and Procedures, which is reviewing every aspect of federal antitrust policy. Members include the FTC chairman, the assistant attorney general for antitrust, three members from each House of Congress, one representative of an independent regulatory agency, one U.S. District Court judge, and five persons from the private sector. *ATRR,* no. 897, 18 January 1979, pp. A–12 to A–15.

72
See articles and commentary by Blake, Adams, Neal, Phillips, Posner, Hart and Hruska in Goldschmid, Mann, and Weston, *Industrial Concentration,* part 7, pp. 339–426; George S. Stigler, "A Theory of Oligopoly," *Journal of Political Economy* 72 (1964): 44.

73
See the proposed Industrial Reorganization Act (the Hart Bill), S.1167, 93rd Cong., 1st sess., 1973. Hart proposed various modifications of the Industrial Reorganization Act. Also see "President Johnson's White House Task Force on Antitrust Policy" (the Neal Report), which proposed *The Concentrated Industies Act* (reprinted in Goldschmid, Mann, and Weston, *Industrial Concentration,* pp. 449–456).

Appendix A
The FTC and the Antitrust Case-Selection Process:
The Organizational Setting

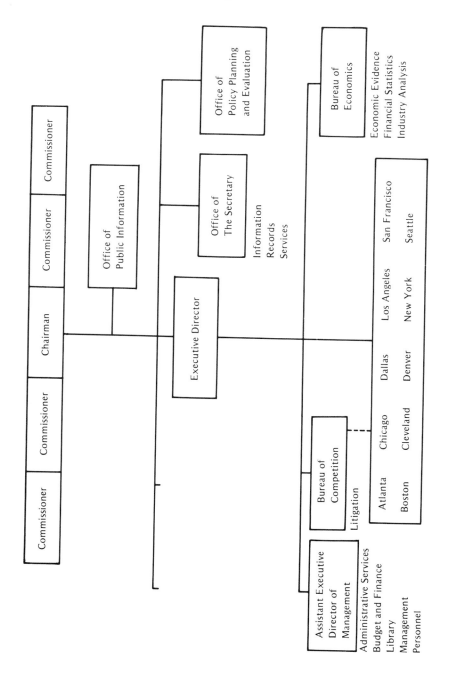

Appendix B
FTC Chairmen

Earl Kintner
June 9, 1959, to March 20, 1961

Paul Rand Dixon
March 21, 1961, to January 12, 1970

Caspar Weinberger
January 13, 1970, to August 6, 1970

Miles Kirkpatrick
September 15, 1970, to February 20, 1973

Lewis Engman
February 20, 1973, to December 31, 1975

Paul Rand Dixon (acting)
January 6, 1976, to March 23, 1976

Calvin Collier
March 24, 1976, to April 20, 1977

Michael Pertschuk
April 21, 1977–

Index